W9-ASP-383

CHARLES BAUDELAIRE

THE PAINTER OF MODERN LIFE AND OTHER ESSAYS

CONSTANTIN GUYS: *In the Row*, *Hyde Park*. Pen and water-colour. London, Mr. Tom Girtin.

THE PAINTER OF MODERN LIFE
AND OTHER ESSAYS

BY

CHARLES BAUDELAIRE

TRANSLATED AND EDITED
BY JONATHAN MAYNE

PHAIDON PRESS

MADE IN GREAT BRITAIN
PRINTED AT THE ABERDEEN UNIVERSITY PRESS

CONTENTS

EDITOR'S NOTE AND ACKNOWLEDGEMENTS

The present translation has been made from the Conard editions of Curiosités esthétiques (*1923*) *and* L'Art romantique (*1925*), *both edited by the late Jacques Crépet. Reference has also been made to the Pléiade edition of the* Oeuvres complètes (*1951*), *edited by M. Y.-G. le Dantec, and to the late André Ferran's fully-annotated edition of the* Salon de 1845 (*Toulouse 1933*). *To these editions I am indebted for much of the material contained in those footnotes which are preceded by a numerical reference. All footnotes, or parts of footnotes, included between an asterisk and the initials 'C.B.' are Baudelaire's own. To some of these I have added a further note after the initials.*

Of the works of art mentioned in the text, I have identified as many as I have been able—though by no means as many as I should have liked—either by giving their present whereabouts, or by indicating where reproductions of them can be seen. In certain cases, where neither reproduction nor whereabouts were known to me, I have referred to standard catalogues raisonnés *of the works of the artists concerned. In the matter of translating, or not translating, the titles of pictures, I have found absolute consistency impossible to secure. Where pictures, such as* Dante et Virgile *or* La Mort de Sardanapale, *are well known under their English titles, it is the English form that I have given. In the case of titles of obscure or unidentified pictures, I have generally left them in French, except in a few instances where the point of a criticism depends upon the literal understanding of a title. My guiding motive has been the avoidance of possible misidentification.*

My greatest personal debts are owed to the late Margaret Gilman, of Bryn Mawr College, whose Baudelaire the Critic *has been an invaluable aid and whose kindness was a constant encouragement; and to Mr. Felix Leakey, of Glasgow University, who has been most patient and helpful with advice. Among those others who have assisted me in a variety of ways, and whom I should like to take this opportunity of thanking once again, are: M. Jean Adhémar, of the Bibliothèque Nationale; Mr. John Beckwith, of the Victoria and Albert Museum; Miss Bernice Davidson, of the Frick Collection; Mme Ronald Davis; Mr. Wolf Drost; M. Claude Ferment; Mr. Tom Girtin; M. Armand Godoy; Mrs. Marie-Louise Hemphill; Mr. Peter Mayne; M. Claude Pichois; Mr. Andrew Porter; Mme J. C. Prost; Mr. Peter Quennell; M. Philippe Roberts-Jones; Mr. Denys Sutton; and M. A. Veinstein, of the Bibliothèque de l'Arsénal, Paris. My thanks are also due to the authorities of the following Museums and Galleries who have kindly granted permission for works of art in their care to be reproduced here: the British Museum and the Victoria and Albert Museum, London; the Bibliothèque*

Nationale, the Musée des Arts Décoratifs, the Petit Palais and the Musée du Louvre, Paris; the Metropolitan Museum, New York; the Musées Royaux, Brussels; the Musée des Beaux-Arts and the Faculté des Lettres, Lyon, and the Stadtmuseum, Munich.

J.M.

EDITOR'S INTRODUCTION

THE present selection of Baudelaire's critical articles forms the first of two volumes designed to cover the poet's preoccupation with the visual arts of his time and with his major artistic heroes—Delacroix, Poe, Wagner and Constantin Guys. It contains some material—the important obituary panegyric of Delacroix and the articles 'On the Essence of Laughter' and on French and foreign caricaturists—which first appeared in English some years ago in *The Mirror of Art.* The second volume will consist of the remainder of the articles contained in that book, which is now out of print, with the addition of the pieces on 'The Museum of Classics' and 'Painters and Etchers'. Thus, while the present volume concerns itself more with personalities and general ideas, its successor will cover the series of Salons and other exhibitions of which from time to time Baudelaire wrote extended accounts. Baudelaire's critical work, which was mostly written for periodicals, was first collected after his death in two volumes entitled *Curiosités esthétiques* (1868) and *L'Art romantique* (1869), from which the articles now translated have been taken. The following Introduction sketches the main lines of the poet's critical method: it is thus inevitably concerned with the contents of the succeeding as well as of the present volume, and was first printed, with some differences of detail, in *The Mirror of Art.*

'*Glorifier le culte des images* (*ma grande, mon unique, ma primitive passion*)', wrote Baudelaire in a famous passage of his autobiographical commonplace-book, *Mon cœur mis à nu.* And perhaps not the least rewarding approach to his art-criticism is to regard it as a kind of lifelong glorification of this chosen cult. Early in his *Salon of 1846* Baudelaire inserted a brief manifesto of what he meant by criticism; in this he was quick to reject a cold, mathematical, heartless type of criticism, and to require in its place a criticism which should be 'partial, passionate and political'—and, he added, 'amusing and poetic'. 'Thus,' he went on to say, 'the best account of a picture may well be a sonnet or an elegy'—a type of 'criticism' of which we find several examples among the *Fleurs du mal.*

But this, of course, is not all. To find the simplest and most revealing exposition of Baudelaire's critic alattitude, it is best to turn to the long article which he wrote some fifteen years later in defence of Wagner. 'All great poets naturally and fatally become critics,' he wrote there. 'I pity those poets who are guided by instinct alone: I regard them as incomplete. But in the spiritual life of the former [i.e. the great poets] a crisis inevitably occurs when they feel the need to reason about their art, to discover the obscure laws in virtue of which they have created, and to extract from this study a set of precepts whose divine aim is infallibility in poetic creation. It would be unthinkable for a critic to become a poet; and it is impossible for a poet not to contain within him a critic. Therefore the reader will not be surprised at my regarding the poet as the best of all critics.' The poet—that is, the creative artist, whatever his medium—is thus a double man who both feels and analyses his feelings; and the movement of his critical thought will be powered by the same central force which is also behind his creation. For Baudelaire, the distinction between criticism and creation in this way breaks down; they turn out to be merely different aspects of the same process.

Earlier in the same article he had written, '*Je résolus de m'informer du pourquoi, et de transformer ma volupté en connaissance*' and this, as several writers have already observed, is at the very core of Baudelaire's critical method. The starting-point is nearly always *volupté*—the shock of pleasure experienced in front of a work of art; the poet-critic then proceeds to examine and analyse the *pourquoi*—the why and the wherefore—until finally he is able to transform the initial shock of pleasure into knowledge—the *volupté* into *connaissance*. Knowledge gained in this way, however, is far from being the same thing as the cold, textbook knowledge which he had long ago rejected as a critical instrument; it is a knowledge charged and quickened by the pleasure which has logically preceded it, and, as we have seen, it is far more likely to take the form of a sonnet than an algebraic equation—a witty and suggestive interpretation than a piece of scientific, or pseudo-scientific, analysis.

Baudelaire made his literary début with a work of art-criticism—the *Salon of 1845*. In later years he became dissatisfied with this early and admittedly imperfect work, although we have the authority of Théodore de Banville that it made a striking effect on publication. Nevertheless it would certainly be worth preserving if only because it provides a kind of preliminary sketch—an *ébauche*, so to speak—for many of the critical attitudes that he was later to adopt and develop. Furthermore it contains his earliest tribute to the genius of Delacroix, whose art and ideas were to inform and interpenetrate so much of what he was to write in the future on the subject of art.

The *Salon of 1845* is set out in a conventional way, and when it touches on general topics, it does so *en passant*. Pictures are arranged neatly within their genres, and each artist is dealt with in his place, with a paragraph or a series of paragraphs to himself. The *Salon of 1846*, however, is composed with great originality and brilliance. It begins with a series of chapters on fundamental aesthetic questions, and by the time that we are presented with the first artist (again Delacroix), a whole critical background has been adumbrated. It is in this general introduction, and in the further 'general' chapters and observations with which this *Salon* is interspersed, that we find the first of the great Baudelairean key-words, themselves defining key-positions in his critical strategy. Individualism, Romanticism, *naïveté*, the Ideal—all of them are paraded before the reader and redefined in a new, exact and highly personal fashion. Nowhere, indeed, could we have a better example of Baudelaire's extraordinary gift for taking already-existing concepts and reanimating them so that they are still recognizable, but, in an essential sense, fresh and surprising. Take Romanticism, for example. 'Few people today will want to give a real and positive meaning to this word,' we are told. And then, after showing us the various ways in which the idea of Romanticism has been misunderstood and perverted, Baudelaire proceeds, in a few short sentences, to give his own definition. 'Romanticism is precisely situated neither in choice of subject nor in exact truth . . . To say the word Romanticism is to say modern art—that is, intimacy, spirituality, colour, aspiration towards the infinite, expressed by every means available to the arts.' Or *naïveté*; 'By the *naïveté* of the genius,' he writes, 'you must understand a complete knowledge of technique combined with the *Know thyself!* of the Greeks, but with knowledge modestly surrendering the leading role to temperament.' Even the old-fashioned, classic shibboleth of 'the Ideal' is given an honoured and important place in this renovated vocabulary of art. 'I am not claiming that there are as many fundamental ideals as there are individuals, for a mould gives several impressions: but in the painter's soul there are just as many ideals as individuals, because a portrait is a *model complicated by an artist*.'

From this necessarily brief résumé of a few of the leading ideas to be encountered in the *Salon of 1846*, it will be apparent that Baudelaire was by no means setting out to make a sudden and shocking breach with the past. What he was doing was to take a series of dead or dying concepts and to breathe a new life into them; and if, in the process, he found it necessary (as he did) to denounce certain fashionable heresies by which, in his opinion, the integrity of art was endangered, this was not because his views were the views of a self-conscious *enfant terrible*. He was living at a time when artistic anarchy and its natural counterpart, artistic puritanism, were both rampant; when the 'great tradition' had been lost, and the new tradition had not yet been discovered; when 'wit' and 'anecdote' and 'erudition' were already beginning to flourish on the soil left vacant by 'history'—and his deeply serious aim was to attempt to call back the visual arts to what he held to be their proper functions. Hence his lifelong devotion to Delacroix who, by his indomitable adherence to classical values of order and artistic purity amid the turbulence of his Romantic imagination, was, in Baudelaire's view, the true painter of the age.

It has often been observed of Baudelaire's poetry that it reveals an extraordinary fusion of a lapidary, Classical permanence and an intimate, Romantic contingency—and this is only one of the striking parallels between Baudelaire and Delacroix as creative and critical artists. Both believed that every nation and every age possessed, and must possess, its own Beauty. Baudelaire analysed these various and varying manifestations of Beauty into two separate elements—the eternal, which was common to all, and the transitory, which resulted from the changing modes of feeling characteristic of different ages. In this, it may be argued, he showed no great originality; the idea was already implicit in Stendhal, and doubtless in other theorists too (for the successful tracing back of individual aspects of Baudelaire's thought to former authors has of recent years become a minor industry of literary scholarship). But in going a step further and asserting that without the co-existence of both elements there could be no Beauty at all, he was asserting something both new and significant. This was but another way of saying that the 'ideal' had now become a relative concept. And if we remember that, in a mechanically progressive age, Baudelaire had the deepest possible contempt for material 'progress', it will only make his understanding of the central aesthetic problem by so much the more prophetic of our own.

It is in the articles on the *Exposition Universelle*, of some nine years later, that we first encounter the concept which may be said to epitomize and develop to their logical conclusion all those that we have already considered. This is the concept of the 'imagination', which makes a brief but telling début in the course of an analysis of the fundamental defects of Ingres. But it is not until the *Salon of 1859* that Baudelaire's idea of the imagination finds its full statement. It is to some extent linked to his doctrine of 'correspondences' (which is also first mentioned by name in the *Exposition Universelle* articles), but it is not necessary to accept that esoteric doctrine in all its implications in order to appreciate the real value of the idea. As with all of Baudelaire's key-words, the word 'imagination' has a very special meaning attached to it. It is an all-informing faculty, which must be allowed to dominate and to order all the others. Furthermore, it is essentially creative—and here, as Miss Gilman has pointed out, Baudelaire comes very close to the doctrine of the creative imagination as developed by Coleridge in the *Biographia Literaria*, though it is in a high degree doubtful that he was aware of this relationship. (If a literary parentage for Baudelaire's Imagination is required, we need look no further than Poe—although it is now fashionable to deplore his influence—and Poe, as is readily admitted even by his friends, owed much to the ideas of Coleridge.)

But Imagination is also the 'most scientific of the faculties'. By this seemingly paradoxical statement Baudelaire meant that the Imagination alone is, by its nature, capable of penetrating beneath the surface of appearances and detecting hidden analogies between different material manifestations, different modes of perception, and different levels of existence. The Imagination, in fact, is that capital faculty of the creative artist whereby he is enabled to see all in one synoptic glance, and thus to order his work in such a way that the topical shall co-exist with the eternal, the natural with the supernatural and the moral with the metaphysical. It is through the Imagination, in short, that the universal correspondences are discerned and the 'ideal' brought to light. Baudelaire is nevertheless careful to insist that the Imagination must have at its service a refined sensibility and a practised technical equipment. He is, indeed, scornful of technical ineptitude (though, as in the case of Corot, he does not always agree that criticism on this score has been correctly applied); but he is, if anything, even more contemptuous of a purely manual dexterity, undirected by Imagination or the 'Soul'.

There is one idea of fundamental importance, however, which we have not yet touched on, although it runs through all of Baudelaire's art-criticism, from the very first *Salon* to the essay on Guys of almost twenty years later, and may be said to emerge naturally from his doctrine of the Imagination and of Beauty. This is the idea of the 'Heroism of Modern Life'. Starting with his definition of Romanticism as intimacy, spirituality and the rest, and feeling (as we know so well from his poetry that he felt) that modern life was presenting a challenge and an obligation to the creative artist which few of his contemporaries seemed willing to meet, Baudelaire concluded his *Salon of 1845* with an impassioned appeal, which he took up again and developed in the following year. This was an appeal for a painter who could interpret the age to itself, with a complete imaginative grasp of its occasional and paradoxical acts of a protesting heroism amid a setting of moral and spiritual desolation. Delacroix, for all that he was in other essentials the 'painter of the age', had scarcely touched modern life, and even though Baudelaire claimed to find a contemporary, sickly type of beauty in his women (somewhat to the consternation of Delacroix himself, it must be admitted), this was hardly enough to qualify him as the almost Messianic genius whom Baudelaire was crying in the wilderness. Courbet might perhaps suggest himself to us as a possible candidate; but this would be to forget that Baudelaire, after a brief flirtation with socialist ideas (and thus with the possibility of a popular, realist art), and in spite of a personal friendship with Courbet himself which lasted longer than is often supposed—Baudelaire, the sworn anti-materialist, had early declared his enmity for the realist ideal. Realism (associated by him with Positivism) was for Baudelaire a flat negation of the Imagination—it was little less than a blasphemy; hence his somewhat curious coupling of the names of Ingres and Courbet in one of his *Exposition Universelle* articles, for both of these he regarded as having sacrificed the imaginative faculty on the altars of other gods—'the great tradition' and 'external nature', respectively.

Another possibility might have been Daumier, for whom Baudelaire expressed a wholehearted admiration in his article on the French caricaturists; or the young Manet, whom he admired in private (if with certain reservations), but never in fact, praised publicly, save on one occasion—in the article on *Painters and Etchers*, in which he joined the name of Manet with that of Alphonse Legros (to the shocked surprise of posterity). When, however, the time came, it was none of these, but the modest, morbidly self-conscious Constantin Guys in whom Baudelaire discovered his 'painter of modern life'; it was around this delightfully gifted but essentially minor artist that he built his fully-developed theory of the relationship of art to modern life.

Whether or not we agree that Baudelaire was justified in glorifying Guys to this extent, it is generally conceded that the *Peintre de la vie moderne* is one of his prose masterpieces. For our present purpose, however, we may perhaps confine ourselves to a single one of the ideas of which it is composed—a crucial idea, nevertheless, not only in its context, but in the whole fabric of Baudelaire's aesthetic and metaphysical opinion. To reduce it to its fundamental statement, this was a passionately-held belief in the Fall of Man, and Original Sin. The essay, *On the Essence of Laughter*, had already made it clear that Baudelaire based his whole theory of the Comic on this idea; and I think that it would be possible to maintain that in the final analysis his whole aesthetic was similarly founded. Good—whether in art or morality—can only be achieved by conscious (and, one might add, imaginative) effort; by striving after an ideal virtue or beauty, and constantly battling against the powerful, but senseless and undirected impulses of Nature. Hence the moving aphorisms of personal morality in *Mon cœur mis à nu*; and hence, as extreme statements, the glorification of the Dandy and the '*éloge du maquillage*' in the *Peintre de la vie moderne*. Transferred to the criticism of the arts in the mid-nineteenth century, the doctrine has a corollary of the greatest importance. For it is precisely this contempt (and also perhaps this fear) of Nature that explains Baudelaire's impatience with all current naturalistic trends—with the landscapes of the Barbizon painters no less than the realism of Courbet. The idea of copying nature, which was at that time more than usually in the air, was to Baudelaire an even greater artistic heresy than was the idea of adding something extraneous ('style', for example) to nature. He remained consistent from first to last in his belief that the immanent, individual ideal—whether expressed by the detachment of the Dandy, the make-up of the courtesan, or the imagination of the poet—was the only thing with which man should concern himself. In the sphere of art the realization of this ideal would always be the result of a collaboration—a sort of fusion, rather—of two separate entities. 'What is pure art, according to the modern idea?', asks Baudelaire in the unfinished article, *L'Art philosophique*. 'It is the creation of an evocative magic containing at once the object and the subject, the world external to the artist and the artist himself.'

In the course of the preceding sketch of Baudelaire's general attitude towards the problems of art, several examples of his practical sympathies and antipathies have already been touched on. As has often been pointed out, Delacroix was from first to last his touchstone of greatness—the Turner to his Ruskin. It is very nearly true to say that Baudelaire's published criticism begins and ends with the name of Delacroix; and it is certain that the idea of Delacroix can almost always be felt hovering in the background through the intervening pages. Some modern critics have indeed come to reproach Baudelaire for this special and all-absorbing devotion, on the grounds that it blinded him to those progressive trends in contemporary painting which were already leading in the direction of Impressionism and thus of Modern Art as we now know it. They are shocked at his severe criticisms of Ingres and Courbet; they note his fundamentally imperfect sympathy for Rousseau, and his damaging dislike of Millet; and finally he is rebuked for omitting to 'discover' Manet at a time when he was in a position to do so, and instead lavishing praise on a host of minor painters who are now almost entirely forgotten—and in most cases deservedly so.

Such is the case against him, as stated by M. Philippe Rebeyrol,[1] for example. But it is necessary first of all to view this kind of criticism in its historical context—to see it as a reaction from a modern devotion to Baudelaire no less fervent than was his own devotion to Delacroix. It has for some time indeed been conventional to hold that Baudelaire was the only art-critic of the nineteenth century who never made mistakes; and if by the phrase 'never made mistakes' we mean that he exactly anticipated the verdicts of posterity in all his

[1] See his article 'Baudelaire et Manet' in *Les Temps modernes*, Oct. 1949.

judgements, it must at once be owned by anyone who has taken the trouble to read what he wrote that this conventional belief is not founded strictly on fact. Other critics of his time—the serious and business-like Thoré, for example, or even a gifted progressive like Champfleury—may be instanced as more accurate prophets of the dawn. Other critical attitudes than his belief in a purified and re-stated Romanticism may now seem to have been more in the mainstream of the theory of art as it has since developed.

But though such practical criticisms must indeed be admitted to have some force, it is legitimate to ask whether it is not perhaps a little crude to attempt to place a critic such as Baudelaire—or any critic, for that matter, who is also a creative artist—in accordance with a simple score-card of 'hits' and 'misses', and particularly when those hits and misses are themselves not so much verifiable facts as elements in a constantly changing complex of opinion. It is necessary at once to state that we do not read Baudelaire in order to dazzle ourselves with the shafts of his prophetic gaze; we may even perhaps allow ourselves to hazard the guess that, if he did look forward to a future art, it may well have been to that of Gustave Moreau rather than of Renoir or Cézanne, to that of Beardsley rather than of Toulouse-Lautrec. But against the enormous positive importance of his work, any such possible shortcomings are fundamentally insignificant. When we call Baudelaire the 'father of modern art-criticism' or the 'first aesthetician of his age' we are referring not to his anticipation of any one of our particular judgements and fashionable cults; we are thinking of his whole approach to the art of art-criticism. For Baudelaire was perhaps the first to detect the dangerous fallacy of a 'party-line' in art, to perceive the 'admirable, eternal and inevitable relationship between form and function' and to apprehend the delicate distinction between anarchy and autonomy in an artist of genius. Even his strictures on artists with whom he was naturally out of sympathy are more often than not conceived in such a way as to throw light on virtues no less than on vices; and in spite of M. Rebeyrol's carefully-arranged texts, he seldom failed to discern greatness, or even 'importance', where it existed, even though he may then have proceeded to enquire why it was not greater or more important still.

But it is above all to Baudelaire's passionately-held belief in the purity of art that we find ourselves returning. Just as his Romanticism transcends the historical reality of that movement, so his belief in the purity or integrity of art transcends the concept of 'Art for Art's sake'. Painting (or poetry, or music) exists in its own right; it has nothing to do with politics (or philosophy, or archaeology), even though in certain conditions it may appeal, in a greater or a lesser degree, to a spectator who is concerned with these things. 'Painting is an evocation, a magical operation' which makes its effect by means of a fusion of colour and line, and which has its own principles of life, to be found nowhere else but in the 'soul' of the artist. If it were nothing more than the constant re-affirmation of this point of view, Baudelaire's criticism would remain a landmark in the development of our understanding of the arts. Add to it all those other qualities—the poetic insight, the wit, the brilliance of description and the underlying humanity—and the result is a critic with whom we may on occasions disagree, but one whom we cannot forget once we have read him.

JONATHAN MAYNE

BIBLIOGRAPHICAL NOTE

THE PAINTER OF MODERN LIFE

This article first appeared in the *Figaro* in instalments on 26 and 28 November and 3 December 1863. It had however been written several years earlier, between November 1859 and February 1860, and had been promised, or offered, to several other periodicals in the meantime. From the available evidence it seems that Baudelaire's relations with his 'sitter' were more or less confined to the period of composition of his portrait. Crépet plausibly suggests that this article may have been intended as part of a general work, never completed, on 'la peinture des moeurs'.

THE LIFE AND WORK OF EUGÈNE DELACROIX

This article, in the form of a long letter to the editor, was published in the *Opinion Nationale* in three parts (2 September, 14 and 22 November 1863). Delacroix had died on 13 August 1863. Baudelaire also used the article as a lecture in Brussels (2 May 1864), when he preceded it with a short passage of introduction (see Crépet's edn. of *L'Art Romantique*).

EDGAR ALLAN POE

This study, entitled 'Edgar Poe, sa vie et ses oeuvres', figured as introduction to the first volume of the *Histoires extraordinaires*, in Baudelaire's translation, which appeared in 1856. It was in fact a revised version of the essay, 'Edgar Allan Poe, sa vie et ses ouvrages', which appeared in the *Revue de Paris*, March and April 1852. Until recently it had been generally assumed that the major source for both versions was the Redfield edition of Poe's works (with Griswold's *Memoir*), the first three volumes of which were published in 1850. Professor W. T. Bandy, however, has established that the first version was in fact largely based not on the original text (with which we must now assume that Baudelaire was not at that time familiar), but on an unsigned review (by John M. Daniel) which was published in the *Southern Literary Messenger* for March 1850; according to Professor Bandy's calculations, more than half of Baudelaire's first version was little more than a word-for-word translation of Daniel's review! There are other echoes, too, from an obituary notice on Poe by John R. Thompson, published also in the *Messenger*, November 1849. By the time he came to revise his essay to form the version here translated, Baudelaire had of course seen the Redfield edition, with the Griswold *Memoir*.

Professor Bandy published his findings, and drew important deductions from them with reference to Poe's influence on Baudelaire as a poet, in his extremely interesting article, 'New Light on Baudelaire and Poe', in *Yale French Studies*, no. 10 (1953).

FURTHER NOTES ON POE

This essay, entitled in French 'Notes nouvelles sur Edgar Poe', is the Introduction to Baudelaire's second collected volume of Poe translations, the *Nouvelles histoires extraordinaires* (1857).

RICHARD WAGNER

This article first appeared in the *Revue européenne*, 1 April 1861. It was published in the form of a booklet, with the addition of the last section, here entitled 'A Few Words More', early in the following month. In the meantime a good part of the article was re-published in the *Presse théâtrale et musicale*.

Crépet (*L'Art Romantique*, p. 509) quotes an unpublished letter of July 1849 to show that already at that early date Baudelaire was an admirer of Wagner's; Newman, however (*Richard Wagner*, 1933–47, vol. III, p.19, n.12), questions whether this date can be correct. At all events the two men did not enter into personal contact until 1860 when, after the *Théâtre italien* concerts, Baudelaire sent Wagner a long letter of appreciation; he did not give his address, 'as you might perhaps think that I had some request to make of you'. Wagner, however, was impressed by the letter, and soon found the means of getting to know its author. See Gilman, pp. 168 ff.

ON THE ESSENCE OF LAUGHTER

Earliest traced publication in *Le Portefeuille*, 8 July 1855; reprinted with minor variations, in *Le Présent*, 1 September 1857, with the addition of the succeeding articles on French (1 October) and Foreign (15 October) Caricaturists. There is evidence, however, that all three articles were part of a larger whole, conceived and perhaps written some years before publication. A work to be entitled 'De la Caricature' was announced 'pour paraître prochainement' as early as 1845, and there are several references in Baudelaire's correspondence of 1851–2 to a work on caricature being finished, or nearly finished.

A PHILOSOPHY OF TOYS

This article first appeared, with minor differences, in the *Monde littéraire*, 17 April 1853. It was twice reprinted in other journals (in 1855 and 1857), before being included in *L'Art Romantique*. Its title in French is 'Morale du Joujou'.

PHILOSOPHIC ART

'This article, found among the author's papers, was evidently not ready for the press. Nevertheless, in spite of lacunae, it seemed to us to be sufficiently finished in its major portions of exposition and analysis to be included here [i.e., in *L'Art Romantique*]. It rounds off Baudelaire's studies on contemporary art by giving us his ideas on a subject with which he was for long preoccupied and which often came up in his conversation.' (Note by the 1868 editors.)

Baudelaire referred to an article on this subject many times in his correspondence, from 1857 onwards; various titles were suggested—'Les Peintres raisonneurs', 'Les Peintres qui pensent', etc. At the end of this article we print a translation of some further sets of notes which were not used by the 1868 editors.

Margaret Gilman's *Baudelaire the Critic* (New York 1943) contains a list of works on Baudelaire's criticism. To this may be added Nino Barbantini's important article 'Baudelaire Critico d'Arte' in his *Scritti d'Arte* (Venice 1953). Martin Turnell's *Baudelaire* (London 1953) contains a good general bibliography, as does Henri Lemaître's edition of *Curiosités esthétiques* and *L'Art romantique* (Paris 1962). For a detailed examination of the art-criticism of the period 1848–70, see Joseph C. Sloane's *French Painting between the Past and the Present* (Princeton 1951).

ABBREVIATIONS USED IN THE FOOTNOTES

Delteil	Loys Delteil. *Honoré Daumier* (in the series 'Le peintre-graveur illustré'). 10 volumes. Paris, 1925–30
Gilman	Margaret Gilman. *Baudelaire the Critic*. New York, 1943
Illustr.	*L'Illustration. Journal universel*
Newman	Ernest Newman. *Richard Wagner*. 3 vols. London, 1933–47.
Robaut	Alfred Robaut. *L'Oeuvre complet d'Eugène Delacroix*. Paris, 1885

THE PAINTER OF MODERN LIFE AND OTHER ESSAYS

THE PAINTER OF MODERN LIFE

I. BEAUTY, FASHION AND HAPPINESS

THE world—and even the world of artists—is full of people who can go to the Louvre, walk rapidly, without so much as a glance, past rows of very interesting, though secondary, pictures, to come to a rapturous halt in front of a Titian or a Raphael—one of those that have been most popularized by the engraver's art; then they will go home happy, not a few saying to themselves, 'I know my Museum.' Just as there are people who, having once read Bossuet and Racine, fancy that they have mastered the history of literature.

Fortunately from time to time there come forward righters of wrong, critics, amateurs, curious enquirers, to declare that Raphael, or Racine, does not contain the whole secret, and that the minor poets too have something good, solid and delightful to offer; and finally that however much we may love *general* beauty, as it is expressed by classical poets and artists, we are no less wrong to neglect *particular* beauty, the beauty of circumstance and the sketch of manners.

It must be admitted that for some years now the world has been mending its ways a little. The value which collectors today attach to the delightful coloured engravings of the last century proves that a reaction has set in in the direction where it was required; Debucourt, the Saint-Aubins and many others have found their places in the dictionary of artists who are worthy of study. But these represent the past: my concern today is with the painting of manners of the present. The past is interesting not only by reason of the beauty which could be distilled from it by those artists for whom it was the present, but also precisely because it is the past, for its historical value. It is the same with the present. The pleasure which we derive from the representation of the present is due not only to the beauty with which it can be invested, but also to its essential quality of being present.

I have before me a series of fashion-plates[1] dating from the

[1] Early in 1859 Baudelaire was writing to his friend and publisher Poulet-Malassis, to thank him for sending him fashion-plates.

Revolution and finishing more or less with the Consulate. These costumes, which seem laughable to many thoughtless people—people who are grave without true gravity—have a double-natured charm, one both artistic and historical. They are often very beautiful and drawn with wit; but what to me is every bit as important, and what I am happy to find in all, or almost all of them, is the moral and aesthetic feeling of their time. The idea of beauty which man creates for himself imprints itself on his whole attire, crumples or stiffens his dress, rounds off or squares his gesture, and in the long run even ends by subtly penetrating the very features of his face. Man ends by looking like his ideal self. These engravings can be translated either into beauty or ugliness; in one direction, they become caricatures, in the other, antique statues.

The women who wore these costumes were themselves more or less like one or the other type, according to the degree of poetry or vulgarity with which they were stamped. Living flesh imparted a flowing movement to what seems to us too stiff. It is still possible today for the spectator's imagination to give a stir and a rustle to this 'tunique' or that 'schall'.[1] One day perhaps someone will put on a play in which we shall see a resurrection of those costumes in which our fathers found themselves every bit as fascinating as we do ourselves in our poor garments (which also have a grace of their own, it must be admitted, but rather of a moral and spiritual type).[2] And then, if they are worn and given life by intelligent actors and actresses, we shall be astonished at ever having been able to mock them so stupidly. Without losing anything of its ghostly attraction, the past will recover the light and movement of life and will become present.

If an impartial student were to look through the *whole* range of French costume, from the origin of our country until the present day, he would find nothing to shock nor even to surprise him. The transitions would be as elaborately articulated as they are in the animal kingdom. There would not be a single gap: and thus, not a single surprise. And if to the fashion plate representing each age he were to add the philosophic thought with which that age was most preoccupied or concerned—the thought being inevitably suggested by the fashion-plate—he would see

[1] An alternative form of the word 'châle'. Cashmere shawls became fashionable in France somewhat later than in England.

[2] See the remarks at the end of the *Salon of 1845* and the section of the *Salon of 1846* entitled 'On the Heroism of Modern Life'.

what a profound harmony controls all the components of history, and that even in those centuries which seem to us the most monstrous and the maddest, the immortal thirst for beauty has always found its satisfaction.

This is in fact an excellent opportunity to establish a rational and historical theory of beauty, in contrast to the academic theory of an unique and absolute beauty; to show that beauty is always and inevitably of a double composition, although the impression that it produces is single—for the fact that it is difficult to discern the variable elements of beauty within the unity of the impression invalidates in no way the necessity of variety in its composition. Beauty is made up of an eternal, invariable element, whose quantity it is excessively difficult to determine, and of a relative, circumstantial element, which will be, if you like, whether severally or all at once, the age, its fashions, its morals, its emotions. Without this second element, which might be described as the amusing, enticing, appetizing icing on the divine cake, the first element would be beyond our powers of digestion or appreciation, neither adapted nor suitable to human nature. I defy anyone to point to a single scrap of beauty which does not contain these two elements.

Let me instance two opposite extremes in history. In religious art the duality is evident at the first glance; the ingredient of eternal beauty reveals itself only with the permission and under the discipline of the religion to which the artist belongs. In the most frivolous work of a sophisticated artist belonging to one of those ages which, in our vanity, we characterize as civilized, the duality is no less to be seen; at the same time the eternal part of beauty will be veiled and expressed if not by fashion, at least by the particular temperament of the artist. The duality of art is a fatal consequence of the duality of man. Consider, if you will, the eternally subsisting portion as the soul of art, and the variable element as its body. That is why Stendhal—an impertinent, teasing, even a disagreeable critic, but one whose impertinences are often a useful spur to reflection—approached the truth more closely than many another when he said that 'Beauty is nothing else but a promise of happiness.'[1] This definition doubtless overshoots the mark; it makes Beauty far too subject to the infinitely variable ideal of Happiness; it strips Beauty too

[1] Crépet refers to *De l'Amour*, chap. XVII; cf. also the footnote in chap. 110 of the *Histoire de la Peinture en Italie:* 'La beauté est l'expression d'une certaine manière habituelle de chercher le bonheur.'

neatly of its aristocratic quality: but it has the great merit of making a decided break with the academic error.

I have explained these things more than once before.[1] And these few lines will already have said enough on the subject for those who have a taste for the diversions of abstract thought. I know, however, that the majority of my own countrymen at least have but little inclination for these, and I myself am impatient to embark upon the positive and concrete part of my subject.

II. THE SKETCH OF MANNERS

FOR the sketch of manners, the depiction of bourgeois life and the pageant of fashion, the technical means that is the most expeditious and the least costly will obviously be the best. The more beauty that the artist can put into it, the more valuable will be his work; but in trivial life, in the daily metamorphosis of external things, there is a rapidity of movement which calls for an equal speed of execution from the artist. The coloured engravings of the eighteenth century have once again won the plaudits of fashion, as I was saying a moment ago. Pastel, etching and aquatint have one by one contributed their quota to that vast dictionary of modern life whose leaves are distributed through the libraries, the portfolios of collectors and in the windows of the meanest of print shops. And then lithography appeared, at once to reveal itself as admirably fitted for this enormous, though apparently so frivolous a task. We have some veritable monuments in this medium. The works of Gavarni and Daumier have been justly described as complements to the *Comédie Humaine*.[2] I am satisfied that Balzac himself would not have been averse from accepting this idea, which is all the more just in that the genius of the painter of manners is of a mixed nature, by which I mean that it contains a strong literary element. Observer, philosopher, *flâneur*—call him what you will; but whatever words you use in trying to define this kind of artist, you will certainly be led to bestow upon him some adjective which you could not apply to the painter of eternal, or at least more lasting things, of heroic or religious subjects. Sometimes

[1] E.g. in the article on 'Critical Method' on the occasion of the *Exposition Universelle*, of 1855.

[2] See p. 183 below.

he is a poet; more often he comes closer to the novelist or the moralist; he is the painter of the passing moment and of all the suggestions of eternity that it contains. Every country, to its pleasure and glory, has possessed a few men of this stamp. In the present age, to Daumier and Gavarni (the first names which occur to the memory) we may add Devéria, Maurin, Numa, historians of the more wanton charms of the Restoration; Wattier, Tassaert, Eugène Lami—the last of these almost an Englishman in virtue of his love for aristocratic elegance; and even Trimolet and Traviès, those chroniclers of poverty and the humble life.

III. THE ARTIST, MAN OF THE WORLD, MAN OF THE CROWD, AND CHILD

TODAY I want to discourse to the public about a strange man, a man of so powerful and so decided an originality that it is sufficient unto itself and does not even seek approval. Not a single one of his drawings is signed, if by signature you mean that string of easily forgeable characters which spell a name and which so many other artists affix ostentatiously at the foot of their least important trifles. Yet all his works are signed—with his dazzling *soul*; and art-lovers who have seen and appreciated them will readily recognize them from the description that I am about to give.

A passionate lover of crowds and incognitos, Monsieur C. G.[1] carries originality to the point of shyness. Mr. Thackeray, who, as is well known, is deeply interested in matters of art, and who himself executes the illustrations to his novels, spoke one day of Monsieur G. in the columns of a London review.[2] The latter was furious, as though at an outrage to his virtue. Recently again, when he learnt that I had it in mind to write an appreciation of his mind and his talent, be begged me—very imperiously, I must admit—to suppress his name, and if I must speak of his works, to speak of them as if they were those of an anonymous artist. I will humbly comply with this singular request. The reader and I will preserve the fiction that Monsieur G. does not exist, and we shall concern ourselves with his drawings and his watercolours (for which he professes a patrician scorn) as though we were scholars who had to pronounce upon precious historical documents, thrown up by chance,

[1] Constantin Guys (1802–92). [2] The reference has not been traced.

whose author must remain eternally unknown. And finally, to give complete reassurance to my conscience, it must be supposed that all that I have to say of his strangely and mysteriously brilliant nature is more or less justly suggested by the works in question—pure poetic hypothesis, conjecture, a labour of the imagination.

Monsieur G. is an old man. Jean-Jacques is said to have reached the age of forty-two before he started writing. It was perhaps at about the same age that Monsieur G., obsessed by the throng of pictures which teemed in his brain, was first emboldened to throw ink and colours on to a white sheet of paper.[1] Truth to tell, he drew like a barbarian, or a child, impatient at the clumsiness of his fingers and the disobedience of his pen. I have seen a large number of these primitive scribbles, and I must own that the majority of those who are, or claim to be, connoisseurs in this matter, might well have been pardoned for failing to discern the latent genius which abode in such murky daubs. Today, after discovering by himself all the little tricks of his trade and accomplishing, without advice, his own education, Monsieur G. has become a powerful master in his own way, and of his early artlessness he has retained no more than what was needed to add an unexpected seasoning to his rich gifts. When he comes across one of those early efforts of his, he tears it up or burns it with a most comical show of bashfulness and indignation.

For ten years I had wanted to get to know Monsieur G., who is by nature a great traveller and cosmopolitan. I knew that for some time he had been on the staff of an English illustrated journal,[2] and that engravings after his travel-sketches, made in Spain, Turkey and the Crimea, had been published there. Since then I have seen a considerable quantity of those drawings, hastily sketched on the spot, and thus I have been able to *read*, so to speak, a detailed account of the Crimean campaign which is much preferable to any other that I know. The same paper had also published, always without signature, a great number of his illustrations of new ballets and operas. When at last I ran him to earth, I saw at once that it was not precisely an *artist*, but rather a *man of the world* with whom I had to do. I ask you to understand the word *artist* in a very restricted sense, and *man of the world* in a very broad one. By the second I mean a

[1] Baudelaire must be mistaken here. Guys was already working for the *Illustrated London News* as early as 1843, and it is hardly likely that he would have been so employed if he had been quite without experience.

[2] *The Illustrated London News.*

man of the whole world, a man who understands the world and the mysterious and lawful reasons for all its uses; by the first, a specialist, a man wedded to his palette like the serf to the soil. Monsieur G. does not like to be called an artist. Is he not perhaps a little right? His interest is the whole world; he wants to know, understand and appreciate everything that happens on the surface of our globe. The artist lives very little, if at all, in the world of morals and politics. If he lives in the Bréda district, he will be unaware of what is going on in the Faubourg Saint-Germain. Apart from one or two exceptions whom I need not name, it must be admitted that the majority of artists are no more than highly skilled animals, pure artisans, village intellects, cottage brains. Their conversation, which is necessarily limited to the narrowest of circles, becomes very quickly unbearable to the *man of the world*, to the spiritual citizen of the universe.[1]

And so, as a first step towards an understanding of Monsieur G., I would ask you to note at once that the mainspring of his genius is *curiosity*.

Do you remember a picture (it really is a picture!), painted—or rather written—by the most powerful pen of our age, and entitled *The Man of the Crowd*?[2] In the window of a coffee-house there sits a convalescent, pleasurably absorbed in gazing at the crowd, and mingling, through the medium of thought, in the turmoil of thought that surrounds him. But lately returned from the valley of the shadow of death, he is rapturously breathing in all the odours and essences of life; as he has been on the brink of total oblivion, he remembers, and fervently desires to remember, everything. Finally he hurls himself headlong into the midst of the throng, in pursuit of an unknown, half-glimpsed countenance that has, on an instant, bewitched him. Curiosity has become a fatal, irresistible passion!

Imagine an artist who was always, spiritually, in the condition of that convalescent, and you will have the key to the nature of Monsieur G.

Now convalescence is like a return towards childhood. The convalescent, like the child, is possessed in the highest degree of the faculty of keenly interesting himself in things, be they apparently of the most trivial. Let us go back, if we can, by a retrospective effort of the imagination,

[1] For an elaboration of this idea, and a note on the exceptions, see the *Salon of 1859*.
[2] A story by Edgar Allan Poe, included among his *Tales* (1845), and translated by Baudelaire in the *Nouvelles Histoires Extraordinaires*.

towards our most youthful, our earliest, impressions, and we will recognize that they had a strange kinship with those brightly coloured impressions which we were later to receive in the aftermath of a physical illness, always provided that that illness had left our spiritual capacities pure and unharmed. The child sees everything in a state of newness; he is always *drunk*. Nothing more resembles what we call inspiration than the delight with which a child absorbs form and colour. I am prepared to go even further and assert that inspiration has something in common with a convulsion, and that every sublime thought is accompanied by a more or less violent nervous shock which has its repercussion in the very core of the brain. The man of genius has sound nerves, while those of the child are weak. With the one, Reason has taken up a considerable position; with the other, Sensibility is almost the whole being. But genius is nothing more nor less than *childhood recovered* at will[1]—a childhood now equipped for self-expression with manhood's capacities and a power of analysis which enables it to order the mass of raw material which it has involuntarily accumulated. It is by this deep and joyful curiosity that we may explain the fixed and animally ecstatic gaze of a child confronted with something new, whatever it be, whether a face or a landscape, gilding, colours, shimmering stuffs, or the magic of physical beauty assisted by the cosmetic art. A friend of mine once told me that when he was quite a small child, he used to be present when his father dressed in the mornings, and that it was with a mixture of amazement and delight that he used to study the muscles of his arms, the gradual transitions of pink and yellow in his skin, and the bluish network of his veins. The picture of external life was already filling him with awe and taking hold of his brain. He was already being obsessed and possessed by form. Predestination was already showing the tip of its nose. His sentence was sealed. Need I add that today that child is a well-known painter?

I asked you a moment ago to think of Monsieur G. as an eternal convalescent. To complete your idea, consider him also as a man-child, as a man who is never for a moment without the genius of childhood—a genius for which no aspect of life has become *stale*.

I have told you that I was reluctant to describe him as an artist pure and simple, and indeed that he declined this title with a modesty touched

[1] An idea taken up and developed by Baudelaire in *Les Paradis artificiels* ('Le Génie Enfant').

with aristocratic reserve. I might perhaps call him a dandy, and I should have several good reasons for that; for the word 'dandy' implies a quintessence of character and a subtle understanding of the entire moral mechanism of this world; with another part of his nature, however, the dandy aspires to insensitivity, and it is in this that Monsieur G., dominated as he is by an insatiable passion—for seeing and feeling—parts company decisively with dandyism. '*Amabam amare*,' said St. Augustine. 'I am passionately in love with passion,' Monsieur G. might well echo. The dandy is blasé, or pretends to be so, for reasons of policy and caste. Monsieur G. has a horror of blasé people. He is a master of that only too difficult art—sensitive spirits will understand me—of being sincere without being absurd. I would bestow upon him the title of philosopher, to which he has more than one right, if his excessive love of visible, tangible things, condensed to their plastic state, did not arouse in him a certain repugnance for the things that form the impalpable kingdom of the metaphysician. Let us be content therefore to consider him as a pure pictorial moralist, like La Bruyère.

The crowd is his element, as the air is that of birds and water of fishes. His passion and his profession are to become one flesh with the crowd. For the perfect *flâneur*, for the passionate spectator, it is an immense joy to set up house in the heart of the multitude, amid the ebb and flow of movement, in the midst of the fugitive and the infinite. To be away from home and yet to feel oneself everywhere at home; to see the world, to be at the centre of the world, and yet to remain hidden from the world—such are a few of the slightest pleasures of those independent, passionate, impartial natures which the tongue can but clumsily define. The spectator is a *prince* who everywhere rejoices in his incognito. The lover of life makes the whole world his family, just like the lover of the fair sex who builds up his family from all the beautiful women that he has ever found, or that are—or are not—to be found; or the lover of pictures who lives in a magical society of dreams painted on canvas. Thus the lover of universal life enters into the crowd as though it were an immense reservoir of electrical energy. Or we might liken him to a mirror as vast as the crowd itself; or to a kaleidoscope gifted with consciousness, responding to each one of its movements and reproducing the multiplicity of life and the flickering grace of all the elements of life. He is an 'I' with an insatiable appetite for the 'non-I', at every instant rendering and explaining it in pictures more living than life itself, which is always unstable and fugitive. 'Any man,' he said one day, in the course of one of those conversations which he illumines with burning glance and evocative gesture,[1] 'any man who is not crushed by one of those griefs whose nature is too real not to monopolize all his capacities, and who can yet be *bored in the heart of the multitude*, is a blockhead! a blockhead! and I despise him!'

When Monsieur G. wakes up and opens his eyes to see the boisterous sun beating a tattoo upon his window-pane, he reproaches himself remorsefully and regretfully: 'What a peremptory order! what a bugle-blast of life! Already several hours of light—everywhere—lost by my sleep! How many *illuminated* things might I have seen and have missed

[1] The following passage from the Goncourts' Journal (23 April 1858) gives an interesting account of Guys at about the same time:

'We came back from Gavarni's with Guys, the draughtsman of the ILLUSTRATED LONDON.

'A little man with an animated face, a grey moustache, looking like an old soldier; hobbling along, constantly hitching up his sleeves on his bony arms with a sharp slap of the hand, diffuse, exuberant with parentheses, zigzagging from idea to idea, going off at tangents and getting lost, but retrieving himself and regaining your attention with a metaphor from the gutter, a word from the vocabulary of the German philosophers, a technical term from art or industry, and always holding you under the thrall of his highly-coloured, almost *visible* utterance. He evoked a thousand memories on that walk, throwing into the conversation handfuls of ironical observations, sketches, landscapes, cities riddled with cannon-balls, blood-soaked, gutted, and ambulances with rats beginning to gnaw at the wounded.

'Then on the other side, rather like in an album in which you find a quotation from Balzac on the back of a design by Decamps, there issued from the mouth of this extraordinary fellow social silhouettes, reflections on the French and the English races, all new, not one that had grown mouldy in a book, two-minute satires, one-word pamphlets, a comparative philosophy of the national genius of the peoples.

'Now we were at the taking of Janina, a river of blood with dogs splashing about in it, flowing between the legs of the young Guys. . . .

'Now it was Dembinski, wearing a blue shirt, his last shirt, tossing a coin, his last coin, on to a green table and nonchalantly forcing the betting up to 40,000 francs.

'And now it was an English castle, with immemorial oaks, a hunt, three *toilettes* a day and a ball every evening, a royal life led, conducted and paid for by a gentleman called Simpson or Tompson (sic), whose twenty-year-old daughter travels to the Mediterranean to inspect her father's eighteen ships of which not one is less than two thousand tons, 'a fleet such as Egypt never had', says Guys. Then he compared *us* to the English—us!—and cries: 'A Frenchman who does nothing, who is in London quietly to spend money—an unheard-of thing! The French travel in order to get over an unhappy love-affair or a gambling-loss, or perhaps to sell textiles, but to see a Frenchman in London riding in a carriage, a Frenchman who is neither an actor nor an ambassador, a Frenchman with a woman at his side who might be his mother or his sister, and not a whore, an actress or a dressmaker—no, that could never be!'

1. Photograph of Guys as an old man, by Nadar. Paris, Bibliothèque Nationale.

2. GUYS: *The Balaklava Railway reaching the Church of Kadiculi, Crimea.* Pen and ink with sepia and water-colour. Paris, Mme J. C. Prost.

3. GUYS: *'My humble self'. The Artist in Conversation with two Sisters of Mercy in the Hospital at Pera.* Pen and wash. Paris, Musée des Arts Décoratifs.

4. GUYS: *The Tchengoan Tower beyond the Tchernaya*. Pen and water-colour. Paris, Mme J. C. Prost.

5. GUYS: *Two Prisoners or Deserters taken in the Plain of Balaklava, brought to General Vinois by English Dragoons.* Pen and ink and water-colour. Paris, Mme J. C. Prost.

6. After Guys: *Procession of the Sultan at the Festival of the Bairam, Constantinople.* Wood-engraving.

7. Guys: *Ramadhan in the Mosque of Top Hane, Constantinople.* Pencil, pen and brown ink, and water-colour. London, British Museum.

8. GUYS: *The Sultan's Wives in their Carriage*. Pen and water-colour. Paris, Musée des Arts Décoratifs.

seeing!' So out he goes and watches the river of life flow past him in all its splendour and majesty. He marvels at the eternal beauty and the amazing harmony of life in the capital cities, a harmony so providentially maintained amid the turmoil of human freedom. He gazes upon the landscapes of the great city—landscapes of stone, caressed by the mist or buffeted by the sun. He delights in fine carriages and proud horses, the dazzling smartness of the grooms, the expertness of the footmen, the sinuous gait of the women, the beauty of the children, happy to be alive and nicely dressed—in a word, he delights in universal life. If a fashion or the cut of a garment has been slightly modified, if bows and curls have been supplanted by cockades, if *bavolets* have been enlarged and *chignons* have dropped a fraction towards the nape of the neck, if waists have been raised and skirts have become fuller, be very sure that his eagle eye will already have spotted it from however great a distance. A regiment passes, on its way, as it may be, to the ends of the earth, tossing into the air of the boulevards its trumpet-calls as winged and stirring as hope; and in an instant Monsieur G. will already have seen, examined and analysed the bearing and external aspect of that company. Glittering equipment, music, bold determined glances, heavy, solemn moustaches—he absorbs it all pell-mell; and in a few moments the resulting 'poem' will be virtually composed. See how his soul lives with the soul of that regiment, marching like a single animal, a proud image of joy in obedience!

But now it is evening. It is that strange, equivocal hour when the curtains of heaven are drawn and cities light up. The gas-light makes a stain upon the crimson of the sunset. Honest men and rogues, sane men and mad, are all saying to themselves, 'The end of another day!' The thoughts of all, whether good men or knaves, turn to pleasure, and each one hastens to the place of his choice to drink the cup of oblivion. Monsieur G. will be the last to linger wherever there can be a glow of light, an echo of poetry, a quiver of life or a chord of music; wherever a passion can *pose* before him, wherever natural man and conventional man display themselves in a strange beauty, wherever the sun lights up the swift joys of the *depraved animal*![1] 'A fine way to fill one's day, to be sure,' remarks a certain reader whom we all know so well. 'Which one of us has not every bit enough genius to fill it in the same way?' But no!

[1] The expression derives from Rousseau; cf. also Brierre de Boismont (*De l' Ennui*): 'L'homme qui pense est un animal dépravé.'

Few men are gifted with the capacity of seeing; there are fewer still who possess the power of expression. So now, at a time when others are asleep, Monsieur G. is bending over his table, darting on to a sheet of paper the same glance that a moment ago he was directing towards external things, skirmishing with his pencil, his pen, his brush, splashing his glass of water up to the ceiling, wiping his pen on his shirt, in a ferment of violent activity, as though afraid that the image might escape him, cantankerous though alone, elbowing himself on. And the external world is reborn upon his paper, natural and more than natural, beautiful and more than beautiful, strange and endowed with an impulsive life like the soul of its creator. The phantasmagoria has been distilled from nature. All the raw materials with which the memory has loaded itself are put in order, ranged and harmonized, and undergo that forced idealization which is the result of a childlike perceptiveness—that is to say, a perceptiveness acute and magical by reason of its innocence!

IV. MODERNITY

AND so away he goes, hurrying, searching. But searching for what? Be very sure that this man, such as I have depicted him—this solitary, gifted with an active imagination, ceaselessly journeying across the great human desert—has an aim loftier than that of a mere *flâneur*, an aim more general, something other than the fugitive pleasure of circumstance. He is looking for that quality which you must allow me to call 'modernity'; for I know of no better word to express the idea I have in mind. He makes it his business to extract from fashion whatever element it may contain of poetry within history, to distil the eternal from the transitory. Casting an eye over our exhibitions of modern pictures, we are struck by a general tendency among artists to dress all their subjects in the garments of the past. Almost all of them make use of the costumes and furnishings of the Renaissance, just as David employed the costumes and furnishings of Rome. There is however this difference, that David, by choosing subjects which were specifically Greek or Roman, had no alternative but to dress them in antique garb, whereas the painters of today, though choosing subjects of a general nature and applicable to all ages, nevertheless persist in rigging them out in the costumes of the Middle Ages, the Renaissance or the Orient.[1] This is clearly symptomatic of a great degree of laziness; for it is much easier to decide outright that everything about the garb of an age is absolutely ugly than to devote oneself to the task of distilling from it the mysterious element of beauty that it may contain, however slight or minimal that element may be. By 'modernity' I mean the ephemeral, the fugitive, the contingent, the half of art whose other half is the eternal and the immutable. Every old master has had his own modernity; the great majority of fine portraits that have come down to us from former generations are clothed in the costume of their own period. They are perfectly harmonious, because everything—from costume and coiffure down to gesture, glance and smile (for each age has a deportment, a glance and a smile of its own)—everything, I say, combines to form a completely viable whole. This transitory, fugitive element, whose metamorphoses are so rapid, must on no account be despised or dispensed with. By neglecting it, you cannot fail to tumble into the abyss of an abstract and indeterminate beauty, like that of the first woman before the fall of man. If for the necessary and inevitable costume of the age you substitute another, you will be guilty of a mistranslation only to be excused in the case of a masquerade prescribed by fashion. (Thus, the goddesses, nymphs and sultanas of the eighteenth century are still convincing portraits, *morally* speaking.)

It is doubtless an excellent thing to study the old masters in order to learn how to paint; but it can be no more than a waste of labour if your aim is to understand the special nature of present-day beauty. The draperies of Rubens or Veronese will in no way teach you how to depict *moire antique*, *satin à la reine* or any other fabric of modern manufacture, which we see supported and hung over crinoline or starched muslin petticoat. In texture and weave these are quite different from the fabrics of ancient Venice or those worn at the court of Catherine. Furthermore the cut of skirt and bodice is by no means similar; the pleats are arranged according to a new system. Finally the gesture and the bearing of the woman of today give to her dress a life and a special character which are not those of the woman of the past. In short, for any 'modernity' to be worthy of one day taking its place as 'antiquity', it is necessary for the mysterious beauty which human life accidentally puts into it to be

[1] These ideas are developed in the sixth section of the *Salon of 1859*.

distilled from it. And it is to this task that Monsieur G. particularly addresses himself.

I have remarked that every age had its own gait, glance and gesture. The easiest way to verify this proposition would be to betake oneself to some vast portrait-gallery, such as the one at Versailles. But it has an even wider application. Within that unity which we call a Nation, the various professions and classes and the passing centuries all introduce variety, not only in manners and gesture, but even in the actual form of the face. Certain types of nose, mouth and brow will be found to dominate the scene for a period whose extent I have no intention of attempting to determine here, but which could certainly be subjected to a form of calculation. Considerations of this kind are not sufficiently familiar to our portrait-painters; the great failing of M. Ingres, in particular, is that he seeks to impose upon every type of sitter a more or less complete, by which I mean a more or less despotic, form of perfection, borrowed from the repertory of classical ideas.

In a matter of this kind it would be easy, and indeed legitimate, to argue *a priori*. The perpetual correlation between what is called the 'soul' and what is called the 'body' explains quite clearly how everything that is 'material', or in other words an emanation of the 'spiritual', mirrors, and will always mirror, the spiritual reality from which it derives. If a painstaking, scrupulous, but feebly imaginative artist has to paint a courtesan of today and takes his 'inspiration' (that is the accepted word) from a courtesan by Titian or Raphael, it is only too likely that he will produce a work which is false, ambiguous and obscure. From the study of a masterpiece of that time and type he will learn nothing of the bearing, the glance, the smile or the living 'style' of one of those creatures whom the dictionary of fashion has successively classified under the coarse or playful titles of 'doxies', 'kept women', *lorettes*, or *biches*.

The same criticism may be strictly applied to the study of the military man and the dandy, and even to that of animals, whether horses or dogs; in short, of everything that goes to make up the external life of this age. Woe to him who studies the antique for anything else but pure art, logic and general method! By steeping himself too thoroughly in it, he will lose all memory of the present; he will renounce the rights and privileges offered by circumstance—for almost all our originality comes from the seal which Time imprints on our sensations. I need hardly tell you that I could easily support my assertions with reference to many objects other than women. What would you say, for example, of a marine-painter (I am deliberately going to extremes) who, having to depict the sober and elegant beauty of a modern vessel, were to tire out his eyes by studying the overcharged, involved forms and the monumental poop of a galleon, or the complicated rigging of the sixteenth century? Again, what would you think if you had commissioned an artist to paint the portrait of a thoroughbred, famed in the annals of the turf, and he then proceeded to confine his researches to the Museums and contented himself with a study of the horse in the galleries of the past, in Van Dyck, Borgognone or Van der Meulen?

Under the direction of nature and the tyranny of circumstance, Monsieur G. has pursued an altogether different path. He began by being an observer of life, and only later set himself the task of acquiring the means of expressing it. This has resulted in a thrilling originality in which any remaining vestiges of barbarousness or *naïveté* appear only as new proofs of his faithfulness to the impression received, or as a flattering compliment paid to truth. For most of us, and particularly for men of affairs, for whom nature has no existence save by reference to utility, the fantastic reality of life has become singularly diluted. Monsieur G. never ceases to drink it in; his eyes and his memory are full of it.

V. MNEMONIC ART

The word 'barbarousness', which may seem to have slipped rather too often from my pen, might perhaps lead some few people to suppose that we are here concerned with defective drawings, only to be transformed into perfect things with the aid of the spectator's imagination. This would be to misunderstand me. What I mean is an inevitable, synthetic, childlike barbarousness, which is often still to be discerned in a perfected art, such as that of Mexico, Egypt or Nineveh, and which comes from a need to see things broadly and to consider them above all in their total effect. It is by no means out of place here to remind my readers that all those painters whose vision is synthesizing and abbreviative have been accused of barbarousness—M. Corot, for example, whose initial concern is always to trace the principal lines of a landscape—its bony structure, its physiognomy, so to speak. Likewise Monsieur

G. brings an instinctive emphasis to his marking of the salient or luminous points of an object (which may be salient or luminous from the *dramatic* point of view) or of its principal characteristics, sometimes even with a degree of exaggeration which aids the human memory; and thus, under the spur of so forceful a prompting, the spectator's imagination receives a clear-cut image of the impression produced by the external world upon the mind of Monsieur G. The spectator becomes the translator, so to speak, of a translation which is always clear and thrilling.

There is one circumstance which adds much to the living force of this *legendary* translation of external life. I refer to Monsieur G's method of draughtsmanship. He draws from memory and not from the model, except in those cases—the Crimean War is one of them—when it may be urgently necessary to take immediate, hasty notes, and to fix the principal lines of a subject. As a matter of fact, all good and true draughtsmen draw from the image imprinted on their brains, and not from nature. To the objection that there are admirable sketches of the latter type by Raphael, Watteau and many others, I would reply that these are notes—very scrupulous notes, to be sure, but mere notes, none the less. When a true artist has come to the point of the final execution of his work, the model would be more of an embarrassment than a help to him. It even happens that men such as Daumier and Monsieur G., for long accustomed to exercising their memory and storing it with images, find that the physical presence of the model and its multiplicity of details disconcerts and as it were paralyses their principal faculty.

In this way a struggle is launched between the will to see all and forget nothing and the faculty of memory, which has formed the habit of a lively absorption of general colour and of silhouette, the arabesque of contour. An artist with a perfect sense of form but one accustomed to relying above all on his memory and his imagination will find himself at the mercy of a riot of details all clamouring for justice with the fury of a mob in love with absolute equality. All justice is trampled under foot; all harmony sacrificed and destroyed; many a trifle assumes vast proportions; many a triviality usurps the attention. The more our artist turns an impartial eye on detail, the greater is the state of anarchy. Whether he be long-sighted or short-sighted, all hierarchy and all subordination vanishes. This is an accident often conspicuous in the works of one of our most fashionable painters[1]—a painter, by the way,

[1] Certainly Meissonier is intended.

whose faults are so well attuned to the faults of the masses that they have singularly assisted his popularity. The same analogy may be observed in the art of the actor, that art so mysterious and so profound, which today has fallen into such a slough of decadence. M. Frédérick Lemaître[1] builds up a role with the breadth and fullness of genius. However studded with luminous details may be his playing of a part, it always remains synthetic and sculptural. M. Bouffé on the other hand creates his roles with the minute precision of a myopic and a bureaucrat. With him everything flashes forth but nothing tells, nothing demands a lodging in the memory.

Thus two elements are to be discerned in Monsieur G.'s execution: the first, an intense effort of memory that evokes and calls back to life—a memory that says to everything, 'Arise, Lazarus'; the second, a fire, an intoxication of the pencil or the brush, amounting almost to a frenzy. It is the fear of not going fast enough, of letting the phantom escape before the synthesis has been extracted and pinned down; it is that terrible fear which takes possession of all great artists and gives them such a passionate desire to become masters of every means of expression so that the orders of the brain may never be perverted by the hesitations of the hand and that finally execution, ideal execution, may become as unconscious and spontaneous as is digestion for a healthy man after dinner. Monsieur G. starts with a few slight indications in pencil, which hardly do more than mark the position which objects are to occupy in space. The principal planes are then sketched in tinted wash, vaguely and lightly coloured masses to start with, but taken up again later and successively charged with a greater intensity of colour. At the last minute the contour of the objects is once and for all outlined in ink. Without having seen them, it would be impossible to imagine the astonishing effects he can obtain by this method which is so simple that it is almost elementary. It possesses one outstanding virtue, which is that, at no matter what stage in its execution, each drawing has a sufficiently 'finished' look; call it a 'study' if you will, but you will have to admit that it is a perfect study. The values are all entirely harmonious, and if the artist should decide to take them further, they will continue to march in step towards the desired degree of completion. He works

[1] Baudelaire had already put on record his admiration for Frédérick Lemaître (1800–76), one of the great French actors of the Romantic generation, in the *Salon of 1846*. H.-D.-M. Bouffé (1800–88) was a well-known comic actor.

in this way on twenty drawings at a time, with an impatience and a delight that are a joy to watch—and amusing even for him. The sketches pile up, one on top of the other—in their tens, hundreds, thousands. Every now and then he will run through them and examine them, and then select a few in order to carry them a stage further, to intensify the shadows and gradually to heighten the lights.

He attaches an enormous importance to his backgrounds, which, whether slight or vigorous, are always appropriate in nature and quality to the figures. Tonal scale and general harmony are all strictly observed, with a genius which springs from instinct rather than from study. For Monsieur G. possesses by nature the colourist's mysterious talent, a true gift that may be developed by study, but which study by itself is, I think, incapable of creating. To put the whole thing in a nutshell, this extraordinary artist is able to express at once the attitude and the gesture of living beings, whether solemn or grotesque, and their luminous *explosion* in space.

VI. THE ANNALS OF WAR

BULGARIA, Turkey, the Crimea, and Spain have all in turn ministered lavishly to the eye of Monsieur G.—or rather to the eye of that imaginary artist whom we have agreed so to call, for every now and then I am reminded that, to give continued reassurance to his modesty, I have promised to pretend that he does not exist. I have studied his archives of the Eastern War—battlefields littered with the débris of death, baggage-trains, shipments of cattle and horses; they are *tableaux vivants* of an astonishing vitality, traced from life itself, uniquely picturesque fragments which many a renowned painter would in the same circumstances have stupidly overlooked. (I would, however, hasten to make an exception of M. Horace Vernet, a military historian rather than essentially a painter, with whom Monsieur G., albeit a subtler artist, has manifest affinities if you are only considering him as an archivist of life.) I am ready to declare that no newspaper, no written account, no book has unfolded so well, in all its painful detail and melancholy scope, the great epic poem of the Crimea. The eye wanders from the banks of the Danube to the shores of the Bosphorus, from Cape Kerson to the plains of Balaclava, from the plains of Inkermann to the encampments of the English, French, Turks and Piedmontese, from the streets of Constantinople to hospital wards and all the splendour of religious and military ceremonial.

One of these drawings most vividly imprinted on my mind represents the *Consecration of the Burial-ground at Scutari by the Bishop of Gibraltar.*[1] The picturesque essence of the scene, which lies in the contrast between its Eastern setting and the Western uniforms and attitudes of those taking part, is realized in an arresting manner, pregnant with dreams and evocations. The officers and men have that ineradicable air of being gentlemen—a mixture of boldness and reserve—which they carry with them to the ends of the earth, as far as the garrisons of the Cape Colony and the cantonments of India; and the English clergymen give one a vague impression of being beadles or money-changers who have put on caps and gowns.

And now we are at Schumla, enjoying the hospitality of Omer Pasha[2] —Turkish hospitality, pipes and coffee; the guests are all disposed on divans, holding to their lips pipes long as speaking-tubes whose bowls lie on the ground at their feet. And here are the Kurds at Scutari,[3] weird-looking troops whose appearance puts one in mind of some barbarian invasion; or if you prefer, the Bashi-Bazouks, no less extraordinary, with their Hungarian or Polish officers whose dandified faces make a peculiar contrast with the baroquely Oriental character of their men.

I remember a magnificent drawing, which shows a single figure standing, a large, sturdy man, looking at once thoughtful, unconcerned and bold; he wears top-boots which extend to above his knees; his uniform is concealed beneath an enormous, heavy, tightly-buttoned greatcoat; he is gazing through the smoke of his cigar at the threatening misty horizon; a wounded arm is carried in a sling. At the bottom of the drawing is the following scribbled inscription: *Canrobert on the battlefield of Inkermann. Taken on the spot.*

Who is this white-moustached cavalry-officer, with so vividly-drawn an expression, who, with lifted head, seems to be savouring all the dreadful poetry of a battlefield, while his horse, sniffing the ground, is picking its way among the corpses heaped up with feet in air, shrunken

[1] *I.L.N.* 9 June 1855. [2] *I.L.N.* 4 March 1854. [3] *I.L.N.* 24 June 1854.

faces, in weird attitudes? In a corner, at the bottom, can be made out these words: *Myself at Inkermann.*

And then there is M. Baraguay d'Hilliers, with the Seraskier, inspecting the artillery at Bechichtash. I have seldom seen more lifelike a military portrait, traced by a bolder or a more spirited pen.

And now a name that has achieved a sinister repute since the disasters in Syria: *Achmet Pasha, General in Chief to the Kalifat, standing with his staff in front of his hut, receiving two European officers.*[1] For all the amplitude of his vast Turkish paunch, Achmet Pasha possesses, both in face and bearing, that indefinably aristocratic air which commonly characterizes the ruling races.

The Battle of Balaclava recurs several times, and in different aspects, in this extraordinary collection. Among the most striking examples we find that historic cavalry-charge celebrated by the heroic trumpet-blasts of Alfred Tennyson, poet laureate: we see a horde of cavalry galloping away at a prodigious speed towards the horizon, between the heavy smoke-clouds of the artillery. The landscape background is closed by a grassy line of hills.

From time to time religious scenes afford some relief to an eye saddened by all this chaos of gunpowder and slaughter. For example, in the midst of a group of British troops, amongst whom the picturesque uniform of the kilted Scots stands out, an Anglican clergyman is conducting the Sunday Service; his lectern is a pyramid of three drums.[2]

But truth to tell, it is almost impossible with no more than a pen to expound so vast and so complicated a poem composed of such a multitude of sketches, or to communicate the intoxication distilled by all this exotic detail—often melancholy but never sentimental—which is accumulated on several hundred scraps of paper whose very stains and smudges tell in their own way of all the turmoil and confusion in the midst of which our artist must have set down his memories of each day. Towards evening the messenger would come to collect Monsieur G.'s notes and drawings, and often he would thus entrust to the post more than ten sketches, hastily scribbled on the thinnest of paper, which the engravers and the subscribers to the journal were eagerly awaiting in London.

Sometimes we are shown ambulances, in which the very atmosphere seems sick, sad and heavy; at another time we are in the hospital at

[1] Paris, Musée des Arts Décoratifs. [2] *I.L.N.* 7 April 1855.

Pera, where, in conversation with two nuns—tall, pallid and erect, like figures by Lesueur—we notice a casually-dressed visitor, identified by this curious legend: *My humble self.*[1] And now, along rough twisting pathways, strewn with some of the débris of an already past engagement, we watch beasts of burden—mules, donkeys or horses—slowly making their way with the pale and inert bodies of the wounded carried in rude chairs on their backs. Amid wastes of snow we see camels of majestic port, their heads held high, with Tartar drivers; they are transporting ammunition and provisions of all kinds. It is a whole warrior-world—alive, busy and silent; it is a world of encampments, Oriental bazaars displaying samples of every kind of supplies, like barbarian cities improvised for the occasion. Through these huts, along these stony or snowy roads, through these ravines, there move uniforms of several different nations, all more or less scarred by war or transmogrified by the addition of enormous topcoats and heavy boots.

It is to be regretted that this album, which is now scattered in several different places (some of its precious pages having been kept by the engravers whose task it was to reproduce them, others by the publishers of the *Illustrated London News*), should not have been brought to the eyes of the Emperor. I feel sure that he would have graciously perused it, and not without emotion, recognizing therein the deeds and doings of his soldiers, from the most dazzling of military actions to the most trivial occupations of everyday life, all minutely transcribed on the spot by a hand so unerring and so intelligent, the hand of a soldier-artist.

VII. POMPS AND CIRCUMSTANCES

TURKEY too has provided our beloved Monsieur G. with some admirable working-material: the festivals of the Bairam,[2] those gloomy, rain-soaked splendours, in the midst of which, like a pale sun, can be discerned the endless *ennui* of the late sultan; drawn up on the sovereign's left, the officers of the civil order; on his right, those of the army, of whom the leader is Said Pasha, sultan of Egypt, at that time present in Constantinople; solemn processions and cavalcades moving in order towards

[1] Paris, Musée des Arts Décoratifs: pl. 3. [2] *I.L.N.* 29 July 1854: see pl. 6.

the little mosque near the palace, and in the crowd Turkish functionaries, real caricatures of decadence, quite overwhelming their magnificent steeds with the weight of their fantastic bulk; massive great carriages,[1] rather like coaches of the time of Louis XV, but gilded and decked out in a bizarre Oriental manner, from which every now and then there dart curiously feminine glances, peeping out from between the strict interval left by the bands of muslin stuck over the face; the frenzied dances of the tumblers of the 'third sex' (never has Balzac's comical expression been more applicable than in the present instance, for beneath this throbbing, trembling light, beneath the agitation of these ample garments, beneath the blazing rouge on these cheeks, in these hysterical, convulsive gestures, in these floating, waist-long tresses, it would be difficult, not to say impossible, to guess that virility lay hid); finally, the *femmes galantes* (if at least it is possible to speak of 'gallantry' in connection with the East), who generally consist of Hungarians, Wallachians, Jewesses, Poles, Greeks and Armenians—for under a despotic government it is the subject races, and amongst them, those in particular that have the most to endure, that provide most candidates for prostitution. Of these women, some have kept their national costume, embroidered jackets with short sleeves, flowing sashes, enormous trousers, turned-up slippers, striped or spangled muslins, and all the tinsel of their native land; others, and these the more numerous, have adopted the principal badge of civilization, which for a woman is invariably the crinoline, but in some small detail of their attire they always preserve a tiny characteristic souvenir of the East, so that they look like Parisian women who have attempted a fancy-dress.

Monsieur G. excels in treating the pageantry of official functions, national pomps and circumstances, but never coldly and didactically, like those painters who see in work of this kind no more than a piece of lucrative drudgery. He works with all the ardour of a man in love with space, with perspective, with light lying in pools or exploding in bursts, drops or diamonds of it sticking to the rough surfaces of uniforms and court toilettes. A drawing representing *Independence-day in the Cathedral at Athens*[2] provides an interesting example of these gifts. That multitude of little figures, of which each one keeps its place so well, only goes to deepen the space which contains them. The Cathedral itself is immense and adorned with ceremonial hangings. King Otho and his Queen

[1] See pl. 8. [2] *I.L.N.* 20 May 1854.

standing upright on a dais, are dressed in the national garb, which they wear with a marvellous ease, as though to give evidence of the sincerity of their adoption and of the most refined Hellenic patriotism. The king's waist is belted like the most elegant of *palikars*, and his kilt spreads out with all the exaggeration prescribed by the national school of dandyism. Towards them walks the patriarch, a bent old man with a great white beard, his little eyes protected behind green spectacles, betraying in his whole being the signs of a consummate Oriental impassivity. All the figures which people this composition are portraits, one of the most curious, by reason of the unexpectedness of her physiognomy (which is just about as un-Greek as could be) being that of a German lady who is standing beside the Queen and is part of her private suite.

In the collected works of Monsieur G. one often comes across the Emperor of the French,[1] whose face he has learnt to curtail to an unerring sketch which he executes with the assurance of a personal signature, without ever damaging the likeness. Sometimes we see him reviewing his troops, on horse-back at full gallop, accompanied by officers whose features are easily recognizable, or by foreign princes—European, Asiatic or African—to whom he is, so to speak, doing the honours of Paris. Or sometimes he will be sitting motionless on a horse whose hooves are as firmly planted as the legs of a table, with, at his left, the Empress in riding-habit, and at his right the little Imperial Prince, wearing a grenadier's cap and holding himself like a soldier on a little horse as shaggy as the ponies that English artists love to send careering across their landscapes; sometimes disappearing in the midst of a whirlwind of dust and light in one of the rides of the Bois de Boulogne; at others walking slowly through the cheering crowds of the Faubourg Saint-Antoine. There is one of these water-colours whose magical quality has particularly dazzled me. The scene is a theatre. At the front of a box of a massive and princely opulence is seen the Empress in a relaxed and peaceful attitude; the Emperor is leaning forward slightly, so as to get a better view of the stage; below him two personal bodyguards are standing at attention in a military, almost hieratic state of immobility, while their brilliant uniforms reflect the splash and splutter of the footlights. On the far side of the barrier of flame, in the ideal atmosphere of the stage, the actors are singing, declaiming and gesticulating in harmony; on the near side there yawns an abyss of dim

[1] See pl. 20.

light, a circular space crowded with tier upon tier of human figures; it is the great chandelier, and the audience.

The popular movements, the republican clubs and the pageantry of 1848 also provided Monsieur G. with a whole series of picturesque compositions, of which the majority were engraved for the *Illustrated London News*.[1] A few years ago, after a stay in Spain which was very fruitful for his genius, he put together an album of the same kind, of which I have seen no more than a few fragments. The carelessness with which he lends or gives away his drawings often exposes him to irreparable losses.

VIII. THE MILITARY MAN

ONCE more to attempt a definition of the kind of subjects preferred by our artist, we would say that it is the *outward show of life*, such as it is to be seen in the capitals of the civilized world; the pageantry of military life, of fashion and of love. Wherever those deep, impetuous desires, war, love, and gaming, are in full flood, like Orinocos of the human heart; wherever are celebrated the festivals and fictions which embody these great elements of happiness and adversity, our observer is always punctually on the spot. But amongst all of this he shows a very marked predilection for the military man, the soldier, and I think that this fondness may be attributed not only to the qualities and virtues which necessarily pass from the warrier's soul into his physiognomy and his bearing, but also to the outward splendour in which he is professionally clad. M. Paul de Molènes[2] has written a passage no less charming than to the point concerning military coquetry and the moral significance of those glittering costumes in which every government is pleased to dress its troops—a passage to which I feel sure that Monsieur G. would be happy to sign his name.

We have already spoken of the idiomatic beauty peculiar to each age, and have observed that each century has, so to speak, its own

[1] Examples are to be found in *I.L.N.* 1 April 1848.

[2] See the chapter 'Voyages et pensées militaires' in Paul de Molènes, *Histoires Sentimentales et Militaires* (1854), and also the same author's *Commentaires d'un Soldat* (L'hiver devant Sébastopol) (1860).

personal sort of grace. The same idea is applicable to the different professions; each derives its external beauty from the moral laws to which it is subject. In some this beauty will be characterized by energy, in others it will bear the visible stamp of idleness. It is like a characteristic badge, a trade-mark of destiny. Taken as a class, the military man has his beauty, just as the dandy and the courtesan have theirs, though of an essentially different flavour. (You will note that I am deliberately passing over those professions in which an exclusive and violent training distorts the muscles and stamps the face with slavery.) Accustomed to surprises, the military man is with difficulty caught off his guard. The characteristic of his beauty will thus be a kind of martial nonchalance, a curious mixture of calmness and bravado; it is a beauty that springs from the necessity to be ready to face death at every moment. Furthermore the face of the ideal military man will need to be characterized by a great simplicity; for, living a communal life like monks or schoolboys, and accustomed to unburden themselves of the daily cares of life upon an abstract paternity, soldiers are in many things as simple as children; like children too, when their duty is done, they are easily amused and given to boisterous entertainments. I do not think that I am exaggerating when I declare that all these moral considerations spill forth naturally from the sketches and water-colours of Monsieur G. Every type of soldier is there, the essence of each being seized upon with a kind of enthusiastic joy; the old infantry officer, solemn and glum, overloading his horse with his bulk; the exquisite staff-officer, trim of figure, wriggling his shoulders and bending unabashed over ladies' chairs, who, seen from the back, puts one in mind of the slimmest and most elegant of insects; the *zouave* and the sharpshooter, whose bearing reveals an exceptional quality of independence and bravado, and as it were a livelier sense of personal responsibility; the sprightly nonchalance of the light cavalry; the oddly academic, professorial appearance of the special corps—artillery or engineers—which is often confirmed by the somewhat unwarriorlike adjunct of a pair of spectacles: not one of these models, not one of these nuances is overlooked, and each is summed up and defined with the same love and wit.

I have before me as I write one of those compositions whose general character is truly heroic. It represents the head of a column of infantry. Perhaps these men have just returned from Italy and are making a halt upon the boulevards amid the acclamations of the crowd; or perhaps they have just completed a long route-march along the roads of Lombardy; I cannot tell. What however is manifest and fully realized is the bold, resolute character, even in repose, of all these faces burned by the sun, the rain and the wind.

Here we can see that uniformity of expression which is created by suffering and obedience endured in common, that resigned air of courage which has been put to the test by long, wearisome fatigues. Trousers tucked into incarcerating gaiters, greatcoats besmirched with dust, stained and discoloured—in short, the entire equipment of these men has taken upon itself the special personality of beings who are returning from afar after running the gauntlet of extraordinary adventures. All these men give the appearance of being more solidly backed, more squarely set on their feet, more erect than ordinary mortals can be. If this drawing could have been shown to Charlet,[1] who was always on the lookout for this kind of beauty, and who frequently found it, he would have been singularly struck by it.

IX. THE DANDY

THE man who is rich and idle, and who, even if blasé, has no other occupation than the perpetual pursuit of happiness; the man who has been brought up amid luxury and has been accustomed from his earliest days to the obedience of others—he, in short, whose solitary profession is elegance, will always and at all times possess a distinct type of physiognomy, one entirely *sui generis*. Dandyism is a mysterious institution, no less peculiar than the duel: it is of great antiquity, Caesar, Catiline and Alcibiades providing us with dazzling examples; and very widespread, Chateaubriand[2] having found it in the forests and by the lakes of the New World. Dandyism, an institution beyond the laws, itself has rigorous laws which all its subjects must strictly obey, whatever their natural impetuosity and independence of character. The English more than others have cultivated the society-novel, and French writers,

[1] Baudelaire had sharply criticized Charlet in 'Some French Caricaturists' (cf. pp. 168 ff.), and had himself been criticized by Delacroix for doing so. Crépet suggests that the present passage may be a gesture of making amends.

[2] Cf. *Les Natchez*.

9. GUYS: *A Turkish Woman with Parasol.* Pen and water-colour. Paris, Petit Palais.

10, GUYS: *Mounted Soldiers*. Pen and wash. London, British Museum.

11. GUYS: *Standing Soldiers*. Pen and wash. London, British Museum.

12. GUYS: *Meeting in the Park*. Pen and water-colour. New York, Metropolitan Museum.

13. GUYS: *Children playing horse and carriage*. Pen and wash. New York, Metropolitan Museum.

14. GUYS: *A Family walking in the Park.* Pen and ink and water-colour.
Private Collection.

15. GUYS: *Taking the air*. Pen and ink and water-colour. London, Mr. Tom Girtin.

16. GUYS: *Two Spanish Girls on their Balcony*. Wash. Paris, Musée des Arts Décoratifs.

17. GUYS: *Two Courtesans.* Water-colour. Paris, Mme Ronald Davis.

18. Guys: *Rue Maubué, 1840.*
Pencil, pen and black ink, brush and water-colour.
Private Collection.

19. GUYS: *Three Women by a Bar*. Pen and wash and water-colour. Paris, Petit Palais.

20. GUYS: *Napoleon III and his staff on horseback*. Pen and wash, touched with water-colour. Private Collection.

21. GUYS: *Carriage and four*. Pen and wash. Private Collection.

22. GUYS: *Greetings in the Bois de Boulogne*. Pen and wash. Paris, Mme J. C. Prost.

23. GUYS: *The Brighton Coach*. Pen and ink and water-colour. London, Mr. Tom Girtin.

24. GUYS: *The Morning Ride*. Pen and ink and wash. Private Collection.

who, like M. de Custine,[1] have made a speciality of love-stories, have taken immediate and very proper care to endow their characters with fortunes ample enough to pay without thinking for all their extravagances; and they have gone on to dispense them of any profession. These beings have no other calling but to cultivate the idea of beauty in their persons, to satisfy their passions, to feel and to think. They thus possess a vast abundance both of time and money, without which fantasy, reduced to a state of passing reverie, can hardly be translated into action. It is sad but only too true that without the money and the leisure, love is incapable of rising above a grocer's orgy or the accomplishment of a conjugal duty. Instead of being a passionate or poetical caprice, it becomes a repulsive utility.

If I speak of love in connection with dandyism, this is because love is the natural occupation of the idle. The dandy does not, however, regard love as a special target to be aimed at. If I have spoken of money, this is because money is indispensable to those who make a cult of their emotions; but the dandy does not aspire to money as to something essential; this crude passion he leaves to vulgar mortals; he would be perfectly content with a limitless credit at the bank. Dandyism does not even consist, as many thoughtless people seem to believe, in an immoderate taste for the toilet and material elegance. For the perfect dandy these things are no more than symbols of his aristocratic superiority of mind. Furthermore to his eyes, which are in love with *distinction* above all things, the perfection of his toilet will consist in absolute simplicity,[2] which is the best way, in fact, of achieving the desired quality. What then is this passion, which, becoming doctrine, has produced such a school of tyrants? what this unofficial institution which has formed so haughty and exclusive a sect? It is first and foremost the burning need to create for oneself a personal originality, bounded only by the limits of the proprieties. It is a kind of cult of the self which can nevertheless survive the pursuit of a happiness to be found in someone else—in woman, for example; which can even survive all that goes by in

[1] Baudelaire had a particular admiration for the work of Astolphe de Custine (1790–1857), and planned to include him, along with Chateaubriand, Paul de Molènes and Barbey d'Aurevilly, in his *Famille des Dandies* (announced in 1860, but never completed).
[2] Crépet reminds us of Champfleury's anecdote of Baudelaire's ordering a dozen replicas when he was pleased with a new suit—at the period, of course, when he had money. Another anecdote has it that Baudelaire glass-papered his suits so that they should not look too new.

the name of illusions. It is the joy of astonishing others, and the proud satisfaction of never oneself being astonished. A dandy may be blasé, he may even suffer; but in this case, he will smile like the Spartan boy under the fox's tooth.

It can be seen how, at certain points, dandyism borders upon the spiritual and stoical. But a dandy can never be a vulgarian. If he committed a crime, it would perhaps not ruin him; but if his crime resulted from some trivial cause, his disgrace would be irreparable. Let not the reader be scandalized by this gravity amid the frivolous; let him rather recall that there is a grandeur in all follies, an energy in all excess. A weird kind of spiritualist, it must be admitted! For those who are at once its priests and its victims, all the complicated material conditions to which they submit, from an impeccable toilet at every hour of the day and the night to the most perilous feats of the sporting field, are no more than a system of gymnastics designed to fortify the will and discipline the soul. In truth I was not altogether wrong to consider dandyism as a kind of religion. The strictest monastic rule, the inexorable order of the Assassins according to which the penalty for drunkenness was enforced suicide, were no more despotic, and no more obeyed, than this doctrine of elegance and originality, which also imposes upon its humble and ambitious disciples—men often full of fire, passion, courage and restrained energy—the terrible formula: *Perinde ac cadaver!*

Whether these men are nicknamed exquisites, *incroyables*, beaux, lions or dandies, they all spring from the same womb; they all partake of the same characteristic quality of opposition and revolt; they are all representatives of what is finest in human pride, of that compelling need, alas only too rare today, of combating and destroying triviality. It is from this that the dandies obtain that haughty exclusiveness, provocative in its very coldness. Dandyism appears above all in periods of transition, when democracy is not yet all-powerful, and aristocracy is only just beginning to totter and fall. In the disorder of these times, certain men who are socially, politically and financially ill at ease, but are all rich in native energy, may conceive the idea of establishing a new kind of aristocracy, all the more difficult to shatter as it will be based on the most precious, the most enduring faculties, and on the divine gifts which work and money are unable to bestow. Dandyism is the last spark of heroism amid decadence; and the type of dandy discovered by our traveller in North America does nothing to invalidate this idea; for how can we be sure that those tribes which we call 'savage' may not in fact be the *disjecta membra* of great extinct civilizations? Dandyism is a sunset; like the declining daystar, it is glorious, without heat and full of melancholy. But alas, the rising tide of democracy, which invades and levels everything, is daily overwhelming these last representatives of human pride and pouring floods of oblivion upon the footprints of these stupendous warriors. Dandies are becoming rarer and rarer in our country, whereas amongst our neighbours in England the social system and the constitution (the true constitution, I mean: the constitution which expresses itself through behaviour) will for a long time yet allow a place for the descendants of Sheridan, Brummel and Byron, granted at least that men are born who are worthy of such a heritage.

What to the reader may have seemed a digression is not so in truth. The moral reflections and considerations provoked by an artist's drawings are in many cases the best translation of them that criticism can make; such suggestions form part of an underlying idea which begins to emerge as they are set out one after the other. It is hardly necessary to say that when Monsieur G. sketches one of his dandies on the paper, he never fails to give him his historical personality—his legendary personality, I would venture to say, if we were not speaking of the present time and of things generally considered as frivolous. Nothing is missed: his lightness of step, his social aplomb, the simplicity in his air of authority, his way of wearing a coat or riding a horse, his bodily attitudes which are always relaxed but betray an inner energy, so that when your eye lights upon one of those privileged beings in whom the graceful and the formidable are so mysteriously blended, you think: 'A rich man perhaps, but more likely an out-of-work Hercules!'

The distinguishing characteristic of the dandy's beauty consists above all in an air of coldness which comes from an unshakeable determination not to be moved; you might call it a latent fire which hints at itself, and which could, but chooses not to burst into flame. It is this quality which these pictures express so perfectly.

X. WOMAN

THE being who, for the majority of men, is the source of the liveliest and even—be it said to the shame of philosophic pleasures—of the most lasting delights; the being towards whom, or on behalf of whom, all their efforts are directed; that being as terrible and incommunicable as the Deity (with this difference, that the Infinite does not communicate because it would thereby blind and overwhelm the finite, whereas the creature of whom we are speaking is perhaps only incomprehensible because it has nothing to communicate); that being in whom Joseph de Maistre saw a graceful animal whose beauty enlivened and made easier the serious game of politics; for whom, and through whom, fortunes are made and unmade; for whom, but above all *through whom*, artists and poets create their most exquisite jewels; the source of the most exhausting pleasures and the most productive pains—Woman, in a word, for the artist in general, and Monsieur G. in particular, is far more than just the female of Man. Rather she is a divinity, a star, which presides at all the conceptions of the brain of man; a glittering conglomeration of all the graces of Nature, condensed into a single being; the object of the keenest admiration and curiosity that the picture of life can offer its contemplator. She is a kind of idol, stupid perhaps, but dazzling and bewitching, who holds wills and destinies suspended on her glance. She is not, I must admit, an animal whose component parts, correctly assembled, provide a perfect example of harmony; she is not even that type of pure beauty which the sculptor can mentally evoke in the course of his sternest meditations; no, this would still not be sufficient to explain her mysterious and complex spell. We are not concerned here with Winckelmann and Raphael; and I hope that I shall not appear to wrong him when I say that despite the wide range of his intelligence, I feel sure that Monsieur G. would willingly pass over a fragment of antique statuary if otherwise he might let slip an opportunity of enjoying a portrait by Reynolds or Lawrence. Everything that adorns woman, everything that serves to show off her beauty, is part of herself; and those artists who have made a particular study of this enigmatic being dote no less on all the details of the *mundus muliebris* than on Woman herself. No doubt Woman is sometimes a light, a glance, an invitation to happiness, sometimes just a word; but above all she is a general harmony, not only in her bearing and the way in which she moves and walks, but also in the muslins, the gauzes, the vast, iridescent clouds of stuff in which she envelops herself, and which are as it were the attributes and the pedestal of her divinity; in the metal and the mineral which twist and turn around her arms and her neck, adding their sparks to the fire of her glance, or gently whispering at her ears. What poet, in sitting down to paint the pleasure caused by the sight of a beautiful woman, would venture to separate her from her costume? Where is the man who, in the street, at the theatre, or in the park, has not in the most disinterested of ways enjoyed a skilfully composed toilette, and has not taken away with him a picture of it which is inseparable from the beauty of her to whom it belonged, making thus of the two things—the woman and her dress—an indivisible unity? This is the moment, it seems to me, to return to certain questions concerning fashion and finery which I did no more than touch upon at the beginning of this study, and to vindicate the art of the dressing-table from the fatuous slanders with which certain very dubious lovers of Nature have attacked it.

XI. IN PRAISE OF COSMETICS

I REMEMBER a song, so worthless and silly that it seems hardly proper to quote from it in a work which has some pretensions to seriousness, but which nevertheless expresses very well, in its *vaudeville* manner, the aesthetic creed of people who do not think. 'Nature embellishes Beauty', it runs. It is of course to be presumed that, had he known how to write in French, the poet would rather have said 'Simplicity embellishes Beauty', which is equivalent to the following startling new truism: '*Nothing* embellishes *something*.'

The majority of errors in the field of aesthetics spring from the eighteenth century's false premiss in the field of ethics.[1] At that time Nature was taken as ground, source and type of all possible Good and Beauty. The negation of original sin played no small part in the general blindness of that period. But if we are prepared to refer simply to the facts, which are manifest to the experience of all ages no less than to the readers of the Law Reports, we shall see that Nature teaches us nothing, or practically nothing. I admit that she *compels* man to sleep, to eat, to drink, and to arm himself as well as he may against the inclemencies of the weather: but it is she too who incites man to murder

[1] Here Baudelaire is following the ideas expressed by Joseph de Maistre in *Les Soirées de Saint-Pétersbourg*. On Baudelaire's general debt to the ideas of de Maistre, see Gilman, pp. 63–66.

his brother, to eat him, to lock him up and to torture him; for no sooner do we take leave of the domain of needs and necessities to enter that of pleasures and luxury than we see that Nature can counsel nothing but crime. It is this infallible Mother Nature who has created patricide and cannibalism, and a thousand other abominations that both shame and modesty prevent us from naming. On the other hand it is philosophy (I speak of good philosophy) and religion which command us to look after our parents when they are poor and infirm. Nature, being none other than the voice of our own self-interest, would have us slaughter them. I ask you to review and scrutinize whatever is natural—all the actions and desires of the purely natural man: you will find nothing but frightfulness. Everything beautiful and noble is the result of reason and calculation. Crime, of which the human animal has learned the taste in his mother's womb, is natural by origin. Virtue, on the other hand, is artificial, supernatural, since at all times and in all places gods and prophets have been needed to teach it to animalized humanity, man being powerless to discover it by himself. Evil happens without effort, naturally, fatally; Good is always the product of some art. All that I am saying about Nature as a bad counsellor in moral matters, and about Reason as true redeemer and reformer, can be applied to the realm of Beauty. I am thus led to regard external finery as one of the signs of the primitive nobility of the human soul. Those races which our confused and perverted civilization is pleased to treat as savage, with an altogether ludicrous pride and complacency, understand, just as the child understands, the lofty spiritual significance of the toilet. In their naif adoration of what is brilliant—many-coloured feathers, iridescent fabrics, the incomparable majesty of artificial forms—the baby and the savage bear witness to their disgust of the real, and thus give proof, without knowing it, of the immateriality of their soul. Woe to him who, like Louis XV (the product not of a true civilization but of a recrudescence of barbarism), carries his degeneracy to the point of no longer having a taste for anything but nature unadorned.*

Fashion should thus be considered as a symptom of the taste for the ideal which floats on the surface of all the crude, terrestrial and loath-

* We know that when she wished to avoid receiving the king, Mme Dubarry made a point of putting on rouge. It was quite enough; it was her way of closing the door. It was in fact by beautifying herself that she used to frighten away her royal disciple of nature. (C.B.)

some bric-à-brac that the natural life accumulates in the human brain: as a sublime deformation of Nature, or rather a permanent and repeated attempt at her *reformation*. And so it has been sensibly pointed out (though the reason has not been discovered) that every fashion is charming, relatively speaking, each one being a new and more or less happy effort in the direction of Beauty, some kind of approximation to an ideal for which the restless human mind feels a constant, titillating hunger. But if one wants to appreciate them properly, fashions should never be considered as dead things; you might just as well admire the tattered old rags hung up, as slack and lifeless as the skin of St. Bartholomew, in an old-clothes dealer's cupboard. Rather they should be thought of as vitalized and animated by the beautiful women who wore them. Only in this way can their sense and meaning be understood. If therefore the aphorism 'All fashions are charming' upsets you as being too absolute, say, if you prefer, 'All were once justifiably charming'. You can be sure of being right.

Woman is quite within her rights, indeed she is even accomplishing a kind of duty, when she devotes herself to appearing magical and supernatural; she has to astonish and charm us; as an idol, she is obliged to adorn herself in order to be adored. Thus she has to lay all the arts under contribution for the means of lifting herself above Nature, the better to conquer hearts and rivet attention. It matters but little that the artifice and trickery are known to all, so long as their success is assured and their effect always irresistible. By reflecting in this way the philosopher-artist will find it easy to justify all the practices adopted by women at all times to consolidate and as it were to make divine their fragile beauty. To enumerate them would be an endless task: but to confine ourselves to what today is vulgarly called 'maquillage', anyone can see that the use of rice-powder, so stupidly anathematized by our Arcadian philosophers, is successfully designed to rid the complexion of those blemishes that Nature has outrageously strewn there, and thus to create an abstract unity in the colour and texture of the skin, a unity, which, like that produced by the tights of a dancer, immediately approximates the human being to the statue, that is to something superior and divine. As for the artificial black with which the eye is outlined, and the rouge with which the upper part of the cheek is painted, although their use derives from the same principle, the need to surpass Nature, the result is calculated to satisfy an absolutely opposite need. Red and black represent life, a supernatural and excessive life: its black frame renders the glance more penetrating and individual, and gives the eye a more decisive appearance of a window open upon the infinite; and the rouge which sets fire to the cheek-bone only goes to increase the brightness of the pupil and adds to the face of a beautiful woman the mysterious passion of the priestess.

Thus, if you will understand me aright, face-painting should not be used with the vulgar, unavowable object of imitating fair Nature and of entering into competition with youth. It has moreover been remarked that artifice cannot lend charm to ugliness and can only serve beauty. Who would dare to assign to art the sterile function of imitating Nature? Maquillage has no need to hide itself or to shrink from being suspected; on the contrary, let it display itself, at least if it does so with frankness and honesty.

I am perfectly happy for those whose owlish gravity prevents them from seeking Beauty in its most minute manifestations to laugh at these reflections of mine and to accuse them of a childish self-importance; their austere verdict leaves me quite unmoved; I content myself with appealing to true artists as well as to those women themselves who, having received at birth a spark of that sacred flame, would tend it so that their whole beings were on fire with it.

XII. WOMEN AND PROSTITUTES

HAVING taken upon himself the task of seeking out and expounding the beauty in *modernity*, Monsieur G. is thus particularly given to portraying women who are elaborately dressed and embellished by all the rites of artifice, to whatever social station they may belong. Moreover in the complete assemblage of his works, no less than in the swarming ant-hill of human life itself, differences of class and breed are made immediately obvious to the spectator's eye, in whatever luxurious trappings the subjects may be decked.

At one moment, bathed in the diffused brightness of an auditorium, it is young women of the most fashionable society, receiving and reflecting the light with their eyes, their jewelry and their snowy, white shoulders, as glorious as portraits framed in their boxes. Some are grave and serious, others blonde and brainless. Some flaunt precocious bosoms with an aristocratic unconcern, others frankly display the chests of young boys. They tap their teeth with their fans, while their gaze is vacant or set; they are as solemn and stagey as the play or opera that they are pretending to follow.

Next we watch elegant families strolling at leisure in the walks of a public garden, the wives leaning calmly on the arms of their husbands, whose solid and complacent air tells of a fortune made and their resulting self-esteem. Proud distinction has given way to a comfortable affluence. Meanwhile skinny little girls with billowing petticoats, who by their figures and gestures put one in mind of little women, are skipping, playing with hoops or gravely paying social calls in the open air, thus rehearsing the comedy performed at home by their parents.[1]

Now for a moment we move to a lowlier theatrical world where the little dancers, frail, slender, hardly more than children, but proud of appearing at last in the blaze of the limelight, are shaking upon their virginal, puny shoulders absurd fancy-dresses which belong to no period, and are their joy and their delight.

Or at a café door, as he lounges against the windows lit from within and without, we watch the display of one of those half-wit peacocks whose elegance is the creation of his tailor and whose head of his barber. Beside him, her feet supported on the inevitable footstool, sits his mistress, a great baggage who lacks practically nothing to make her into a great lady—that 'practically nothing' being in fact 'practically everything', for it is *distinction*. Like her dainty companion, she has an enormous cigar entirely filling the aperture of her tiny mouth. These two beings have not a single thought in their heads. Is it even certain that they can see? Unless, like Narcissuses of imbecility, they are gazing at the crowd as at a river which reflects their own image. In truth, they exist very much more for the pleasure of the observer than for their own.

And now the doors are being thrown open at Valentino's, at the Prado, or the Casino (where formerly it would have been the Tivoli, the Idalie, the Folies and the Paphos)—those Bedlams where the exuberance of idle youth is given free rein. Women who have exaggerated the fashion to the extent of perverting its charm and totally destroying its aims, are ostentatiously sweeping the floor with their trains and the fringes of their shawls; they come and go, pass and repass,

[1] See pl. 14.

opening an astonished eye like animals, giving an impression of total blindness, but missing nothing.

Against a background of hellish light, or if you prefer, an *aurora borealis*—red, orange, sulphur-yellow, pink (to express an idea of ecstasy amid frivolity), and sometimes purple (the favourite colour of canonesses, like dying embers seen through a blue curtain)—against magical backgrounds such as these, which remind one of variegated Bengal Lights, there arises the Protean image of wanton beauty. Now she is majestic, now playful; now slender, even to the point of skinniness, now cyclopean; now tiny and sparkling, now heavy and monumental. She has discovered for herself a provocative and barbaric sort of elegance, or else she aspires, with more or less success, towards the simplicity which is customary in a better world. She advances towards us, glides, dances, or moves about with her burden of embroidered petticoats, which play the part at once of pedestal and balancing-rod; her eye flashes out from under her hat, like a portrait in its frame. She is a perfect image of the savagery that lurks in the midst of civilization. She has her own sort of beauty, which comes to her from Evil always devoid of spirituality, but sometimes tinged with a weariness which imitates true melancholy. She directs her gaze at the horizon, like a beast of prey; the same wildness, the same lazy absent-mindedness, and also, at times, the same fixity of attention. She is a sort of gipsy wandering on the fringes of a regular society, and the triviality of her life, which is one of warfare and cunning, fatally grins through its envelope of show. The following words of that inimitable master, La Bruyère, may be justly applied to her: 'Some women possess an artificial nobility which is associated with a movement of the eye, a tilt of the head, a manner of deportment, and which goes no further.'[1]

These reflections concerning the courtesan are applicable within certain limits to the actress also; for she too is a creature of show, an object of public pleasure. Here however the conquest and the prize are of a nobler and more spiritual kind. With her it is a question of winning the heart of the public not only by means of sheer physical beauty, but also through talents of the rarest order. If in one aspect the actress is akin to the courtesan, in another she comes close to the poet. We must never forget that quite apart from natural, and even artificial, beauty, each human being bears the distinctive stamp of his trade, a

[1] See pl. 18.

characteristic which can be translated into physical ugliness, but also into a sort of 'professional' beauty.

In that vast picture-gallery which is life in London or Paris, we shall meet with all the various types of fallen womanhood—of woman in revolt against society—at all levels. First we see the courtesan in her prime, striving after patrician airs, proud at once of her youth and the luxury into which she puts all her soul and all her genius, as she delicately uses two fingers to tuck in a wide panel of silk, satin or velvet which billows around her, or points a toe whose over-ornate shoe would be enough to betray her for what she is, if the somewhat unnecessary extravagance of her whole toilette had not done so already. Descending the scale, we come down to the poor slaves of those filthy stews which are often, however, decorated like cafés; hapless wretches, subject to the most extortionate restraint, possessing nothing of their own, not even the eccentric finery which serves as spice and setting to their beauty.

Some of these, examples of an innocent and monstrous self-conceit, express in their faces and their bold, uplifted glances an obvious joy at being alive (and indeed, one wonders why). Sometimes, quite by chance, they achieve poses of a daring and nobility to enchant the most sensitive of sculptors, if the sculptors of today were sufficiently bold and imaginative to seize upon nobility wherever it was to be found, even in the mire; at other times they display themselves in hopeless attitudes of boredom, in bouts of tap-room apathy, almost masculine in their brazenness, killing time with cigarettes, orientally resigned—stretched out, sprawling on settees, their skirts hooped up in front and behind like a double fan, or else precariously balanced on stools and chairs; sluggish, glum, stupid, extravagant, their eyes glazed with brandy and their foreheads swelling with obstinate pride. We have climbed down to the last lap of the spiral, down to the *femina simplex* of the Roman satirist.[1] And now, sketched against an atmospheric background in which both tobacco and alcohol have mingled their fumes, we see the emaciated flush of consumption or the rounded contours of obesity, that hideous health of the slothful. In a foggy, gilded chaos, whose very existence is unsuspected by the chaste and the poor, we assist at the Dervish dances of macabre nymphs and living dolls whose childish eyes betray a sinister glitter, while behind a bottle-laden counter there lolls in state an enormous Xanthippe whose head, wrapped in a dirty

[1] Juvenal, Satire VI.

kerchief, casts upon the wall a satanically pointed shadow, thus reminding us that everything that is consecrated to Evil is condemned to wear horns.[1]

Please do not think that it was in order to gratify the reader, any more than to scandalize him, that I have spread before his eyes pictures such as these; in either case this would have been to treat him with less than due respect. What in fact gives these works their value and, as it were, sanctifies them is the wealth of thoughts to which they give rise—thoughts however which are generally solemn and dark. If by chance anyone should be so ill-advised as to seek here an opportunity of satisfying his unhealthy curiosity, I must in all charity warn him that he will find nothing whatever to stimulate the sickness of his imagination. He will find nothing but the inevitable image of vice, the demon's eye ambushed in the shadows or Messalina's shoulder gleaming under the gas; nothing but pure art, by which I mean the special beauty of evil, the beautiful amid the horrible. In fact, if I may repeat myself in passing, the general feeling which emanates from all this chaos partakes more of gloom than of gaiety. It is their moral fecundity which gives these drawings their special beauty. They are heavy with suggestion, but cruel, harsh suggestion which my pen, accustomed though it is to grappling with the plastic arts, has perhaps interpreted only too inadequately.

XIII. CARRIAGES

AND so they run on, those endless galleries of high and low life, branching off at intervals into innumerable tributaries and backwaters. For the few minutes that remain, let us leave them for a world which, if not exactly pure, is at any rate more refined; a world where we shall breathe perfumes not perhaps more healthful, but at least more delicate. I have already remarked that the brush of Monsieur G., like that of Eugène Lami, is marvellously skilled at portraying the rites of dandyism and the elegance of foppery. The physical attitudes of the rich are familiar to him; with a light stroke of the pen and a sureness of touch which never deserts him, he is able to give us that assurance of glance, gesture

[1] See pl. 19.

and pose which is a result of a life of monotony in good fortune. In the particular series of drawings of which I am thinking we are shown a thousand aspects and episodes of the outdoor life—racing, hunting, drives in the woods, proud 'ladies' and frail 'misses' expertly controlling their exquisitely graceful steeds, themselves no less dazzling and dainty than their mistresses. For Monsieur G. is not only a connoisseur of horses in general, but has also a happy gift for expressing the personal beauty of the individual horse. At one moment it is wayside halts, bivouacs, as it were, of innumerable carriages, from which slim young men and women garbed in the eccentric costumes authorized by the season, hoisted up on cushions, on seats, or on the roof, are assisting at some ceremony of the turf which is going on in the distance; at another, a rider is seen galloping gracefully alongside an open barouche, and even his horse seems, by his prancing curtseys, to be paying his respects in his own way. The carriage drives off at a brisk trot along a pathway zebra'd with light and shade, carrying its freight of beauties couched as though in a gondola, lying back idly, only half listening to the gallantries which are being whispered in their ears, and lazily giving themselves up to the gentle breeze of the drive.

Fur or muslin lap around their chins, billowing in waves over the carriage-doors. Their servants are stiff and erect, motionless and all alike. It is always the same monotonous and self-effacing image of servility, punctual and disciplined; its distinctive quality is to have none. The woods in the background are green or russet, dusty or gloomy, depending upon the time of day and the season. Their glades are filled with autumnal mists, blue shadows, golden shafts of light, effulgences of pink, or sudden flashes which cut across the darkness like rapier-thrusts.

If Monsieur G.'s powers as a landscape-painter had not already been revealed to us in his countless water-colours dealing with the Eastern War, these would most certainly be enough to do so. Here however we are no longer concerned with the butchered countryside of the Crimea or the operatic shores of the Bosphorus; instead we are back in those intimate, familiar landscapes which fringe the skirts of a great city, where the light creates effects which no truly Romantic artist could disregard.

Another merit which deserves to be noticed at this point is our artist's remarkable understanding of harness and coachwork. He draws and paints each and every kind of carriage with the same care and ease as an expert marine-painter all sorts of ships. His coachwork is always consummately accurate; each detail is in its place, and no fault can be found with it. In whatever attitude it may be caught, at whatever speed it may be running, a carriage, like a ship, derives from its movement a mysterious and complex grace which is very difficult to note down in shorthand. The pleasure which it affords the artist's eye would seem to spring from the series of geometrical shapes which this object, already so intricate, whether it be ship or carriage, cuts swiftly and successively in space.

I am convinced that in a few years' time Monsieur G.'s drawings will have taken their place as precious archives of civilized life. His works will be sought after by collectors as much as those of the Debucourts, the Moreaus, the Saint-Aubins, the Carle Vernets, the Devérias, the Gavarnis, and all those other delightful artists who, though depicting nothing but the familiar and the charming, are in their own way no less of serious historians. A few of them have even sacrificed too much to charm, and have sometimes introduced into their compositions a classic style alien to the subject; some have deliberately rounded their angles, smoothed the rough edges of life and toned down its flashing highlights. Less skilful than they, Monsieur G. retains a remarkable excellence which is all his own; he has deliberately fulfilled a function which other artists have scorned and which it needed above all a man of the world to fulfil. He has everywhere sought after the fugitive, fleeting beauty of present-day life, the distinguishing character of that quality which, with the reader's kind permission, we have called 'modernity'. Often weird, violent and excessive, he has contrived to concentrate in his drawings the acrid or heady bouquet of the wine of life.

THE LIFE AND WORK OF EUGÈNE DELACROIX

To the Editor of the *Opinion Nationale*

SIR,

Once more and for the last time I wish to pay homage to the genius of Eugène Delacroix, and I beg you to be so kind as to extend the hospitality of your journal to the following few pages in which I shall attempt to bring together, as briefly as possible, the history of his talent, the reasons for his pre-eminence (which in my opinion is still not sufficiently recognized) and finally a few anecdotes and observations upon his life and his character.

I had the good fortune to be associated at a very early age with the illustrious deceased (from the year 1845, as far as I can remember); and this association, from which reverence on my part and indulgence on his in no wise excluded mutual confidence and familiarity, enabled me to form the most accurate notions not only upon his method, but also upon the most intimate qualities of his great soul.

You would not expect me, Sir, to carry out here a detailed analysis of the works of Delacroix. Quite apart from the fact that each of us has already performed the task in accordance with his own powers and by gradual degrees as the great painter revealed to the public the successive labours of his brain, the list is such a long one that, even if only a few lines each were to be allotted to his chief works, an analysis of this kind would fill almost a whole volume. Let it be enough for us to confine ourselves here to a brisk summary.

His monumental paintings are there for all to see in the 'Salon du Roi'[1] and the library[2] at the Chambre des députés; in the library at the Palais du Luxembourg[3]; in the 'Galerie d'Apollon'[4] at the Louvre; and in the 'Salon de la Paix' at the Hôtel de Ville.[5] These decorations comprehend an enormous mass of allegorical, religious and historical subjects, all of them belonging to the noblest realms of the intelligence. As for his easel-pictures, his sketches, his *grisailles*, his water-colours, etc., the reckoning amounts to an approximate total of two hundred and thirty-six.

[1] 1833–7. [2] 1838–47. [3] 1840–6. [4] 1849–51.
[5] 1851–3: destroyed during the Commune.

The great subject-pictures exhibited at various Salons reach the number of seventy-seven. (I am taking these figures from the catalogue which M. Théophile Silvestre has placed at the end of his excellent account of Eugène Delacroix in his *Histoire des artistes vivants*.[1])

I myself have tried more than once to draw up this enormous catalogue[2]; but my patience was always exhausted by the incredible fecundity of the man, and finally, for the sake of peace and quiet, I gave it up. If M. Théophile Silvestre has made mistakes, they can only be mistakes of omission.

I believe, Sir, that the important thing for me to do here is to search for, and to try and define, the characteristic quality of Delacroix's genius; to seek to discover in what it is that he differs from his illustrious ancestors, while equalling them; and finally to show, as far as the written word is capable of showing, the magical art with whose help he has been able to translate the *word* by means of plastic images more vivid and more appropriate than those of any other creative artist of the same profession—to discover, in short, what was the *speciality*[3] with which Providence had charged Eugène Delacroix in the historical development of painting.

I

WHAT is Delacroix? What role did he come into this world to play, and what duty to perform? That is the first question that we must examine. I shall be brief, and I look for immediate conclusions. Flanders has Rubens, Italy Raphael and Veronese; France has Lebrun, David and Delacroix.

A superficial mind may well be shocked, at first glance, by the coupling of these names which represent such differing qualities and methods. But a keener mental eye will see at once that they are united by a common kinship, a kind of brotherhood or cousinage which derives from their love of the great, the national, the immense and the universal—a love which had always expressed itself in the kind of

[1] Published 1856: the catalogues were by L. de Virmond.

[2] Robaut (*L'Oeuvre complet de Delacroix*, 1885) lists 1968 works in all.

[3] Gilman (p. 250, n. 27) suggests that Baudelaire's italicizing of this word may reflect Swedenborg's and Balzac's use of it to denote a state of intuitive and immediate vision of all things, both material and spiritual, 'in their original and consequential ramifications'; it would amount, therefore, to a full understanding of the '*correspondances*'.

painting which is called 'decorative', or in what are known as great *machines*.

Many others, of course, have painted great *machines*; those that I have mentioned, however, painted them in the way most suited to leave an eternal trace upon the memory of mankind. Which is the greatest of these great men who differ so much from one another? Each must decide as he pleases, according as whether his temperament urges him to prefer the prolific, radiant, almost jovial abundance of Rubens; the mild dignity and eurythmic order of Raphael; the paradisal —one might almost say the *afternoon* colour of Veronese; the austere and strained severity of David; or the dramatic and almost literary rhetoric of Lebrun.

None of these men is replaceable; aiming, all of them, at a like goal, they yet used different means, drawn from their individual natures. Delacroix, the last to come upon the scene, expressed with an admirable vehemence and fervour what the others had translated but incompletely. To the detriment of something else, perhaps, as they too had done? It may be; but that is not the question that we have to examine.

Many others apart from myself have gone out of their way to pontificate on the subject of the fatal consequences of an essentially personal genius; and it may also be quite possible, after all, that the finest expressions of genius, elsewhere than in Heaven—that is to say, on this poor earth, where perfection itself is imperfect—could only be secured at the price of an unavoidable sacrifice.

But doubtless, Sir, you will be asking what is this strange, mysterious quality which Delacroix, to the glory of our age, has interpreted better than anyone else. It is the invisible, the impalpable, the dream, the nerves, the *soul*; and this he has done—allow me, please, to emphasize this point—with no other means but colour and contour; he has done it better than anyone else—he has done it with the perfection of a consummate painter, with the exactitude of a subtle writer, with the eloquence of an impassioned musician. It is, moreover, one of the characteristic symptoms of the spiritual condition of our age that the arts aspire if not to take one another's place, at least reciprocally to lend one another new powers.

Delacroix is the most *suggestive* of all painters; he is the painter whose works, even when chosen from among his secondary and inferior productions, set one thinking the most and summon to the memory the greatest number of poetic thoughts and sentiments which, although once known, one had believed to be for ever buried in the dark night of the past.

The achievement of Delacroix sometimes appears to me like a kind of *mnemotechny* of the grandeur and the native passion of universal man. This very special and entirely new merit, which has permitted the artist to express, simply with contour, the gesture of man, no matter how violent it may be, and with colour what one might term the atmosphere of the human drama, or the state of the creator's soul—this utterly original merit has always earned him the support of all poets; and if it were permissible to deduce a philosophical proof from a simple material manifestation, I would ask you, Sir to observe that amongst the crowd that assembled to pay him his last honours, you could count many more men of letters than painters. To tell the blunt truth, these latter have never perfectly understood him.

II

AND WHAT is so very surprising in that, after all? Do we not know that the age of Raphael, Michelangelo and Leonardo—not to speak of the age of Reynolds—is already long past, and that the general intellectual level of artists has singularly dropped? It would doubtless be unfair to look for philosophers, poets and scholars among the artists of the day; but it would seem legitimate to demand from them a little more interest in religion, poetry and science than in fact they show.

Outside of their studios, what do they know? what do they love? what ideas have they to express? Eugène Delacroix, however, at the same time as being a painter in love with his craft, was a man of general education, as opposed to the other artists of today, who for the most part are little more than illustrious or obscure daubers, sad specialists, old or young—mere artisans, possessing some the ability to manufacture academic figures, others fruit and others cattle. Eugène Delacroix loved and had the ability to paint *everything*, and knew also how to appreciate every kind of talent.

His was of all minds the most open to every sort of idea and impression; he was the most eclectic and the most impartial of voluptuaries.

A great reader, it is hardly necessary to mention. The reading of the poets left him full of sublime, swiftly-defined images—ready-made pictures, so to speak. However much he differed from his master Guérin both in method and in colour, he inherited from the great Republican and Imperial school a love of the poets and a strangely impulsive spirit of rivalry with the written word. David, Guérin and Girodet kindled their minds at the brazier of Homer, Virgil, Racine and Ossian. Delacroix was the soul-stirring translator of Shakespeare, Dante, Byron and Ariosto. The resemblance is important; the difference but slight.

But let us enter a little further, if you please, into what one might call the *teaching* of the master—a teaching which, for me, results not only from the successive contemplation of all his works and from the simultaneous contemplation of certain of them (as we had the opportunity of enjoying at the *Exposition Universelle* of 1855), but also from many a conversation that I had with him.

III

DELACROIX was passionately in love with passion, and coldly determined to seek the means of expressing it in the most visible way. In this duality of nature—let us observe in passing—we find the two signs which mark the most substantial geniuses—-extreme geniuses who are scarce made to please those timorous, easily-satisfied souls who find sufficient nourishment in flabby, soft and imperfect works. An immense passion, reinforced with a formidable will—such was the man.

Now he used continually to say:

'Since I consider the impression transmitted to the artist by nature as the most important thing of all for him to translate, is it not essential that he should be armed in advance with all the most rapid means of translation?'

It is evident that in his eyes the imagination was the most precious gift, the most important faculty, but that this faculty remained impotent and sterile if it was not served by a resourceful skill which could follow it in its restless and tyrannical whims. He certainly had no need to stir the fire of his always-incandescent imagination; but the day was never long enough for his study of the material means of expression.

It is this never-ceasing preoccupation that seems to explain his endless investigations into colour and the quality of colours, his lively interest in matters of chemistry, and his conversations with manufacturers of colours. In that respect he comes close to Leonardo da Vinci, who was no less a victim of the same obsessions.

In spite of his admiration for the fiery phenomena of life, never will Eugène Delacroix be confounded among that herd of vulgar artists and scribblers whose myopic intelligence takes shelter behind the vague and obscure word 'realism'. The first time that I saw M. Delacroix—it was in 1845, I think (how the years slip by, swift and greedy!)—we chatted much about commonplaces—that is to say, about the vastest and yet the simplest questions; about Nature, for example. Here, Sir, I must ask your permission to quote *myself*, for a paraphrase would not be the same thing as the words which I wrote on a former occasion, almost at the dictation of the master[1]:

> 'Nature is but a dictionary, he kept repeating. Properly to understand the extent of meaning implied in this sentence, you should consider the numerous ordinary uses of a dictionary. In it you look for the meaning of words, their genealogy and their etymology—in brief, you extract from it all the elements that compose a sentence or a narrative; but no one has ever thought of his dictionary as a *composition*, in the poetic sense of the word. Painters who are obedient to the imagination seek in their dictionary the elements which suit with their conception; in adjusting those elements, however, with more or less of art, they confer upon them a totally new physiognomy. But those who have no imagination just copy the dictionary. The result is a great vice, the vice of banality, to which those painters are particularly prone whose speciality brings them closer to what is called inanimate nature—landscape-painters, for example, who generally consider it a triumph if they can contrive not to show their personalities. By dint of contemplating and copying, they forget to feel and think.
>
> 'For this great painter, however, no element of art, of which one man takes this and another that as the most important, was—I should rather say, *is*—anything but the humblest servant of a unique and superior faculty. If a very neat execution is called for, that is so that the language of the dream may be translated as neatly as possible; if it should be very rapid, that is lest anything be

[1] The following two passages are quoted from Baudelaire's *Salon de 1859*, sections iv and v; they contain a few minor verbal discrepancies.

lost of the extraordinary vividness which accompanied its conception; if the artist's attention should even be directed to something so humble as the material cleanliness of his tools, that is easily intelligible, seeing that every precaution must be taken to make his execution both deft and unerring.'

I might mention in passing that never have I seen a palette as meticulously and delicately prepared as that of Delacroix. It was like an expertly-matched bouquet of flowers.

'With such a method, which is essentially logical, all the figures, their relative disposition, the landscape or interior which provides them with horizon or background, their garments—everything, in fact, must serve to illuminate the general idea, must wear its original colour, its livery, so to speak. Just as a dream inhabits its own proper, coloured atmosphere, so a conception which has become a composition needs to move within a coloured setting which is peculiar to itself. Obviously a particular tone is allotted to whichever part of a picture is to become the key and to govern the others. Everyone knows that yellow, orange and red inspire and express the ideas of joy, richness, glory and love; but there are thousands of different yellow or red atmospheres, and all the other colours will be affected logically and to a proportionate degree by the atmosphere which dominates. In certain of its aspects the art of the colourist has an evident affinity with mathematics and music.

'And yet its most delicate operations are performed by means of a sentiment or perception, to which long practice has given an absolute sureness. We can see that this great law of general harmony condemns many instances of dazzling or crude colour, even in the work of the most illustrious painters. There are paintings by Rubens which not only make one think of a coloured firework, but even of several fireworks set off on the same platform. It is obvious that the larger a picture, the broader must be its *touch*; but it is better that the individual touches should not be materially fused, for they will fuse naturally at a distance determined by the law of sympathy which was brought them together. Colour will thus achieve a greater energy and freshness.

'A good picture, which is a faithful equivalent of the dream which has begotten it, should be brought into being like a world.

Just as the creation, as we see it, is the result of several creations, in which the preceding ones are always completed by the following, so a harmoniously-conducted picture consists of a series of pictures superimposed on one another, each new layer conferring greater reality upon the dream and raising it by one degree towards perfection. On the other hand, I remember having seen in the studios of Paul Delaroche and Horace Vernet huge pictures, not sketched but actually begun—that is to say, with certain passages completely finished, while others were only indicated with a black or a white outline. You might compare this kind of work to a piece of purely manual labour—so much space to be covered in a given time—or to a long road divided into a great number of stages. As soon as each stage is reached, it is finished with; and when the whole road has been run, the artist is delivered of his picture.

'It is clear that all these rules are more or less modifiable in accordance with the varying temperaments of artists. Nevertheless I am convinced that what I have described is the surest method for men of rich imagination. Consequently, if an artist's divergences from the method in question are too great, there is evidence that an abnormal and undue importance is being set upon some secondary element of art.

'I have no fear that anyone may consider it absurd to presuppose a single method to be employed by a crowd of different individuals. For it is obvious that systems of rhetoric or prosody are no arbitrarily invented tyrannies, but rather they are collections of rules demanded by the very constitution of the spiritual being. And systems of prosody and rhetoric have never yet prevented originality from clearly emerging; the contrary—namely, that they have assisted the birth of originality—would be infinitely more true.

'To be brief, I must pass over a whole crowd of corollaries resulting from my principal formula in which is contained, so to speak, the entire formulary of the true aesthetic, and which may be expressed thus: The whole visible universe is but a store-house of images and signs to which the imagination will give a relative place and value; it is a sort of pasture which the imagination must digest and transform. All the faculties of the human soul must be subordinated to the imagination, which puts them in requisition all at once. Just as a good knowledge of the dictionary does not necessarily imply a knowledge of the art of composition, and just as the art of composition does not itself imply a *universal* imagination, in the same way a *good* painter need not be a *great* painter. But a great painter is perforce a good painter, because the universal imagination embraces the understanding of all means of expression and the desire to acquire them.

'As a result of the ideas which I have just been making as clear as I have been able (but there are still so many things that I could have mentioned, particularly concerning the concordant aspects of all the arts, and their similarities in method!), it is clear that the vast family of artists—that is to say, of men who have devoted themselves to the expression of beauty—can be divided into two quite distinct camps. There are those who call themselves 'realists'—a word with a double meaning, whose sense has not been properly defined, and so, in order the better to characterize their error, I propose to call them 'positivists'; and *they* say, 'I want to represent things as they are, or rather as they would be, supposing that I did not exist.' In other words, the universe without man. The others, however—the 'imaginatives'—say, 'I want to illuminate things with my mind, and to project their reflection upon other minds.' Although these two absolutely contrary methods could magnify or diminish any subject, from a religious scene to the most modest landscape, nevertheless the man of imagination has generally tended to express himself in religious painting and in fantasy, while landscape and the type of painting called 'genre' would appear to offer enormous opportunities to those whose minds are lazy and excitable only with difficulty . . .'

'Delacroix's imagination! Never has it flinched before the arduous peaks of religion! The heavens belong to it, no less than hell, war, Olympus and love. In him you have the model of the painter-poet. He is indeed one of the rare elect, and the scope of his mind embraces religion in its domain. His imagination blazes with every flame and every shade of crimson, like the banks of glowing candles before a shrine. All that there is of anguish in the Passion impassions him; all that there is of splendour in the Church casts its glory upon him. On his inspired canvases he pours blood, light and darkness in turn. I believe that he would willingly bestow his own natural magnificence upon the majesties of the Gospel itself, out of superabundance.

'I remember seeing a little *Annunciation* by Delacroix in which the angel visiting Mary was not alone, but was escorted in ceremony by two other angels, and the effect of this celestial retinue was powerful and touching. One of his youthful pictures, the *Christ in the Garden of Olives* ('O my Father, if it be possible, let this cup pass from me') positively melts with feminine sensibility and poetic unction. Anguish and Splendour, which ring forth so sublimely in religion, are never without an echo in his mind.'

And more recently still, when writing on the subject of the chapel of the Holy Angels at Saint-Sulpice (*Heliodorus*[1] and *Jacob and the Angel*), his last great labour, and one so stupidly criticized, I said[2]:

'Never, not even in the *Justice of Trajan*, or in the *Entry of the Crusaders*, has Delacroix displayed a palette more splendidly or more scientifically supernatural; never a draughtsmanship more *deliberately* epic. I know very well that some people—bricklayers no doubt, or possibly architects—have uttered the word 'decadence' in connection with this last work. This is the moment to recall that the great masters, whether poets or painters, Hugo or Delacroix, are always several years ahead of their timid admirers.

'In relation to genius, the public is like a slow-running clock. Who among the ranks of the discerning does not understand that the master's very first picture contained all his others in embryo? But that he should be ceaselessly perfecting and diligently sharpening his natural gifts, that he should extract new effects from them and should himself drive his nature to its utmost limits—that is inevitable, foredoomed and worthy of praise. The principal characteristic of Delacroix's genius is precisely the fact that he knows not decadence; he only displays progress. The only thing is that his original qualities were so forceful and so rich, and they have left such a powerful impression upon even the most commonplace of minds, that day-

[1] See pl. 28.

[2] The following passage is taken from an article published in the *Revue Fantaisiste*, 15 September 1861. The remainder of the article—little more than a description of the paintings—was published in *L'Art Romantique* as 'Peintures murales d'Eugène Delacroix à Saint-Sulpice'.

to-day progress is imperceptible for the majority; it is only the dialecticians of art that can discern it clearly.

'I spoke a moment ago of the remarks of certain *bricklayers*.[1] By this word I wish to characterize that class of heavy and boorish spirits (their number is legion) who appraise objects solely by their contour, or worse still, by their three dimensions, length, breadth and height—for all the world like savages and rustics. I have often heard people of that kind laying down a hierarchy of qualities which to me was absolutely unintelligible; I have heard them declare, for example, that the faculty that enables one man to produce an exact contour, or another a contour of a supernatural beauty, is superior to the faculty whose skill it is to make an enchanting assemblage of *colours*.[2] According to those people, colour has no power to dream, to think or to speak. It would seem that when I contemplate the works of one of those men who are specifically called 'colourists', I am giving myself up to a pleasure whose nature is far from a noble one; they would be delighted to call me 'materialistic', reserving for themselves the aristocratic title of 'spiritual'.

'It seems not to have occurred to those superficial minds that the two faculties can never be entirely separated, and that they are both of them the result of an original seed that has been carefully cultivated. External nature does nothing more than provide the artist with a constantly-renewed opportunity of cultivating that seed; it is nothing but an incoherent heap of raw materials which the artist is invited to group together and put in order—a stimulant, a kind of alarum for the slumbering faculties. Strictly speaking there is neither line nor colour in nature. It is man that creates line and colour. They are twin abstractions which derive their equal status from their common origin.

'A born draughtsman (I am thinking of him as a child) observes in nature, whether at rest or in motion, certain undulations from which he derives a certain thrill of pleasure, and which he amuses

[1] The French word *maçon* is sometimes used in such a figurative sense, to denote crass stupidity of one kind or another.

[2] Although the text as originally printed in the *Revue Fantaisiste* reads 'couleurs' at this point, until very recently all editions of *L'Art Romantique* have contained the obvious misprint 'contours'.

himself in fixing by means of lines on paper, exaggerating or moderating their inflexions at his will. He learns thus to achieve stylishness, elegance and character in drawing. But now let us imagine a child who is destined to excel in that department of art which is called colour; it is the collision or the happy marriage of two tones, and his own pleasure resulting therefrom, that will lead him towards the infinite science of tonal combinations. In neither case has nature been other than a pure *excitant.*

'Line and colour both of them have the power to set one thinking and dreaming; the pleasures which spring from them are of different natures, but of a perfect equality and absolutely independent of the subject of the picture.

'A picture by Delacroix will already have quickened you with a thrill of supernatural pleasure even if it be situated too far away for you to be able to judge of its linear graces or the more or less dramatic quality of its subject. You feel as though a magical atmosphere has advanced towards you and already envelops you. This impression, which combines gloom with sweetness, light with tranquillity—this impression, which has taken its place once and for all in your memory, is certain proof of the true, the perfect colourist. And when you come closer and analyse the subject, nothing will be deducted from, or added to, that original pleasure, for its source lies elsewhere and far away from any material thought.

'Let me reverse my example. A well-drawn figure fills you with a pleasure which is absolutely divorced from its subject. Whether voluptuous or awe-inspiring, this figure will owe its entire charm to the arabesque which it cuts in space. So long as it is skilfully drawn, there is nothing—from the limbs of a martyr who is being flayed alive, to the body of a swooning nymph—that does not admit of a kind of pleasure in whose elements the subject-matter plays no part. If it is otherwise with you, I shall be forced to believe that you are either a butcher or a rake.

'But alas! what is the good of continually repeating these idle truths?'

But perhaps, Sir, your readers will set much less store upon all this rhetoric than upon the details which I myself am impatient to give them concerning the person and the habits of our late-lamented genius.

IV

It is Eugène Delacroix's writings[1] above all that reveal that duality of nature which I have mentioned. I need hardly remind you, Sir, that many people were astonished at the sagacity of his written opinions and at the moderation of his style, some finding this a matter for regret, and others for approval. The *Variations du Beau*, the studies on Poussin, Prud'hon and Charlet, and other pieces published either in *L'Artiste* (whose proprietor at that time was M. Ricourt) or in the *Revue des Deux-Mondes*, only go to confirm that two-sidedness of great artists which drives them, as critics, to praise and to analyse more zestfully those qualities which, in their capacity as creators, they need the most, and which form a kind of antithesis to those they already possess in superabundance. If Eugène Delacroix had praised and magnified the qualities which we admire pre-eminently in him—his violence and abruptness in gesture, his turbulence of composition and the magic of his colour—that would indeed have been a matter for astonishment. Why look for what one already has almost to excess? and how can one fail to praise what seems rarer and more difficult to acquire? You will always observe the same phenomenon occurring with creative geniuses, be they painters or writers, whensoever they apply their faculties to criticism. At the time of the great struggle between the two schools, the Classic and the Romantic, simple souls were amazed to hear Eugène Delacroix ceaselessly extolling Racine, La Fontaine and Boileau. I could name a poet, by nature always stormy and restless, whom a line of Malherbe, with its balanced and symmetrical melody, will throw into long ecstasies.

Nevertheless, however judicious, however sound, however compact of expression and intention we find the great painter's literary fragments, it would be absurd to suppose that they were written easily or with the bold assurance of his brush. His feeling of confidence that he was *writing* what he really thought about a canvas was always balanced by his concern that he was not able to *paint* his thoughts upon the paper. 'The pen,' he used often to say, 'is not my tool. I am conscious of the justness of my thought, but the need for order, to which I am obliged to submit, I find quite terrifying. Would you believe it, but the necessity

[1] The articles mentioned below by Baudelaire are included in the two volumes of *Oeuvres Littéraires d'Eugène Delacroix* (Paris 1923).

of writing a page gives me a sick headache!' It is this awkwardness, which results from lack of practice, that may perhaps explain certain slightly threadbare forms of words—outworn clichés, even—which too often escaped this naturally distinguished pen.

The most manifest characteristic of Delacroix's style is its concision and a kind of unobtrusive intensity—the customary result of a concentration of the entire mental powers upon a given point. 'The hero is he who is immovably centred,' says the transatlantic moralist, Emerson,[1] who, in spite of his reputation as the leader of the wearisome Bostonian school, has nevertheless a certain flavour of Seneca about him, which effectively stimulates meditation. 'The hero is he who is immovably centred.' But this maxim, which the leader of American *Transcendentalism* applies to the conduct of life and the sphere of business, can equally well be applied to the sphere of poetry and art. You might equally well say, 'The literary hero, i.e. the true writer, is he who is immovably centred.' It will therefore hardly seem surprising to you, Sir, when I tell you that Delacroix had a very marked sympathy for concise and concentrated writers—for writers whose simple, unadorned prose seems to imitate the swift movements of thought, and whose sentences are like gestures—Montesquieu, for example. Let me offer you a curious example of this pregnant and poetic brevity. Like me, you must recently have read a very admirable and interesting study by M. Paul de Saint-Victor on the ceiling of the Galerie d'Apollon. It appeared in *La Presse*.[2] The various different conceptions of the flood, the way in which the legends relating to the flood should be interpreted, the moral significance of the episodes and actions which make up the ensemble of that wonderful picture—everything was there; and the picture itself was minutely described in that delightful style, as witty as it is highly-coloured, of which the author has already shown us so many samples. And yet all this will leave no more than a shadowy phantom in the memory—like something dimly seen through a telescope. Now compare that vast essay with the following few lines which, in my opinion, are much more forceful and much better adapted to conjure up a picture, even assuming that the picture which they summarize did not already exist. I am simply copying the programme which M. Delacroix distributed to his friends when he invited them to inspect the work in question:

[1] In the *Conduct of Life*, 'Considerations by the Way' (*Prose Works*, Boston 1870, vol. II, p. 463).
[2] 13 September 1863.

APOLLO VICTORIOUS OVER THE SERPENT PYTHON

'Mounted upon his chariot, the god has already shot a portion of his arrows; his sister Diana is flying at his heels and holding his quiver out to him. Already transfixed by the shafts of the god of warmth and life, the bloody monster writhes as it breathes forth the last remnants of its life and impotent rage in a flaming cloud. The waters of the flood are beginning to run dry, leaving the bodies of men and animals upon the mountain-tops, or sweeping them away with it. The gods are wrathful to see the earth abandoned to misshapen monsters, foul products of the primeval slime. Like Apollo, they have taken up arms; Minerva and Mercury leap forth to their destruction, until the time comes for eternal Wisdom to repeople the solitude of the universe. Hercules is crushing them with his club; Vulcan, the god of fire, is driving the night and the foul mists before him, while Boreas and the Zephyrs dry up the waters with their breath and finally dispel the clouds. The nymphs of the rivers and the streams have regained their reedy bed and their urn, still soiled by filth and débris. A few of the more timid divinities are standing aside and watching this combat between the gods and the elements. Meanwhile from the summit of the heavens Victory is flying down to crown Apollo the conqueror, and Iris, the messenger of the gods, is unfolding her veil in the airs—a symbol of the triumph of light over darkness and the revolt of the waters.'[1]

I know that the reader will be obliged to use his imagination a great deal—to collaborate, so to speak, with the author of the note. But do you really think, Sir, that my admiration for the painter is making me see visions in this matter? Tell me, am I totally mistaken in pretending to discover here the evidence of aristocratic habits acquired in good reading, and of that rectitude of thought which has enabled men of rank, soldiers, adventurers, or even simple courtiers, to write—sometimes even to *dash off*—very excellent books which even we, who are writers by trade, are constrained to admire?

V

EUGÈNE DELACROIX was a curious mixture of scepticism, politeness, dandyism, burning determination, craftiness, despotism, and finally of

[1] See pl. 29

a sort of personal kindness and tempered warmth which always accompanies genius. His father belonged to that race of strong men of whom we knew the last in our childhood—half of them fervent apostles of Jean-Jacques, and the other half resolute disciples of Voltaire, though they all collaborated with an equal zeal in the French Revolution, and their survivors, whether Jacobins or Cordeliers, all rallied with a perfect integrity (it is important to note) to the aims of Bonaparte.

Eugène Delacroix never lost the traces of his revolutionary origin. It may be said of him, as of Stendhal, that he had a great dread of being made a fool of. Sceptical and aristocratic, he only knew passion and the supernatural through his forced intimacy with the world of dreams. A hater of the masses, he really only thought of them as iconoclasts, and the acts of violence perpetrated upon several of his works in 1848[1] were ill-suited to convert him to the political sentimentalism of our times. There was even something of Victor Jacquemont[2] about him, as regards style, manners and opinions. I know that the comparison is just a little offensive, and therefore I should only wish it to be applied with an extreme discretion; for there is a touch of the rebellious bourgeois wit in Jacquemont—a kind of churlish sarcasm which is just as likely to mystify the ministers of Brahma as those of Jesus Christ, while Delacroix, cautioned by the *taste* which is always inherent in genius, could never fall into such vulgar crudities. My comparison only relates therefore to the sense of prudence and sobriety which characterized them both. In the same way, the hereditary marks which the eighteenth century had left upon his nature seemed to have been borrowed above all from that class which is just as far removed from the utopians as from the fanatics—I mean from the class of the polished sceptics, the victors and the survivors, who, generally speaking, stemmed more from Voltaire than from Jean-Jacques. And so, at first glance Eugène Delacroix simply gave the impression of an *enlightened* man, in the honorable acceptance of the word—of a perfect *gentleman*,[3] with neither prejudices nor passions. It was only by seeking his company more assiduously that one could penetrate beneath the varnish, and guess at the hidden corners

[1] His *Richelieu disant la Messe* was destroyed in the Palais-Royal, and his *Corps de garde marocain* was somewhat damaged at the Tuileries.

[2] The botanist and traveller, who visited America and India. He was well known through the two volumes of his correspondence which were published in 1834, two years after his death. See David Stacton, *A Ride on a Tiger* (London 1954).

[3] This word is used in the original.

of his soul. A man to whom one could compare him more justly, both in his outward appearance and in his manners, would be M. Mérimée.[1] There we find the same apparent, slightly affected, coldness, the same icy mantle which cloaked a bashful sensitivity and a burning passion for the good and the beautiful; beneath the same hypocritical pretence of egotism, we find the same devotion to his private friends and his pet ideas.

There was much of the *savage* in Eugène Delacroix—this was in fact the most precious part of his soul, the part which was entirely dedicated to the painting of his dreams and to the worship of his art. There was also much of the man of the world; that part was destined to disguise and excuse the other. It was, I think, one of the great concerns of his life to conceal the rages of his heart and not to seem to be a man of genius. His spirit of dominance, which was quite legitimate and even a part of his destiny, had almost entirely disappeared beneath a thousand kindnesses. You might have called him a volcanic crater artistically concealed behind bouquets of flowers.

Another feature of resemblance with Stendhal was his propensity for simple formulas, brief maxims for the proper conduct of life. Like all men whose passion for method is all the more intense as their ardent and sensitive temperaments seem to deflect them from it, Delacroix loved to construct those little catechisms of practical morality which the thoughtless and the idle (who practise nothing) would scornfully attribute to M. de la Palisse,[2] but which genius does not despise, because genius is allied with simplicity—I mean sound, strong, simple and firm maxims, which serve as buckler and cuirass to the man whom the fatality of his genius hurls into an endless battle.

Need I tell you that the same spirit of inflexible and contemptuous wisdom inspired M. Delacroix's opinions in political matters also? He believed that nothing changes, although everything appears to change, and that certain climacteric moments in the history of the nations will invariably bring with them analogous phenomena. On the whole, his thinking in matters of this kind came very close (particularly in its attitude of cold and sorrowful resignation) to the thinking of a historian for whom I for my part have a quite special respect, and whom you, Sir, who are so perfectly familiar with these arguments, and know how to

[1] Baudelaire's admiration for Mérimée was not reciprocated.

[2] The phrase 'une vérité de la Palisse' means a stale truism.

assess talent even when it contradicts you, must have felt constrained to admire more than once, I feel sure. I am referring to M. Ferrari,[1] the subtle and learned author of the *Histoire de la raison d'Etat*. And so the speaker who, in M. Delacroix's presence, gave way to childish utopian enthusiasms had very soon to suffer the effect of his bitter laugh, shot through with a sarcastic pity; and if anyone was imprudent enough in his company to launch forth the great chimera of modern times, the monster-balloon of perfectibility and indefinite progress, he would be swift to ask, 'Where then are your Pheidiases? where are your Raphaels?'

Be assured, however, that this gruff good sense did not divest M. Delacroix of any of his graces. This zest of incredulity, and this refusal to be taken in, seasoned his conversation—already so poetic and so colourful—like a dash of Byronic salt. He owed also to himself, far more than to his long familiarity with the world of society—to himself, that is to his genius and the consciousness of his genius—a sureness, a marvellous ease of manner, combined with a politeness which, like a prism, admitted every nuance, from the most cordial good nature to the most irreproachable rudeness. He possessed quite twenty different ways of uttering the words '*mon cher Monsieur*', which, for a practised ear, represented an interesting range of sentiments. For finally it must be said—since to me this seems but one more reason for praise—that Eugène Delacroix, for all that he was a man of genius, or *because* he was a man of *complete* genius, had much of the dandy about him. He himself used to admit that in his youth he had thrown himself with delight into the most material vanities of dandyism, and he used to tell with a smile, but not without a certain touch of conceit, how, with the collaboration of his friend Bonington, he had laboured energetically to introduce a taste for English cut in clothes and shoes among the youth of fashion. I take it that this will not seem to you an idle detail, for there is no such thing as a superfluous detail when one has the nature of certain men to portray.

I have told you that what most struck the attentive observer was the *natural* part of Delacroix's soul, in spite of the softening veil of a civilized refinement. He was all energy, but energy which sprang from the nerves and from the will—for physically he was frail and delicate. The tiger intent upon his prey has eyes less bright and muscles less impatiently

[1] Giuseppe Ferrari (1811–76), philosopher, politician, and editor of Vico. His *Histoire de la Raison d'Etat* was published in Paris in 1860.

25. EUGENE LAMI: *Portrait of Delacroix*. Water-colour after a pastel by Eugène Giraud. France, Private Collection.

26. DELACROIX: *The Massacre at Chios.* Oil on canvas. Paris, Louvre.

27. DELACROIX: *The Death of Sardanapalus* (detail). Oil on canvas. Paris, Louvre.

28. DELACROIX: *The Expulsion of Heliodorus from the Temple.* Wall painting. Paris, Church of St. Sulpice.

29. DELACROIX: *Apollo Victorious over the Serpent Python*. Sketch. Brussels, Musée des Beaux-Arts.

30. DELACROIX: *Study for the Figure of Liberty*. Pencil. Paris, Louvre.

31. DELACROIX: *Portrait of Jenny Le Guillou.* Oil on canvas. Paris, Louvre.

32. MEISSONIER: *The Barricade*. Oil on canvas. Paris. Louvre.

a-quiver than could be observed when the whole spiritual being of our great painter was hurled upon an idea or was struggling to possess itself of a dream. Even the physical character of his countenance, his Peruvian or Malay-like colouring, his great black eyes (which, however, the blinkings of concentration made appear smaller, so that they seemed to do no more than *sip* at the light), his abundant and glossy hair, his stubborn brow, his tight lips, to which an unceasing tension of will gave an expression of cruelty—his whole being, in short, suggested the idea of an exotic origin. More than once, when looking at him, I have found myself thinking of those ancient rulers of Mexico, of Montezuma, whose hand, with sacrificial skill, could immolate three thousand human creatures in a single day upon the pyramidal altar of the Sun, or perhaps of some oriental potentate who, amid the splendours of the most brilliant of feasts, betrays in the depths of his eyes a kind of unsatisfied craving and an inscrutable nostalgia—something like the memory and the regret of things not known. I would ask you to observe too that even the general colour of Delacroix's pictures has something of the colour proper to oriental landscapes and interiors, and that it produces a somewhat similar impression to that which is experienced in tropical lands by a sensitive eye; I mean that there, in spite of the intensity of local tones, the immense diffusion of light creates a general effect which is almost crepuscular. The *morality* of his works—if it is at all permissible to speak of ethics in painting—is also visibly marked with Molochism. His works contain nothing but devastation, massacres, conflagrations; everything bears witness against the eternal and incorrigible barbarity of man. Burnt and smoking cities, slaughtered victims, ravished women, the very children cast beneath the hooves of horses or menaced by the dagger of a distracted mother—the whole body of this painter's works, I say, is like a terrible hymn composed in honour of destiny and irremediable anguish. Occasionally he found it possible to devote his brush to the expression of tender and voluptuous feelings—for certainly he was not lacking in tenderness; but even into these works an incurable bitterness was infused in strong measure, and carelessness and joy—the usual companions of simple pleasure—were absent from them. Once only, I believe, did he make an experiment in the role of clown or comedian, and as though he had guessed that this was both beyond and below his nature, he never more returned to it.[1]

[1] Delacroix published a few lithographic caricatures in *Le Miroir* in 1821.

6

VI

I KNOW several people who have a right to say '*Odi profanum vulgus*'; but which among them can triumphantly add '*et arceo*'? Too much hand-shaking tends to cheapen the character. But if ever a man had an *ivory tower*, well protected by locks and bolts, that man was Eugène Delacroix. And who has ever had a greater love for his *ivory tower*—that is, for his privacy? He would even, I believe, have liked to arm it with artillery and transport it bodily into a forest or to the top of an inaccessible rock! Who has had a greater love for the *home*[1]—both sanctuary and den? As others seek privacy for their debauches, he sought it for inspiration, and once he had gained it, he would give himself up to veritable drunken orgies of work. 'The one prudence in life is concentration; the one evil is dissipation,' says the American philosopher whom we have already quoted.[2]

M. Delacroix might almost have written that maxim; but certainly he austerely practised it. He was too much a man of the world not to scorn the world; and the efforts to which he went in order not to be too visibly *himself* drove him naturally to prefer our society. The word 'our' is not intended to imply only the humble author of these lines, but others as well, young or old, journalists, poets and musicians, in whose company he could freely relax and be himself.

In his delightful study of Chopin, Liszt puts Delacroix among the poet-musician's most assiduous visitors, and tells how he loved to fall into deep reverie at the strains of that tenuous and impassioned music which is like a brilliant bird fluttering above the horrors of an abyss.

That is how it came about that, thanks to the sincerity of our admiration, we were able, though still very young, to penetrate the fortifications of that studio where, in spite of the rigours of our climate, an equatorial temperature prevailed, and where the eye was immediately struck by a sober solemnity and by the classic austerity of the old school. We had seen such studios in our childhood, belonging to the late rivals of David—those touching heroes long since departed. One felt instinctively that this retreat could not be the habitation of a frivolous mind, titillated by a thousand incoherent fancies.

There were no rusty panoplies to be seen there, not a single Malayan

[1] This word is used in the original.

[2] In the *Conduct of Life*, 'Power' (p. 353).

kris, no ancient Gothic scrap-iron, no jewellery, no old clothes, no bric-à-brac, nothing of what indicts its owner of a taste for toys and the desultory wanderings of childish day-dreaming. A marvellous portrait by Jordaens, which he had unearthed somewhere or other, and several studies and copies, made by the master himself, sufficed to decorate that vast studio, in which a softened and subdued light illumined self-communion.

These copies will probably be seen at the sale of Delacroix's drawings and pictures which is fixed, I am told, for next January.[1] He had two very distinct manners of copying. The first, which was broad and free, was a mixture of fidelity and betrayal of the model, and into this he put much of himself. The result of this method was a fascinating mongrel-compound which threw the mind into a state of delightful uncertainty. It is in that paradoxical light that I remember a large copy of Rubens's *Miracles of St Benedict*.[2] In his other manner Delacroix made himself the humblest and most obedient slave of his model, and he achieved an exactness of imitation of which those who have not seen these miracles may well be incredulous. Such, for example, are the copies which he made after two heads by Raphael[3] in the Louvre—copies in which expression, style and manner are imitated with such a perfect simplicity that one could reciprocally and in turn mistake the originals for the translations.

After a luncheon lighter than an Arab's, and with his palette arranged with the meticulous care of a florist or a cloth-merchant, Delacroix would set himself to grapple with the interrupted idea; but before launching out into his stormy task, he often experienced those feelings of languor, fear and prostration which make one think of the Pythoness fleeing the god, or which remind one of Jean-Jacques Rousseau dilly-dallying, rummaging among his papers and turning over his books for an hour before attacking paper with pen. But as soon as the artist's special magic had started to work, he never stopped until overcome by physical fatigue.

One day, when we happened to be talking about that question which always has such an interest for artists and writers—I mean, about the *hygienics* of work and the conduct of life—he said to me:

'Formerly, in my youth, I was unable to get down to work unless I had the promise of some pleasure for the evening—some music,

[1] In fact it took place in February 1864. [2] Now in the Brussels Museum.
[3] Robaut lists three such copies; nos. 1925–7.

dancing, or any other conceivable diversion. But today I have ceased to be like a schoolboy, and I can work without stopping and without any hope of reward. And then (he added), if only you knew how unremitting work makes one indulgent and easy to satisfy where pleasures are concerned! The man who has filled his day well will be prepared to find a sufficiency of wit even in the local postman, and will be quite content to spend his evening playing cards with him!'

This remark made me think of Machiavelli playing dice with the peasants. Now one day (a Sunday it was) I caught sight of Delacroix at the Louvre in the company of his old servant,[1] she who so devotedly looked after and cared for him for thirty years; and he, the elegant, the exquisite, the erudite, was not too proud to point out and to explain the mysteries of Assyrian sculpture to that excellent woman, who, moreover, was listening to him with an artless concentration. The memory of Machiavelli and of our former conversation leapt immediately into my mind.

The truth is that during his latter years everything that one normally calls pleasure had vanished from his life, having all been replaced by a single harsh, exacting, terrible pleasure, namely *work*, which by that time was not merely a passion but might properly have been called a madness.

After having dedicated the hours of the day to painting, either in his studio or upon the scaffolding whither he was summoned by his great decorative tasks, Delacroix found strength yet remaining in his love of art, and he would have judged that day ill-filled if the evening hours had not been employed at the fire-side, by lamp-light, in drawing, in covering paper with dreams, ideas, or figures half-glimpsed amid the random accidents of life, and sometimes in copying drawings by other artists whose temperament was as far as possible removed from his own; for he had a passion for notes, for sketches, and he gave himself up to it wherever he happened to be. For quite a long time he made a habit of drawing at the house of friends to whom he went to spend his evenings. That is how it comes about that M. Villot[2] possesses a considerable quantity of drawings from that fertile pen.

He once said to a young man of my acquaintance: 'If you have not sufficient skill to make a sketch of a man throwing himself out of a

[1] There is a portrait by Delacroix of his servant, Jenny le Guillou, in the Louvre; see pl. 31.

[2] Delacroix's Journals contain many references to his friend Frédéric Villot.

window, in the time that it takes him to fall from the fourth floor to the ground, you will never be capable of producing great *machines*.' This enormous hyperbole seems to me to contain the major concern of his whole life, which was, as is well known, to achieve an execution quick and sure enough to prevent the smallest particle of the intensity of action or idea from evaporating.

Delacroix was, as many others have been in a position to observe, a man of conversation. But the humorous side of it is that he was as frightened of conversation as he was of a debauch, a dissipation in which he ran the risk of wasting his strength. When you entered into his presence he began by saying:

'I think perhaps that we had better not talk this morning, don't you? or only a very, very little.'

And then he would chatter away for three hours! His talk was brilliant and subtle, but full of facts, memories and anecdotes—in short, 'the word that nourisheth'.

When he was roused by contradiction, he drew back momentarily, and instead of a frontal assault upon his adversary (a thing which runs the risk of introducing the brutalities of the hustings into the skirmishes of the drawing-room), he played for some time with him, and then returned to the attack with unexpected arguments or facts. It was indeed the conversation of a man who loved a tussle, but was the slave of courtesy, shrewd, giving way on purpose, and full of sudden feints and attacks.

In the intimacy of his studio he freely relaxed so far as to deliver his opinions upon his contemporaries, and it was on these occasions that we often had to admire that special forbearance of genius which derives perhaps from a particular kind of simplicity or of readiness to appreciate.

He had an astonishing weakness for Decamps, who today has fallen very low, but who doubtless was still enthroned in his mind through the power of memory. And the same for Charlet. He once sent for me to come and see him on purpose to rap me sharply over the knuckles about a disrespectful article[1] that I had perpetrated on the subject of that spoiled child of chauvinism. In vain did I try to explain to him that it was not the Charlet of the early days that I was censuring, but the Charlet of the decadence—not the noble historian of the old campaigners, but the tavern-wit. But I never managed to win my pardon.

[1] See pp. 168-171.

He admired Ingres in certain of his aspects, and assuredly he must have had great critical stamina to admire by reason what he can only have rejected by temperament. He even carefully copied some photographs which had been made of a few of those meticulous pencil-portraits in which we see the relentless and searching talent of M. Ingres at its best, for he is all the more resourceful as he is the more cramped for space.

Horace Vernet's detestable colour did not prevent him from feeling the personal potentiality with which most of his pictures are charged, and he hit upon some amazing expressions in order to praise their scintillation and their indefatigable passion. His admiration for Meissonier went a little too far. He had appropriated, almost by violence, the drawings which had been used in the preparation of *La Barricade*,[1] the best picture of an artist whose talent, nevertheless, finds far more energetic expression with the simple pencil than with the brush. Of Meissonier he often used to say, as though anxiously dreaming of the future, 'After all, he is the most certain of us all to live!' Is it not strange to see the author of such great works showing something very like jealousy of the man who only excels in small ones?

The only man whose name had the power to wring an abusive word or two from those aristocratic lips was Paul Delaroche. In that man's works there was obviously not a single extenuating circumstance to be found, and he never rid himself of the memory of the distress which had been caused him by all that sour and muddy painting, executed with 'ink and boot-polish', as Théophile Gautier once observed in an unusual access of independence.

But his favourite choice as his travelling-companion on vast *exiles* of talk was the man who resembled him least of all in talent as in ideas, his veritable opposite pole—a man who has not yet received all the justice which is his due, and whose brain, although as fog-ridden as the fuliginous sky of his native city, contains a whole host of admirable things. I am describing M. Paul Chenavard.[2]

The abstruse theories of the painter-philosopher of Lyons made Delacroix smile; and that doctrinaire pedagogue held the sensuous pleasures of pure painting to be frivolous, if not blameworthy things. But however remote they may have been from one another, or precisely

[1] Now in the Louvre; see pl. 32.

[2] On Chenavard, see pp. 207ff.

because of that remoteness, they loved to set course for one another, until, like two vessels secured by grappling-irons, they could no longer part company. Both of them, moreover, being highly educated and endowed with a remarkable sense of sociability, met together on the common ground of erudition. It is well known that generally speaking this is not the quality for which artists are conspicuous.

Chenavard was thus a precious resource for Delacroix. It was a real pleasure to watch them set to in innocent struggle, the words of the one marching ponderously like an elephant in full panoply of war, and those of the other quivering like a fencing-foil, equally keen and flexible. During the last hours of his life our great painter expressed the desire to shake the hand of his friendly sparring-partner once more. But he was far from Paris at that time.

VII

SENTIMENTAL and affected women will perhaps be shocked to learn that, like Michelangelo (may I remind you that one of his sonnets ends with the words 'Sculpture! divine Sculpture! thou art my only love!'), Delacroix had made painting his unique muse, his exclusive mistress, his sole and sufficient pleasure.

No doubt he had loved woman greatly in the troubled hours of his youth. Who among us has not sacrificed too much to that formidable idol? And who does not know that it is precisely those that have served her the best that complain of her the most? But a long time before his death he had already excluded woman from his life. Had he been a Mohammedan, he would not perhaps have gone so far as to drive her out of his mosques, but he would have been amazed to see her entering them, not being quite able to understand what sort of converse she could have with Allah.

In this question, as in many others, the oriental idea dominated him keenly and tyrannically. He regarded woman as an object of art, delightful and well suited to excite the mind, but disobedient and disturbing once one throws open the door of one's heart to her, and gluttonously devouring of time and strength.

I remember that once we were in a public place, when I pointed out to him the face of a woman marked with an original beauty and a melancholy character; he was very anxious to be appreciative, but instead, to be self-consistent, he asked with his little laugh, 'How on earth could a woman be melancholy?', doubtless insinuating thereby that, when it comes to understanding the sentiment of melancholia, woman is lacking in some essential ingredient.

This, unfortunately, is a highly insulting theory, and I certainly would not want to advocate defamatory opinions upon a sex which has often exhibited glowing virtues. But you will surely allow that it is a *prudential* theory; and further, that talent could not be too well armed with prudence in a world that is full of ambushes, and that the man of genius is privileged to hold certain doctrines (so long as they are not subversive of order) which would rightly scandalize us in a mere citizen or a simple family man.

At the risk of casting a shadow upon his memory in the estimation of elegiac souls, perhaps I ought to add that neither did he show any affectionate partiality for childhood. He never thought of children except with jam-smeared hands (a thing that dirties canvas and paper), or beating a drum (a thing that interrupts meditation), or as incendiaries and animally dangerous creatures like monkeys.

'I remember very well (he used to say sometimes) that when I was a child, *I was a monster*. The understanding of duty is only acquired very slowly, and it is by nothing less than by pain, chastisement and the progressive exercise of reason that man can gradually diminish his natural wickedness.'

Thus, by the road of simple good sense he reverted towards the Catholic idea. For it is true to say that, generally speaking, the child, in relation to the man, is much closer to original sin.

VIII

YOU WOULD have thought that Delacroix had reserved his entire sensibility, which was manly and deep, for the austere sentiment of friendship. There are people who become easily attached to the first comer; others reserve the use of the divine faculty for great occasions. If he had no love of being bothered over trifles, the famous man about whom I am now talking to you with so much pleasure knew how to be a courageous and zealous ally when important matters were in question. Those who knew him well have had many an opportunity of appreciating his positively English loyalty, punctiliousness and stability in social relations. If he was exacting to others, he was no less severe upon himself.

It is sad and distressing to me to have to say a few words about certain accusations that have been brought against Eugène Delacroix. I have heard people taxing him with egotism and even with avarice. I would ask you to observe, Sir, that this reproach is always directed by the countless tribe of commonplace souls against those that endeavour to bestow their generosity with as much care as their friendship.

Delacroix was very economical; for him it was the only way of being, on occasion, very generous. I could prove this with several examples, but I would hesitate to do so without having been authorized by him, any more than by those who have had good reason to thank him.

Please observe too that for many a long year his paintings sold very badly, and that his decorative works ate up almost the whole of his salary, when he did not actually have to dip into his own purse. He gave innumerable proofs of his scorn for money when needy artists revealed a desire to possess one of his works. Then, like those liberal and generous-minded doctors who sometimes expect to be paid for their professional services, and sometimes give them free, he would give away his pictures, or part with them at a nominal price.

Finally, Sir, we must remember that the superior man, more than any other, is obliged to have an eye to his personal defences. It might be said that the whole of society is at war with him. We have had more than one opportunity of confirming this. His courtesy is called coldness; his irony, however much he may have softened it, is interpreted as spitefulness; and his economy, as avarice. But if, on the other hand, the poor creature turns out to be improvident, society will say, 'Quite right too! His penury is a punishment for his prodigality.'

I am able to assert that, so far as money and economy were concerned, Delacroix completely shared the opinion of Stendhal—an opinion which reconciles greatness and prudence.

'The sensible man,' said Stendhal, 'must devote himself to acquiring what is strictly necessary to him in order not to be dependent upon anyone (in Stendhal's time, this meant an income of 6,000 francs); but if, once he has achieved this security, he wastes his time increasing his fortune, he is a scoundrel.'[1]

[1] See Stendhal *De l'Amour* (Lévy edition), p. 193.

Pursuit of the essential, and scorn of the superfluous—that is the conduct of a wise man and a Stoic.

One of our painter's greatest concerns during his last years was the judgement of posterity and the uncertain durability of his works. One moment his ever-sensitive imagination would take fire at the idea of an immortal glory, and then he would speak with bitterness of the fragility of canvases and colours. At other times he would enviously cite the old masters who almost all of them had the good fortune to be translated by skilful engravers whose needle or burin had learnt to adapt itself to the nature of their talent, and he keenly regretted that he had not found his own translator. This friability of the painted work, as compared with the stability of the printed work, was one of his habitual themes of conversation.

When this man, who was so frail and so stubborn, so highly-strung and so courageous; this man, who was unique in the history of European art; the sickly and sensitive artist who never ceased to dream of covering walls with his grandiose conceptions—when this man, I say, was carried off by one of those inflammations of the lung, of which, it seems, he had a convulsive foreboding, we all of us felt something approximating to that depression of soul, that sensation of growing solitude which the death of Chateaubriand and that of Balzac had already made familiar to us—a sensation which was quite recently renewed by the death of Alfred de Vigny.[1] A great national sorrow brings with it a lowering of general vitality; a clouding of the intellect which is like an eclipse of the sun; a momentary imitation of the end of the world.

I believe however that this impression is chiefly confined to those proud anchorites who can only make themselves a family by means of intellectual relations. As for the rest of the community, it is only gradually that they most of them learn to realize the full extent of their country's loss in losing its great man, and to appreciate what an empty space he has left behind him. And yet it is only right to warn them.

I thank you, Sir, with all my heart for having been so kind as to allow me to say freely all that was suggested to my mind by the memory of one of the rare geniuses of our unhappy age—an age at once so poor and so rich, an age at times too exacting, at times too indulgent—and too often unjust.

[1] Chateaubriand had died in 1848, Balzac in 1850, and Vigny only a few months before Delacroix.

EDGAR ALLAN POE

HIS LIFE AND WORKS

. . . some unhappy master whom unmerciful Disaster
Followed fast and followed faster till his songs one burden bore—
Till the dirges of his Hope that melancholy burden bore—
Of 'Never—nevermore'.

Edgar Allan Poe, *The Raven*

Sur son trône d'airain le Destin, qui s'en raille,
Imbibe leur éponge avec du fiel amer,
Et la Nécessité les tord dans sa tenaille.

Théophile Gautier, *Ténèbres*

I

NOT many years ago there appeared in one of our courts a poor wretch whose brow was tattooed with the following rare and curious device: *Never had a chance!* He was thus wearing upon his face the badge of his life, like a book its title, and the subsequent examination proved that this strange motto was only too cruelly truthful. Literary history has similar destinies to show us, examples of true damnation, men who go through life with the word 'jynx'[1] written in mysterious letters on the tortured lines of their foreheads. The blind angel of expiation has seized hold of them and mercilessly flogs them for the edification of others. In vain may their lives have talents, virtues or grace to show; Society reserves a special curse for them, denouncing those very weaknesses which have resulted from its own persecution.—To what lengths did not Hoffmann go to disarm fate, and what pains did not Balzac take to conjure fortune?—Are we to believe then in the existence of a diabolic Providence which for some brews misfortune from the cradle to the grave, *deliberately* hurling spiritual and angelic natures into hostile surroundings, like Christian martyrs into the circus? Are there then sacrificial souls, dedicated to the altar, doomed to walk to death

[1] The French word is 'guignon'. Readers of the *Fleurs du mal* will recall the sonnet of this title.

and glory through the débris of their own lives? Will these chosen spirits be eternally beset by the nightmare of *Ténèbres*?[1]—Vainly they struggle, vainly try to adapt themselves to the world, its tricks and cautions; let them perfect their vigilance, stop up every gap and bolster the windows against chance missiles: the Devil will enter through the keyhole; some perfection will turn out to be the weak spot in their breast-plate, a superlative quality the seed of their damnation.

> L'aigle, pour le briser, du haut du firmament
> Sur leur front découvert lâchera la tortue,
> Car *ils* doivent périr inévitablement.[2]

Their fate is written in the very tissue of their beings, it shines forth with a lurid brilliance in their glance and their gestures, it flows through their veins with each drop of their blood.

A well-known writer of our times[3] has published a book to show that there can be no proper place for the poet either in a democratic or an aristocratic society, no more in a republic than in an absolute or tempered monarchy. And has any one been able to answer him decisively? Today I offer a new legend in support of his thesis, I am adding a new saint to the martyrology; I have the story to tell of one of those glorious unfortunates, too rich in poetry and passion, who came into this lowly world, following in the footsteps of so many others, to perform the rude apprenticeship of genius among baser spirits.

What a lamentable tragedy was the life of Edgar Poe! His death, a horrible consummation, whose horror is only enhanced by its triviality! —All the accounts that I have read have only helped to convince me that for Poe the United States were nought but a vast prison in which he ran about with the fevered restlessness of a creature born to breathe the air of a sweeter-scented world—nought but a great, gas-lit Barbary— and that his interior, spiritual life as poet, or even as drunkard, was no

[1] Gautier's poem was particularly admired by Baudelaire who, in his essay on the poet (not included here), described it as 'une prodigieuse symphonie' which sometimes reminded him of Beethoven. The quotation below is from this source.

[2] The following is a literal translation of these lines:

'From the heights of the heavens the eagle will drop the tortoise upon their unprotected brow, to shatter it, for *they* (Baudelaire's italics) must perish inevitably.'

In the next stanza the poet tells how the eagle misses its target and hits instead some antique statue which tumbles from its pedestal and crushes and kills them.

[3] Alfred de Vigny, who is explicitly named in the 1852 text; the book is clearly *Stello* (1832).

more than a perpetual effort to escape the influence of that antipathetic atmosphere. What a pitiless dictatorship is that of opinion in a democratic society! Ask of it neither charity nor indulgence, nor any sort of flexibility in the application of its laws to the multiple and complex issues of the moral life. You might think that the impious love of liberty had given birth to a new tyranny, a *bestial* tyranny, or zoocracy,[1] whose savage insensibility recalls the idol of Juggernaut. One biographer—and he is well-intentioned, the good fellow—will solemnly tell us that if Poe had been prepared to regularize his genius and apply his creative gifts in a manner more suited to the climate of America, he had it in him to become a 'money-making author';[2] another—a crude cynic, this one—tells us that however fine may have been his genius, it would have been better for him to have had no more than talent, talent always yielding easier returns than genius.[3] Yet another,[4] who has been a newspaper and magazine editor, and was a friend of the poet's, owns that it was difficult to employ him and that he had to be paid less than others, because he wrote in a style too far above the popular level. *Here we smell the shopkeeper!* as Joseph de Maistre[5] said.

Some became still bolder and, combining the dullest insensibility to his genius with the savagery of bourgeois hypocrisy, vied with one another in insulting him; after his sudden departure from this life, they gave the corpse a severe talking-to—Mr. Rufus Griswold[6] in particular who, to quote Mr. George Graham's[7] avenging words, took this opportunity to commit an act of immortal infamy. Feeling perhaps a sinister presentiment of his sudden end, Poe had appointed Messrs. Griswold and Willis to put his works in order, to write his life and

[1] A word that Baudelaire appears to have borrowed from Alphonse Rabbe.

[2] This phrase, which Baudelaire quotes in English, occurs in Daniel's review (p. 172) as follows: 'Had Mr. Poe possessed mere *talent*, even with his unfortunate moral constitution, he might have been a popular and money-making author.' See Bibliographical Note, p, xviii above.

[3] Perhaps James Russell Lowell (*Graham's Magazine*, February 1845).

[4] No doubt Willis, in his obituary article in the *Home Journal*, October 1849;—'Mr. Poe wrote with fastidious difficulty, and in a style too much above the popular level to be well paid.' See p. 81.

[5] In *Soirées de Saint-Pétersbourg, sixième entretien.*

[6] In a pseudonymous article (the 'Ludwig article') in the *New York Tribune*, 7 October 1849, which formed the basis of the *Memoir* referred to above.

[7] The proprietor of *Graham's Magazine*, of which Poe had been editor; his successor in the chair was Griswold. Graham published his 'Defence of Poe' in his magazine in 1850.

restore his memory. That pedagogue-vampire straightway proceeded to libel his friend at length, in an immense, banal and spiteful article which he printed at the beginning of the posthumous edition of his works.[1]—Is there no by-law then in America to prohibit dogs from entering cemeteries?—As for Mr. Willis, he proved on the contrary that kindness and decorum always go hand in hand with true perception, and that charity towards our fellows, besides being a moral duty, is also one of the dictates of taste.

If you talk to an American about Poe, he will perhaps admit his genius and may even show himself proud of it; but in a superior, sardonical tone which bespeaks the positivist, he will go on to speak of the poet's Bohemian life, his alcoholic breath which would have caught fire at a candle's flame, and his nomadic habits; he will tell you that he was an erratic and uncouth creature, an orbitless planet, ceaselessly on the move between Baltimore and New York, New York and Philadelphia, Philadelphia and Boston, Boston and Baltimore, Baltimore and Richmond. And if, with your heart stirred by the opening bars of this distressing story, you venture the opinion that the individual may not perhaps be solely to blame, and that it must be hard to think and write at one's ease in a country which has millions of rival sovereigns, a country without a capital,[2] properly speaking, and without an aristocracy—then you will see his eyes open wide and flash fire, you will see the spittle of suffering patriotism rise to his lips, and America, through his mouth, will start hurling insults at Europe, her old mother, and at the philosophy of bygone days.

The conclusion, I repeat, has been forced upon me that Poe and his country were not on a level. As a country, the United States is like a gigantic child, naturally jealous of the old continent. Proud of her material, abnormal and well-nigh monstrous development, this newcomer in

[1] There is a point of some, if minor, interest here. The Griswold *Memoir* was printed not at the beginning of the first posthumous edition of his works, but in the third volume (*The Literati*, 1850); in the subsequent edition it was placed *en tête* of the first volume. It appears therefore as if it were the 1853 edition, and not the earlier one, that Baudelaire was using—which is only worth pointing out as it corroborates Bandy's hypothesis that, when he published the first version of his article in 1852, Baudelaire had not read the *Memoir*.

[2] There may be an echo here from Lowell's article referred to above: 'The situation of American literature is anomalous. It has no centre. . . . Our capital city, unlike London or Paris, is not a great central heart. . . .'

history has a simple faith in the all-powerfulness of industry; like some unhappy spirits among us, she is convinced that Industry will end by gobbling up the Devil. Time and money have so great a value over there! Material activity, inflated to the proportions of a national form of madness, leaves the American mind with very little room for the things which are not of the earth. Poe, who was of good stock and who held moreover that his country's great disaster was to have no aristocracy of birth, granted, as he said, that among a people without an aristocracy the cult of Beauty could only be corrupted, cheapened and must finally disappear—Poe, who diagnosed even in the ostentatious and costly luxury of his fellow-citizens all the symptoms of bad taste which characterize the parvenu—Poe, who regarded Progress, that great idea of modern times, as an idiot's delight, and who called the 'perfections' of the human habitation 'scars' and 'rectangular obscenities'[1]—this man found himself singularly alone in America. He believed only in the unchangeable, the eternal, the 'self-same',[2] and—a thing which must be a cruel privilege in a society enamoured of itself!—he possessed that great Machiavellian common sense which marches ahead of the wise man, like a pillar of fire, across the desert of history. What would he have thought, what written, poor man, had he heard the lady-theologian of sentiment[3] doing away with Hell out of kindness for the human race, or the actuarial philosopher[4] proposing an insurance system, a subscription of a penny a head for the suppression of war—and the abolition of the death-penalty[5] and of orthography, those twin forms of madness!—and all those other hospital-cases of thought who, with their ears cocked to the wind, indulge in fantasies as flatulent as the element which dictates them?—If you add to this impeccable eye for Truth (which can be a true weakness in certain circumstances) an exquisite delicacy of perception which a false note tortured, a fineness of taste which all but exact proportion disgusted, and an insatiable love of Beauty which had assumed the potency of a morbid passion, you will hardly be surprised

[1] From the *Colloquy of Monos and Una.*

[2] In English in Baudelaire's text.

[3] George Sand; the point is developed with biting sarcasm in *Mon coeur mis à nu.*

[4] After a long note in which he lists the possible originals of the 'philosophe du chiffre', Crépet admits that he has not been able to identify him satisfactorily. He then tentatively suggests the journalist and politician, Emile de Girardin.

[5] 'The death-penalty is the expression of a mystical idea, totally misunderstood today. The death-penalty does not aim to *save* Society—at least not in the *material* sense. Its aim is to save (*spiritually*) Society and the guilty person. . . .' *Mon coeur mis à nu,* XLIII.

that for such a man life should have become a hell and that he should have ended unhappily; you will marvel rather that he should have been able to hold out for so long.

II

THE Poe family was among the most respectable in Baltimore. The poet's paternal grandfather had served as Quartermaster-general in the War of Independence, and La Fayette held him in high esteem and friendship. At the time of his last visit to the United States, the latter expressed a wish to see the General's widow and convey to her his gratitude for the services which her husband had rendered him. The poet's great-grandfather had married the daughter[1] of an English admiral named McBride, who was related to the noblest houses of England. David Poe, the father of Edgar and son of the Quartermaster-general, fell passionately in love with Elizabeth Arnold,[2] an English actress, famed for her beauty; the couple eloped and were married. To entwine his fate more closely with hers, he too became an actor and appeared with his wife in different theatres in the chief cities of the Union. The couple died at Richmond,[3] within a few weeks of one ano-other, leaving three young children, one of whom was Edgar,[4] in a state of the utmost neglect and destitution.

Edgar Poe was born at Baltimore in 1813—I give this date according to his own testimony, uttered in protest against Griswold's statement that he was born in 1811.[5] If ever the spirit of romance—to use an expression of our poet—has presided over a birth, it certainly presided over this one. It is indeed a stormy, sinister spirit; and Poe was a true child of passion and adventure. A rich merchant of the city, a certain Mr. Allan,[6] was attracted by this pretty waif, so charmingly endowed by nature, and as he had no children of his own, adopted him. From that

[1] She was in fact a sister, not a daughter, of the admiral.

[2] She came to America with her mother in 1796. David Poe, Jr., was her second husband, marrying her in 1805.

[3] This is true of Elizabeth Poe, who died in 1811; she had already separated from her husband, whose known history ends in New York in 1809.

[4] The other two were William Henry and Rosalie.

[5] Neither is correct: Edgar Poe was born in Boston, 19 January 1809.

[6] He was a tobacco-merchant, and it was his wife rather than he who took a fancy to the child. The adoption was never a legal one.

day onward the boy was known as Edgar Allan Poe. He was thus brought up in comfortable surroundings and in the legitimate expectation of one of those fortunes which give a superb assurance to the character. His adoptive parents took him on a journey which they made to England, Scotland and Ireland,[1] and before returning home they left him in the care of a certain Dr. Bransby, who kept an important educational establishment[2] at Stoke Newington, not far from London. In *William Wilson*, Poe himself has left us a description of this quaint old Elizabethan house and has given us his impressions of his schoolboy life.

He returned to Richmond in 1822,[3] to continue his studies under the instruction of the best masters of the region. At the University of Virginia, Charlottesville, which he entered in 1825,[4] he was distinguished not only for a well-nigh miraculous intelligence, but also for an almost alarming superabundance of passion—a truly American precocity—which in the end was the cause of his expulsion.[5] We should note in passing that already at Charlottesville Poe had manifested a quite uncommon aptitude for the physical and mathematical sciences. He was later to draw frequently upon this in his weird stories and to achieve thereby some highly original effects. But I have reason to believe that it was not to this particular branch of his writings that he attached the greatest importance, and that—perhaps even because of this precocious aptitude—he was not far from regarding them as facile conjuring-tricks in comparison with his works of pure imagination. A number of unfortunate gambling-debts led to a temporary quarrel with his adoptive father, and Edgar conceived the idea of taking part in the Greek War of Independence and of going to fight the Turks—a most curious fact which, whatever may have been said to the contrary, argues quite a strong element of chivalrous feeling in his impressionable brain. And so he sailed for Greece.[6] What befell him in the East? what did he do there? did he study the classic shores of the Mediterranean? why, and in what circumstances, do we find him next in St. Petersburg, without a

[1] This was in 1815. Edgar stayed in England for five years.

[2] The Manor House School, where the boy was known as Edgar Allan.

[3] In fact in 1820.

[4] Poe registered at the University in February 1826.

[5] So the early biographies; but there is no evidence that Poe was expelled.

[6] Baudelaire is here following Poe's own *Memorandum*, which on this point is quite misleading. Poe never went to Greece—or to Russia. At this time (1827–9) he was in fact serving in the American army, in the ranks, under the name Edgar A. Perry.

passport and in trouble, forced to appeal to the American minister, Henry Middleton, for help to escape the penalties of the Russian laws and to return home? We know nothing. There is a gap here which he alone could have filled. The life of Edgar Poe, his early years, his adventures in Russia and his Correspondence were long ago announced in the American press, but have never appeared.

He returned to America in 1829 with the wish to enter the West Point Military Academy; he was in fact admitted,[1] and there, as elsewhere, he gave evidence of an admirably endowed but undisciplinable intelligence, and at the end of a few months was expelled.[2]—At the same time an event occurred in his adoptive family that was destined to have the gravest consequences upon his whole life. Mrs. Allan, for whom he seems to have felt a truly filial affection, died,[3] and Mr. Allan married again, quite a young woman. At this point a domestic quarrel occurs—a strange, gloomy story whose details I cannot go into because it is not clearly explained by any of his biographers. For this reason there is no call to be surprised at his breaking once and for all with Mr. Allan, and that the latter, who had children of his own by his second marriage, should have completely cut him off from his inheritance.

A short time after leaving Richmond, Poe published a slim volume of poems;[4] this was in truth a brilliant dawn. Anyone with a feeling for English poetry will find already that unearthly accent, that melancholy calm, that engaging solemnity, that precocious—I was on the point of saying *inborn*—experience which characterize the great poets.

Poverty reduced him for some time to service in the ranks,[5] and it is to be presumed that he made use of the weary monotonies of garrison-life to put in order the materials for his future writings—strange writings which seem to have been created in order to prove to us that strangeness is one of the integral parts of beauty.[6] Returning to the life of letters, the only element in which certain classless beings can breathe, Poe was dying in the uttermost poverty when a happy chance came to his rescue. A magazine[7] had just announced two prizes, one for the best

[1] In July 1830. [2] In February 1831.
[3] In February 1829, more than a year before Poe went to West Point.
[4] *Al Aaraaf, Tamerlane and Minor Poems*, Baltimore, 1829.
[5] This seems to be a misplaced reference to the earlier period of service.
[6] This idea derives, through Poe, from Bacon: 'There is no exquisite beauty without some *strangeness* in the proportion.'
[7] *The Baltimore Saturday Visiter*. This was in 1833.

story, the other for the best poem. An uncommonly beautiful manuscript attracted the eye of Mr. Kennedy, the President of the committee, and made him want to look at the texts himself. As it turned out, Poe won both prizes; but one only[1] was awarded him. The President was curious to see the unknown author. The publisher brought to see him a young man of striking beauty, in rags, buttoned up to the chin, with the air of a nobleman as proud as he was starving. Kennedy acquitted himself well. He arranged for Poe to meet a Mr. Thomas White, who was at the time starting *The Southern Literary Messenger* at Richmond. Mr. White was an enterprising man, but without any literary talent; he needed an assistant. Thus Poe found himself while still quite young—at the age of twenty-two—editor of a magazine whose fortunes were entirely in his hands.[2] Its prosperity was his creation. *The Southern Literary Messenger* has since admitted that it was to this accursed eccentric, to this incorrigible drunkard, that it owed its circulation and its profitable renown. It was this publication that saw the first appearance of *Hans Phaal* and several other stories which our readers will shortly see parading before their eyes. For nigh on two years[3] Edgar Poe, with a wonderful energy, was to keep his public amazed with a series of compositions of a quite novel kind, and with critical articles whose liveliness, precision and reasoned severity could not fail to attract the eye. These articles bore on books of all kinds, and the sound education which the young man had given himself stood him in good stead. It is only right for it to be known that this considerable labour was performed for a salary of five hundred dollars—that is two thousand seven hundred francs—a year. '*Immediately*',—says Griswold, meaning 'So he thought himself rich enough, poor fool!'—he married[4] a beautiful, charming girl, a girl of a loveable and heroic nature, but '*without a cent*'—adds the same Griswold with a nuance of contempt. She was a Miss Virginia Clemm, his cousin.

In spite of his services to the magazine, Mr. White quarrelled with Poe at the end of about two years. The reason for this rupture is evidently to be found in the poet's attacks of melancholia and his crises of drunkenness—characteristic accidents which darkened his spiritual sky like those leaden clouds which suddenly give to the most Romantic landscape an apparently irreparable sense of gloom. From then onwards

[1] For the *Manuscript Found in a Bottle*.

[2] Poe began his editorial connection with the *Messenger* in the summer of 1835.

[3] Until the beginning of 1837. [4] The ceremony took place in May 1836.

we watch the hapless wanderer forever moving his tent, like a desert nomad, and transporting his scant household gods between the principal cities of the Union. Everywhere we shall find him editing magazines or contributing to them with a dazzling brilliance. With lightning swiftness he will be pouring out critical or philosophical articles and those magical stories which appear collected under the title of *Tales of the Grotesque and the Arabesque*[1]—a remarkable and deliberately chosen title, for the grotesque and arabesque ornaments thrust aside the human figure, and indeed we shall see that in many respects Poe's is an extra- or supra-human literature. We learn next, through the medium of wounding and humiliating paragraphs in the newspapers, that Poe and his wife are dangerously ill at Fordham,[2] and in abject poverty. Shortly after the death[3] of his wife, the poet suffers his first attacks of *delirium tremens*. A new, and even crueller, note appears in a paper, denouncing his contempt and disgust of the world and launching one of those underhand attacks, very indictments of public opinion, against which he was always having to defend himself—one of the most pointlessly exhausting struggles that I know of.

No doubt he was earning money, and his literary labours could more or less support him. But I have proof that he was never without sordid difficulties to overcome. As do so many other writers, he dreamt of a Magazine of his own, he wanted to feel *at home*, and indeed his sufferings had been quite stormy enough to make him long for such a haven for his thought. In order to raise enough money to achieve this result, he had recourse to lectures. Everyone knows what these lectures, or readings, are—a kind of speculation, the Collège de France put at the disposal of all *literati*, the author delaying publication of his reading until he has squeezed from it all the profits that it can yield. Poe's New York reading of *Eureka*,[4] his cosmogonic poem, had already given rise to vociferous debate. Now he bethought himself to try his luck in Virginia, his own part of the world. As he wrote to Willis,[5] he planned to make a tour in the West and the South, and he hoped for the support of his literary friends and his former acquaintances from College and

[1] 1840.

[2] In 1846. Fordham was at that time some thirteen miles from New York City; it was near what is now East 192nd Street.

[3] In January 1847.

[4] In 1848, before the Society Library in New York City.

[5] Letter of 22 January 1848.

West Point. And so he visited the chief cities of Virginia,[1] and the people of Richmond saw once again the man whom they had known so young, so poor and so shabby. All those who had not seen Poe since the days of his obscurity crowded round to gaze at their now famous compatriot. There he was, handsome, elegant, correct, every inch the genius. I even believe that some time before he had stooped as far as joining a Temperance Society.[2] He chose a theme as broad as it was lofty, *The Poetic Principle*, and developed it with that lucidity which is one of his great gifts. True poet that he was, he held that the aim and object of poetry is of the same nature as its principle, and that it ought to have nothing else in view but itself.

The good reception accorded him caused his poor heart to overflow with pride and joy; his delight was so manifest that he spoke of making his permanent home at Richmond and of ending his days in the surroundings that his childhood had endeared to him. Nevertheless he had business to attend to in New York, and on 4 October[3] he left, complaining of attacks of shivering and faintness. Still feeling rather unwell on his arrival at Baltimore, he had his luggage taken to the station from which he had to depart for Philadelphia, and went into an inn in search of some sort of stimulant. There, unfortunately, he fell in with some old acquaintances, and lingered. The following morning, in the pale twilight of the dawn, a corpse was found on the roadway—no, it would be more accurate to say a body still living, but already marked with Death's royal imprint. On this body, whose identity was unknown, neither papers nor money were found, and it was taken to the hospital.[4] It was there that Poe died, on the evening of Sunday, 7 October 1849, at the age of

[1] In the summer of 1849.

[2] The 'Sons of Temperance', according to the *Messenger* (p. 177).

[3] Poe left Richmond a week or so earlier than this.

[4] This account of Poe's last hours is evidently romanticized. What we know is that his friend, Dr. J. E. Snodgrass, of Baltimore, received on 3 October the following letter:

> Dear Sir,
>
> There is a gentleman, rather worse for wear, at Ryan's 4th Ward Polls, who goes under the cognomen of Edgar A. Poe, and who appears in great distress, and he says he is acquainted with you, and I assure you he is in need of immediate assistance.

Snodgrass found Poe and took him to the hospital on the afternoon of 3 October. He did not regain consciousness sufficiently to explain what had happened, and died on the morning of 7 October.

thirty-seven, the victim of *delirium tremens*, that dread visitant which had already haunted his brain more than once. Thus the world saw the last of one of its greatest literary heroes, the man of genius who, in *The Black Cat*, had prophetically written 'What disease is like Alcohol!'

Poe's death was almost a suicide—a suicide long prepared. At least it caused a similar scandal. The outcry was great, and *virtue* gave full vent to its pompous *cant*, freely and with voluptuous pleasure. The more charitable funeral orations stood no chance against the inevitable moralizing of the bourgeoisie, which took good care not to let slip so admirable an opportunity. Mr. Griswold uttered slanders; Mr. Willis, who was genuinely distressed, behaved more properly.—Alas, he who had scaled the steepest aesthetic heights and had plumbed the least explored abysses of the human brain, he who, throughout a life which was like a storm without a lull, had discovered new techniques, novel devices to thrill the imagination and to charm minds athirst for Beauty, this man had just died, within the space of a few hours, in a hospital bed—what a fate! Such greatness and such misery to provoke a whirlwind of bourgeois verbiage and to provide food and theme for virtuous journalists! *Ut declamatio fias!*[1]

But there is nothing new in all this; it is unusual for a fresh and illustrious grave to fail to be a rallying-point for scandal-mongers. Moreover Society has no love for these hapless intransigents, and whether it be because they seem like skeletons at its feasts, or whether it frankly regards them as twinges of conscience, it is undoubtedly right. Who does not recall the sermonizing here in Paris at the time of the death of Balzac, who nevertheless died according to the rules?—And more recently still—exactly a year ago today, the 26th January—when a writer of admirable integrity and lofty intelligence, a writer *who was always lucid*, discreetly went off, without disturbing anyone—so discreetly indeed that his discretion looked not unlike contempt—to free his soul in the darkest street that he could find—what revolting homilies!—what a refined act of murder took place![2] A well-known journalist, to whom Our Lord will never teach generosity of manners, found the event sufficiently comic to be celebrated in a crude pun.—Amongst the endless inventories of the *rights of man* which the nineteenth century in its wisdom draws up so often and so smugly, two not unimportant items

[1] Juvenal, *Satire X*, l. 167, about Hannibal.

[2] Gérard de Nerval, who was found hanging in the rue de la Vieille-Lanterne.

have been overlooked—the right to contradict oneself, and the right to *take one's leave*.[1] But Society regards the man who takes his leave as an impudent fellow; its natural impulse is to punish certain selected corpses, like that unfortunate soldier afflicted with vampirism to the extent that the sight of a dead body roused him to a state of frenzy.—And yet it can be said that under the pressure of certain circumstances, after a serious examination of certain incompatibilities, with a firm belief in certain dogmas and doctrines of metempsychosis—it can be said without pomposity or verbal juggling that suicide is sometimes the most reasonable action in life.—And thus we watch forming an already numerous band of ghosts which familiarly haunt us, each member coming to us to boast of his present repose and to pour into our ears his honeyed persuasions.

Let us own nevertheless that the melancholy end of the author of *Eureka* occasioned a few consoling exceptions, without which we should have to abandon hope and the position would no longer be tenable. Mr. Willis, as I have already said, spoke properly, and even with emotion, of the excellent relations he had always had with Poe. Messrs. John Neal[2] and George Graham called Mr. Griswold to shame. Mr. Longfellow was able, in a manner worthy of a poet, to praise his high powers as poet and prose-writer—which was all the more meritorious in him as he had suffered cruelly at Poe's hands. An unknown correspondent wrote that literary America had lost her most powerful brain.

But the heart that was broken, the heart that was rent and pierced with seven swords was that of Mrs. Clemm. Edgar was at once her son and her daughter. It was a hard fate, says Willis, from whom I am taking these details almost word for word, it was a hard fate that she was watching over and protecting. For Edgar Poe was an awkward man to handle; apart from the fact that he wrote with a 'fastidious difficulty' and 'in a style too much above the popular level to be well paid', he was always plunged in money difficulties, and often he and his sick wife were in want of the merest necessaries of life. One day there came into Willis's office an elderly, gentle, grave-looking woman. It was Mrs. Clemm. She was 'in search of employment' for her dear Edgar. The biographer tells us that he was sincerely touched not only by the perfect

[1] At various periods of his life Baudelaire was obsessed with the idea of suicide.
[2] The reference is probably to Neal's review of the first two volumes of the posthumous edition in the *Portland Daily Advertiser*, 23 April 1850.

estimate, the just appreciation that she gave of the talents of her son, but also by her whole physical demeanour—her 'gentle, mournful voice', her 'long-forgotten but habitually and unconsciously refined manners'. And for several years, he adds, we saw this tireless minister to genius, thinly and insufficiently dressed, going from office to office, with now a poem, now an article to sell, saying sometimes that *he* was ill—the unique explanation, the unique reason, the invariable excuse that she gave when her son was momentarily struck down by one of those attacks of sterility which nervous writers know—and never suffering one syllable to escape her lips that could convey a doubt of him or a lessening of pride in the genius and good intentions of her darling. When her daughter died, she attached herself to the survivor of the disastrous struggle with a reinforced maternal ardour; she lived with him, took care of him, watching over him and defending him against life and against himself. Certainly—concludes Willis, with a lofty and impartial reason—if woman's devotion, born with a first love and fed with human passion, glorifies and hallows its object, what does not a devotion like this—pure, disinterested and holy as the watch of an invisible spirit—say for him who inspired it? Poe's detractors would indeed have done well to observe that certain sorts of charm are so potent that they can only be virtues.

We can guess how terrible was the news for this unhappy woman. She wrote to Willis a letter of which the following are a few lines:

'I have this morning heard of the death of my darling Eddie. . . . Can you give me any circumstances or particulars? . . . Oh! do not desert your poor friend in this bitter affliction. . . . Ask Mr. — to come, as I have to deliver a message to him from my poor Eddie. . . . I need not ask you to notice his death and to speak well of him. I know you will. *But say what an affectionate son he was to me*, his poor desolate mother. . . .'

This woman seems to me to be great, greater even than a mother of Antiquity. Struck down by an irreparable blow, she thinks only of the reputation of him who was everything to her, and to content her it is not enough to say that he was a genius; it must be known that he was a man of duty and affection. It is clear to me that this Mother—a flame and a beacon lit by a shaft of light from the highest heaven—has been given as an example to the races of the world, too little heedful as they are to devotion, to heroism, to all that goes beyond duty. Was it not only justice to inscribe at the head[1] of the poet's works the name of the woman who was the moral sun of his life? His glory will embalm the name of the woman whose love could dress his wounds and whose image will forever float above the martyrology of literature.

III

POE's life, his behaviour, his manners, his physical being, all that goes to make up the aggregate of his personality, leaves a final impression at once both dark and dazzling. His physical person was odd, attractive, and, like his works, stamped with an indefinable accent of melancholy. Yet he was a man of remarkable endowments in every way. When young he had shown a singular bent for all kinds of physical activity, and although he was slightly built, with the hands and feet of a woman—indeed his whole being was characterized by a kind of feminine delicacy—he was unusually robust and capable of remarkable feats of strength. In his youth he had won a swimming-wager which went beyond the ordinary bounds of possibility.[2] It would almost appear that Nature makes a point of bestowing a special vigour of temperament upon those of whom she expects great things, just as she gives a rugged vitality to those trees whose function it is to symbolize grief and mourning. Puny as they may sometimes look, these men are built like athletes, framed for the orgy no less than for work, quick to fall into excess and capable of amazing feats of sobriety.

There are several aspects of Edgar Poe on which there is unanimous agreement; for example, his high natural distinction, his eloquence and his physical beauty, of which, it is said, he was more than a little vain. His manners—a strange mixture of hauteur with an exquisite sweetness—were wonderfully assured. His expression, his bearing, his gestures, the way he carried his head, everything proclaimed him—and especially in the days of his prime—as a chosen spirit. His whole being gave forth an aura of penetrating seriousness. He was truly marked by Nature, like those occasional figures in the street which rivet the observer's eye and haunt his memory. Even the sour and pedantic Griswold admits that when he went to visit Poe and found him pale and still under the

[1] The posthumous edition and Baudelaire's first volume of translation were dedicated to Maria Clemm.
[2] See the Griswold *Memoir*, p. x.

blow of the sickness and death of his wife, he was immeasurably struck not only by the perfection of his manners but also by his aristocratic mien and the perfumed atmosphere of his rooms, modestly furnished as they were. Griswold must be unaware that the poet more than any man else shares with the Parisian and the Spanish woman that wonderful gift of self-adornment with a mere nothing, and that Poe, who loved beauty in everything, would have found no difficulty in transforming a cottage into a new kind of palace. Has he not brought the most original and curious wit to the elaboration of his schemes for furniture, plans for country-houses, gardens and landscape-reforms?[1]

There is a charming letter from Mrs. Osgood, one of Poe's friends, which gives us the most interesting details about his habits, his person and his home life. This woman, herself a distinguished writer, courageously denies all the faults and vices with which the poet was charged. 'With men,' she told Griswold, 'perhaps he was as you depict him, and speaking as a man you may be correct. But I maintain that with women he was quite another person, and that no woman has ever been able to know Mr. Poe without his inspiring in her a profound interest. He never struck me as anything but a model of elegance, distinction and generosity. . . .

'My first meeting with the poet was at the Astor House. Willis had handed me, at the *table d'hôte*, that strange and thrilling poem entitled "The Raven", saying that the author wanted my opinion of it. Its effect on me was so singular, so like that of "weird, unearthly music", that it was with a feeling almost of dread, I heard he desired an introduction. . . . With his proud and beautiful head erect, his dark eyes flashing with the elective light of feeling and of thought, a peculiar, an inimitable blending of sweetness and hauteur in his expression and manner, he greeted me calmly, gravely, almost coldly, yet with so marked an earnestness that I could not help being deeply impressed by it. From that moment until his death we were friends. . . . And in his last words, ere reason had forever left her imperial throne in that overtaxed brain, I have a touching memento of his undying faith and friendship.

'It was in his own simple yet poetical home that, to me, the character of Edgar Poe appeared in its most beautiful light. Playful, affectionate, witty, alternately docile and wayward as a petted child—for his young,

[1] See particularly the *Philosophy of Furniture*, *The Domain of Arnheim* and *Landor's Cottage*.

gentle and idolized wife, and for all who came, he had even in the midst of his most harassing literary duties, a kind word, a pleasant smile, a graceful and courteous attention. At his desk beneath the romantic picture of his loved and lost Lenore,[1] he would sit, hour after hour, patient, assiduous and uncomplaining, tracing, in an exquisitely clear chirography and with almost superhuman swiftness, the lightning thoughts—the "rare and radiant" fancies as they flashed through his ever wakeful brain. I recollect one morning, towards the close of his residence in this city, when he seemed unusually gay and light-hearted. Virginia, his sweet wife, had written me a pressing invitation to come to them; and I, who never could resist her affectionate summons and who enjoyed his society far more in his own home than elsewhere, hastened to Amity Street. I found him just completing his series of papers entitled "The Literati of New York." "See," said he, displaying, in laughing triumph, several little rolls of narrow paper (he always wrote thus for the press), "I am going to show you, by the difference of length in these, the different degrees of estimation in which I hold all you literary people. In each of these, one of you is rolled up and fully discussed. Come, Virginia, help me!" And one by one they unfolded them. At last they came to one which seemed interminable. Virginia laughingly ran to one corner of the room with one end, and her husband to the opposite with the other. "And whose lengthened sweetness long drawn out is that?" said I. "Hear her!" he cried, "just as if her little vain heart didn't tell her it's herself!"—

'During that year, while travelling for my health, I maintained a correspondence with Mr. Poe, in accordance with the earnest entreaties of his wife, who imagined that my influence over him had a restraining and beneficial effect. . . . Of the charming love and confidence that existed between his wife and himself, always delightfully apparent to me, in spite of the many little poetical episodes, in which the impassioned romance of his temperament impelled him to indulge; of this I cannot speak too earnestly—too warmly. I believe she was the only woman whom he ever truly loved. . . .'[2]

In Poe's Tales there is never any love. Even *Ligeia* and *Eleonora* are

[1] This was Mrs. Jane Stith Craig Stanard, the mother of one of Poe's schoolfellows and the first of his 'ideal passions'. She died in 1824—when Poe was just fifteen—and the two poems, *To Helen* and *Lenore* were written in her memory.

[2] Mrs. Osgood's letter is taken from the Griswold *Memoir*, pp. xxxvi ff.

not strictly speaking love-stories, the pivotal idea of each being something quite different. Perhaps he thought that the language of prose is not equal to this weird and almost untranslateable sentiment; for his poems, in contrast, are drenched in it. There the divine passion appears in all its magnificence, star-girt and forever veiled in an incurable melancholy. In his articles he sometimes speaks of love, and even as if it were a thing at whose very name his pen starts to tremble. In *The Domain of Arnheim* we shall find him declaring that the four basic conditions of happiness are an open-air life, *the love of a woman*, detachment from all ambition, and the creation of a new Beauty.—Mrs. Osgood's notion of Poe's chivalrous respect for women is borne out by the fact that, in spite of his prodigious talent for the grotesque and the horrible, there is not a single passage in the whole of his works that touches on lewdness or even on the delights of the senses. His portraits of women are, as it were, haloed; they loom forth from the depths of a supernatural mist and are painted in the urgent manner of an adorer.—As for those 'little poetical episodes', have we any right to be surprised that a being so highly-strung, a being whose thirst for Beauty was perhaps his principal trait, should have sometimes, and with a passionate ardour, cultivated the flower of romance, that volcanic and heavy-scented flower for which the seething brain of a poet provides a favourite soil?

Of his singular personal beauty, of which several biographers speak, we can, I think form an approximate idea by calling to mind all the vague yet characteristic notions contained in the word 'romantic'—a word which generally serves to suggest those types of beauty which consist above all in expression. Poe had a vast, dominating brow, in which certain protuberances betrayed the prodigious faculties which it is their function to represent—construction, comparison, causality—and in which was calmly enthroned the proud sense of ideality, the aesthetic sense *par excellence*. Nevertheless in spite of these gifts, or possibly even because of these extravagant endowments, Poe's head was not perhaps seen at its best in profile. As in all things which are excessive in one direction, this very abundance could result in a deficiency, this usurpation in an impoverishment. His large eyes were at once luminous and dark, their colour deep and equivocal, verging on violet; his nose was firm and noble, his mouth sensitive and sad, if gently smiling; his complexion light brown, inclining to sallowness, and his expression a trifle anxious and imperceptibly overcast by an habitual melancholy.

His conversation was quite outstanding and essentially life-giving. He was not what is called 'a good talker'—a horrible thing—and moreover his tongue, like his pen, shrank from the commonplace; but a vast learning, a powerful command of language, a sound background of study and a store of impressions gathered in several different countries made of his utterance an education in itself. An eloquence which was essentially poetic and highly methodical, yet whose sphere of operation was outside that of any known method; an arsenal of imagery drawn from a world but little frequented by the generality of minds; an extraordinary gift for drawing secret and novel insights from evident and absolutely acceptable propositions, for opening up amazing vistas—in a word, the art of spell-binding, of making his listeners think and dream, of snatching their souls from the quagmire of routine:—such were the dazzling qualities which many still remember. But occasionally it happened—at least, so we are told—that the poet, yielding to a destructive whim, would abruptly call his friends back to earth with a harsh piece of ribaldry, thus brutally demolishing his work of spirituality. It is moreover worth notice that he was very far from exacting in his choice of an audience,[1] but I fancy that the reader will have no need to ransack history to recall other great and original minds for whom any company was good company. Certain beings, who live alone in the midst of the crowd and who find their sustenance in monologue, have no use for delicacy in the matter of a public. It is after all a kind of brotherhood based on contempt.

Of Poe's drunkenness, which has been bruited abroad and denounced with an insistence which might lead one to suppose that he was alone among American writers in not being an angel of sobriety—of this subject we must nevertheless speak. Several explanations are plausible, and none excludes the others. First and foremost it is my duty to recall that according to Willis and Mrs. Osgood the very smallest quantity of liquor was sufficient to upset completely his physical and mental balance. It is moreover easy to imagine that a man so genuinely isolated and so deeply unhappy, a man who was often capable of considering the whole social system as a paradox and a fraud, and who, when harassed by a pitiless fate, would often repeat that Society is no more than a gang of thugs (it is Griswold that tells us this, with the shocked horror of a man

[1] Asselineau (*Charles Baudelaire, sa vie et son oeuvre*, 1869) tells us much the same, in almost the same words, about Baudelaire himself. See also p. 62 above.

who can think, but never admit, the same thing)—it is natural, I say, to suppose that this poet who had been hurled while still a child into the free-for-all of life and whose brain was bound by the fetters of a harsh and unremitting toil, should have sometimes sought the delicious oblivion of the bottle. Literary spites, terrors before the infinite, domestic griefs, the insults of poverty—from all these Poe sought refuge in the darkness of drunkenness, as though it were a preliminary tomb. But however satisfactory this explanation may seem, it does not strike me as sufficiently broad, and I distrust it because of its regrettable simplicity.

I am told that he did not drink like an ordinary toper, but like a savage, with an altogether American energy and fear of wasting a minute, as though he was accomplishing an act of murder, as though there was *something* inside him that he had to kill, 'a worm that would not die'.[1] There is in fact a story of how one day, at the moment of his second marriage, when, after the publication of the banns, he was being congratulated on an alliance which was to bring him such favourable conditions of happiness and well-being, he replied, 'It is indeed possible that you have heard the banns read, but make very sure of this: I shall not marry.'[2] And then, desperately drunk, he went off and scandalized the neighbourhood of his future wife, resorting in this way to his vice in order to purge himself of an act of infidelity towards the poor dead woman whose image was always living in his mind and whom he had so admirably sung in his *Annabel Lee*. Therefore in a great number of cases I consider the infinitely valuable fact of *premeditation* as established and proven.

Then again, in a long article in *The Southern Literary Messenger*[3]—that very journal whose fortunes he had founded—I read that the purity and finish of his style, the precision of his thought and his zest for work were never for a moment impaired by this terrible habit; that the composition of the greater part of his admirable writings immediately preceded or followed one of his drinking-bouts; that after the publication of *Eureka* he made a deplorable sacrifice to his weakness, and that

[1] From *Morella*.

[2] This fabricated anecdote, which Baudelaire takes from Griswold, refers to his engagement in 1848 to Mrs. Whitman, an attractive widow and poetess of Providence, Rhode Island. The engagement was broken off because of opposition in the lady's family, whereupon Poe attempted suicide.

[3] This is the article of March 1850, referred to above.

in New York, on the very publication-day of *The Raven*, he staggered across Broadway in the most outrageous state. Note that the words 'preceded or followed' imply that alcohol could provide stimulus as well as respite.

Now there are certain fugitive and striking impressions—all the more striking in their recurrence as they are the more fugitive—which sometimes take their cue from an external signal, a kind of warning like the sound of a bell, a musical note or a forgotten scent, and which are themselves followed by an event similar to an event already familiar which occupied the same place in a previously revealed chain; in the same way, as in those strange recurrent dreams which haunt our sleep, it cannot be denied that drunkenness too has not only its linked chains of dreams but also its rational trains of thought, which, if they are to be repeated, need a repetition of the circumstances which gave them birth. If the reader has followed me as far as this without disgust, he will already have guessed my conclusion; I think that very often, though by no means always, Poe's drunkenness was a mnemonic device, a deliberate method of work, drastic and fatal, no doubt, but suited to his passionate nature. Poe taught himself to drink, just as a careful man of letters makes a deliberate practice of filling his notebooks with notes. He could not resist the desire to return to the marvellous or terrifying visions, the subtle conceptions, which he had encountered in a previous storm; they were old acquaintances which peremptorily called to him, and in order to renew relations with them he took the most perilous but the straightest road. One part of what delights us today was the cause of his death.

IV

Of the works of this rare genius I propose to say but little; the public will let us know what it thinks of them. It would be difficult, perhaps, but by no means impossible, to unravel his methods and anatomize his technique, especially in that part of his writings where the principal effect lies in a well-conducted analysis. I could initiate the reader into the mysteries of his craft, spread myself on the 'American' element in his personality, which leads him to delight in a difficulty overcome, a riddle solved, a *tour de force* successfully accomplished,—which prompts him to revel with a childlike and almost perverse glee in the world of probabilities and conjectures, and to devise *hoaxes* to which his subtle art has given a convincing life. No one will deny that Poe was a wonderful trickster;[1] but I know that it was by another side of his work that he set most store. I have other, more important observations to make, brief though they be.

In spite of the fact that they made his name, it is not these material miracles that will earn him the admiration of thinking men: rather it is his love of Beauty; his poetry, deep and poignant yet wrought to the transparency and perfection of a crystal jewel; his admirable style, eccentric yet pure,—a style compact as the plates of a suit of mail,—a style both urbane and precise, whose slightest nuance only goes to urge the reader gently on towards a desired end; and finally that entirely personal genius, that unique temperament which enables him to paint and to unfold, in an impeccable, thrilling and terrible manner, *all that is exceptional in the moral order*.—Diderot is a sanguine author—to choose one example out of a hundred; Poe is the writer of the nerves, and even of something more—and I can think of none better.

Each one of his opening paragraphs draws the reader in without violence, like a whirlpool. His gravity arrests and keeps the mind alert. We feel immediately that something serious is afoot. And slowly, little by little, a tale unfolds whose entire interest is centred upon some barely perceptible deviation of the intellect, a bold hypothesis, a rash dose of Nature stirred into the amalgam of the faculties. His head thus swimming, the reader has no choice but to follow the author along the train of his deductions.

No man, I repeat, has more magically described the *exceptions* in human life and nature;—convalescence, with its fevers of curiosity; autumnal skies heavy with exhausting splendours, warm, humid, misty days when the south wind loosens and relaxes the nerves like the strings of a musical instrument, when the eyes brim with tears that come not from the heart; hallucination, at first leaving room for doubt, but soon as positive and rational as a book; the perverse enthroning itself in the brain and dominating it with a terrible logic; hysteria supplanting will, nerves and mind at variance, and man himself unstrung to the point of expressing pain by laughter. He analyses whatever is most transitory, weighs the imponderable and describes, in that detailed, scientific manner whose effects are so terrible, the whole imaginary

[1] See p. 95 below. The French word is 'jongleur'.

atmosphere which floats around the man of nerves and leads him on to his downfall.

The very fervour with which he hurls himself into the grotesque for love of the grotesque and the horrible for love of the horrible I regard as proofs of the sincerity of his work and the intimate accord between the man and the poet.—I have already noticed in several men that such a fervour is often the result of a vast store of unused vital energy, sometimes too of an inflexible chastity and of a deep, repressed sensibility. The supernatural rapture which man can feel at the sight of his own blood flowing, those sudden, needless spasms of movement, those piercing cries uttered without the mind's having issued any orders to the throat—all these are phenomena which fall within the same category.

As he breathes the attenuated ether of this world, the reader may feel that vague distress of mind, that fear on the brink of tears, that anguish of the heart which dwell in strange immensities. But admiration is the dominant emotion, and moreover the writer's art is so great! Backgrounds and accessories are all attuned to the feelings of the characters. Whether nature's solitude or urban bustle, everything is described with a high-strung fantasy. Like our own Eugène Delacroix,[1] who has raised his art to the level of great poetry, Edgar Poe loves to set his figures in action against greenish or purplish backgrounds, in which we can glimpse the phosphorescence of decay and sniff the coming storm. So-called inanimate Nature co-operates in the nature of living beings, and like them gives an unearthly and convulsive shudder. Space is extended by opium, which also adds a magical accent to every tint, a more meaningful resonance to every sound. Sometimes magnificent vistas, flooded with colour and light, open out suddenly in the midst of his landscapes, in whose depths loom Oriental cities and fantastic edifices, vaporized by the distance over which the sun pours its showers of golden rain.

Poe's characters, or rather Poe's single character, the man of razor-sharp perceptions and slackened nerves, the man whose burning and patient will hurls defiance at difficulties and whose gaze is fixed with the concentration of a sword upon objects which grow larger as he looks at them—this man is Poe himself.—And his women, all luminous and ailing, dying of strange sicknesses and speaking in a voice which is like music—these are himself again; or at least, in their strange

[1] Delacroix was vexed at the comparison.

aspirations, their learning and their incurable melancholia, they suggest a strong natural kinship with their creator. As for his ideal woman, his Titanide, her face is to be discerned in various different portraits scattered among his all too scanty poems—portraits, or rather ways of apprehending Beauty, which the author's temperament groups and blends in a vague but perceptible unity and in which there is to be found, more delicately embodied perhaps than elsewhere, that insatiable love of the Beautiful which is his great title, or rather the epitome of all his titles to the affection and respect of poets.[1]

[1] The essay, in its second version, concluded with a single paragraph referring to some of the contents of the book and to Baudelaire's hope to be able to write further on Poe's philosophical opinions; this paragraph we have here omitted.

FURTHER NOTES ON EDGAR POE

I

'Literature of the decadence!'—Empty words that we often hear dropping, with all the resonance of a flatulent yawn, from the lips of those sphinxes-without-a-riddle which stand guard before the holy portals of Classical Aesthetics. Each time that the dogmatic oracle echoes forth, you can be certain that you are in the presence of something more entertaining than the Iliad. It is undoubtedly a question of some poem or novel in which all the parts are skilfully interwoven to create surprise, a work superbly rich in style, in which all the resources of language and prosody have been employed by an unerring hand. Whenever I hear this anathema thundering in the air—and perhaps I may observe in passing that it generally falls upon some favourite poet—I am invariably seized with a desire to reply, 'Do you take me for a barbarian like yourselves? Do you really think me capable of taking my pleasures as drearily as you do?' Grotesque comparisons then start up in my brain; I imagine that two women have been introduced to me: one, a rustic matron, bursting with rude health and virtue, quite without style or spirit, a woman, in short, *whose sole debt is to nature unadorned*; the other, one of those beauties who dominate and haunt the memory, crowning a profound and original charm with all the eloquence of the dressing-table, mistress of her bearing, conscious of her own majestic self-assurance, with a voice like a well-tuned instrument and glances charged with thought, letting nothing escape but what they intend. My choice could never be in doubt; and yet there are professorial sphinxes who would criticize me for failing in my duty towards Classic Honour.—But, leaving aside parables for a moment, I think I may be allowed to ask these learned gentlemen if they really understand all the vanity and uselessness of their wisdom. The phrase 'literature of the decadence' implies a scale of literatures, one infantile, one childish, one adolescent, etc., etc. The term, I mean, presupposes something fatal and foreordained, like an ineluctable decree; and it is entirely unfair to blame us for accomplishing such a mysterious law. The only meaning that I can attach to the academic pronouncement is that it is somehow shameful to obey with enjoyment—that we are guilty, in fact, of taking pleasure in our fate.—The sun which, some hours ago, was shattering everything with its harsh white light will soon be flooding the western horizon with multifarious colours.[1] In the restless sport of this dying sun certain poetic spirits will discover new delights—dazzling colonnades, cascades of molten metal, fiery Elysiums, melancholy splendours, the sensuous pleasures of regret, all the magic of dreams, all the memories of opium. And the sunset will in fact seem to them like a wonderful allegory of some life-charged soul dipping below the horizon with a magnificent profusion of thought and dreams.

But what the professional pundits[2] have not considered is that in the midst of the movement of life some complication, some combination may occur which is absolutely undreamt of in their schoolboy wisdom. When this happens their inadequate vocabulary[3] is found to be lacking, as in the case when a nation *begins* with decadence and starts off where the others leave off—a phenomenon which may well repeat itself with variations.

Assuming that new literatures will arise among the immense colonies of the present age, we shall most certainly witness spiritual accidents of a kind to baffle the academic mind. At once young and old, America[4] chatters and gabbles on with an astonishing volubility. Who could number her poets? they are countless. Her blue-stockings? they overwhelm the reviews. Her critics? Make no doubt that she possesses pedants every bit the equal of ours at incessantly recalling the artist to Antique Beauty, at questioning the poet or novelist on the ethics of his aim or the quality of his intentions. America, no less than France—and perhaps even more—has her men of letters who do not know how to spell; her childish, pointless bustle of activity; her compilers galore, literary parrots, plagiarists of plagiaries, and critics of critics. In the midst of this seething ferment of mediocrities, in this world in thrall to material perfection (a new sort of scandal which makes one understand the true greatness of the idle races!), in this society greedy for wonder, in love with life, but especially with a life full of excitements,

[1] See the 'Coucher du Soleil Romantique' in the *Fleurs du mal.*

[2] The expression 'professeurs-jurés' was borrowed from Heine, who had used it in his *Salon* of 1831.

[3] Crépet sees in this a reply to such critics as Pontmartin, Jean Rousseau, and others, who accused Baudelaire of making too frequent a use of neologisms.

[4] Baudelaire's anti-Americanism was associated in his mind with his anti-Progress feelings.

a man has arisen who was great not only by virtue of his metaphysical subtlety, the sinister or enchanting beauty of his conceptions, and the rigour of his analysis, but great also, and no less great, as a *caricature*.— I must explain my meaning with some care; for not long ago an imprudent critic, wishing to denigrate Edgar Poe and to call in question the sincerity of my admiration, made use of the word 'trickster'[1] which I myself had applied to the noble poet almost as a term of praise.

From the midst of a world avid and starving for materialities, Poe has soared up into the element of dreams. Stifled as he was by the atmosphere of America, he wrote in his epigraph to *Eureka*: 'I offer this Book to those who put faith in dreams as in the only realities.' He thus himself acted as an admirable protest; he *was* it and he made it in his own way. The writer who, in the *Colloquy of Monos and Una*, discharges torrents of scorn and disgust upon democracy, progress and *civilization*, is the same who, to capture the credulity, to ravish the idle curiosity of his fellow-countrymen, has most strenuously insisted upon human sovereignty and has most ingeniously concocted *hoaxes*[2] of a kind most flattering to the pride of *modern man*. Seen in this light, Poe seems to me like a slave determined to make his master blush. In a word, to state my opinion even more concisely, Poe was always great, not only in his noble conceptions, but also as a joker.

II

FOR he was never taken in![3]—I do not think that the Virginian who, at the floodtide of democracy, could calmly write: 'The People have nothing to do with the laws but to obey them'[4] could ever have fallen a victim to modern wisdom,—and: 'The nose of a mob is its imagination. By this, at any time, it can be quietly led',[5]—and a hundred other passages in which mockery pours down like a shower of grapeshot—but with haughty nonchalance.—The Swedenborgians congratulate him on his *Mesmeric Revelation*, rather like those simple-minded *Illuminati* who years

[1] Crépet lists at least three such 'imprudent critics', of whom one was Baudelaire's friend, Barbey d'Aurevilly.

[2] See particularly *The Balloon-Hoax*.

[3] Baudelaire was later to apply the same phrase to Gautier.

[4] *Fifty Suggestions*, XLV (Poe, *Works*, ed. J. H. Ingram, vol. III, London 1899, p. 491; this is the edition used in all further references involving page-numbers).

[5] *Marginalia*, CXVIII (p. 409).

ago detected in the author of the *Diable amoureux*[1] a revealer of their mysteries; they thank him for the great truths that he has just revealed—for they have discovered (O verifiers of the unverifiable!) that every statement he has made is absolutely true;—though at first, these fine fellows admit, they suspected that it might well have been no more than a mere piece of fiction. Poe's reply is that as far as he is concerned, he never had any doubt of it.[2]—Should I quote again this little passage which strikes my attention as, for the hundredth time, I skim through his amusing *Marginalia*, which are as it were the secret chamber of his mind? 'The enormous multiplication of books in every branch of knowledge is one of the greatest evils of this age; since it presents one of the most serious obstacles to the acquisition of correct information . . .'[3] An aristocrat by nature even more than by birth, this Virginian, this Southerner, this Byron astray in a wicked world, never lost his philosophic calm, and whether he is defining the nose of a mob, mocking at the fabricators of religions or jeering at libraries, he remains what was and always will be the true poet—a truth clad in singular raiment, an apparent paradox, refusing to be jostled by the crowd and running off to the furthest Orient the moment the fireworks start up in the West.

But now comes the most important thing of all: we shall note that this writer, the product of a self-infatuated age, the child of a nation more self-infatuated than any other, has clearly seen and dispassionately asserted the natural Wickedness of Man. There is in man, he says, a mysterious force which modern philosophy refuses to take into account; and yet, without this nameless force, without this primeval tendency, a whole host of human actions will remain unexplained and inexplicable. The whole fascination of these actions lies in the fact that they are evil, dangerous; they have the lure of the abyss. This primitive, irresistible force is man's natural Perversity,[4] which makes him forever and at once both homicide and suicide, murderer and hangman;—for, he adds with a remarkably Satanic subtlety, the impossibility of finding an adequate

[1] This was Jacques Cazotte, who published his novel in 1772. Crépet refers to A. Viatte, *Les sources occultes du romantisme* (1928). The name 'Illuminés', or 'Illuminati', has been given to various more or less hermetic sects at various times. Baudelaire here is undoubtedly referring to the Martinists (founded 1754), whom Cazotte in fact joined.
[2] *Marginalia*, CXCIV, 'Swedenborgian Credulity' (p. 456).
[3] *Marginalia*, CXXVIII (p. 412).
[4] See Poe's story *The Imp of the Perverse*, which Baudelaire translated as *Le Démon de la perversité*.

rational motive for certain evil and dangerous actions could lead us to regard them as the result of diabolic suggestion, if experience and history did not teach us that God often makes use of them for the establishment of order and the punishment of knaves—*after having used those same knaves as accomplices!* (which is the idea that slips into my mind, I must admit, as an implication no less treacherous than inevitable). But for the moment I wish to confine myself to that great forgotten truth—the primeval perversity of man—and it is not without a certain satisfaction that I see in this some scraps of ancient wisdom floating back to us from a country whence one would have least expected them. It is pleasant that a few explosions of old-established truth should thus be detonating in the faces of all those complimenters of humanity, all those coddlers and cajolers who never cease to repeat with every possible nuance and inflection, 'I was born good, and you too; we were all of us born good!', forgetting, no, pretending to forget, those topsy-turvy egalitarians, that we were all born marked for evil!

By what lie could he be deceived, he who on occasions—by the painful necessity of the circumstances—manipulated them so well himself? What blistering scorn for armchair philosophizing, on his good days, on those days when he was, so to say, illuminated! This poet, some of whose stories seem to have been wantonly composed in order to confirm the alleged omnipotence of man, occasionally felt the desire to administer himself a purge. The day that he wrote 'All certainty is in dreams', he was thrusting back his own Americanism into the limbo of inferior things; at other times, returning to the true road of poets, he heaved the burning sighs of the 'fallen angel mindful of Heaven'; he turned his regretful eye towards the Golden Age and Paradise Lost; he wept for all those glories of Nature, 'shrinking before the hot breath of furnaces'; in a word, in the *Colloquy of Monos and Una*, he threw off those admirable pages which would have charmed and troubled the impeccable De Maistre.

He it was that said, on the subject of Socialism (at a time when that thing had not yet received a name, or at least when that name was not on everybody's lips): 'The world is infested just now by a new sect of philosophers, who have not yet suspected themselves of forming a sect, and who, consequently, have adopted no name. They are the *Believers in everything Old* (which is like saying, "antiquated preachers"). Their High Priest in the East is Charles Fourier, in the West Horace Greeley, and high priests they are to some purpose. The only common bond among the sect is Credulity—let us call it Insanity at once, and be done with it. Ask any one of them *why* he believes this or that, and, if he be conscientious (ignorant people usually are), he will make you very much such a reply as Talleyrand made when asked why be believed in the Bible. "I believe in it first," said he, "because I am Bishop of Autun, and secondly *because I know nothing about it at all.*" What these philosophers call "argument" is a way they have "*de nier ce qui est, et d'expliquer ce qui n'est pas*".'[1]

Progress, that great heresy of the decline, could no more escape his attention. The reader will see for himself, in various different passages, the terms that he used to characterize it. To see the passion which he lavished upon it, you would really think that he felt the need to attack it like a public nuisance, a scourge of the streets. How he would have laughed, with the scornful laugh of the poet who will never swell the band of the empty-heads, if, as happened to me recently, he had hit upon the following miraculous *obiter dictum*, which makes one think of a deliberate piece of circus-ring buffoonery, but which in fact I found treacherously flaunting itself in a more than serious journal. Here it is: 'The uninterrupted progress of Science has enabled us quite recently to recover the long-lost, long-sought secret of . . . (Greek Fire? Copper-tempering? anything you like that has disappeared) whose most perfect usages date back to a *barbarous* and very ancient period'!![2]—Here you have a sentence that might itself be called a real find, a dazzling discovery, even in an age of *uninterrupted progress*; and yet I fancy that the Mummy Allamistakeo[3] would hardly have failed to enquire, in those gentle guarded tones of authority, if it was thanks also to *uninterrupted progress*—to the fatal, irresistible law of progress—that this famous secret had originally come to be lost.—Moreover, to be serious for a moment, on a subject which contains as much food for tears as for laughter, is it not a truly astounding thing to see a nation, several nations, soon the whole of humanity, saying to its wise men, to its magicians: 'I will love you and make you great if you can persuade me that we progress without willing it, inevitably—while we sleep; relieve us of responsibility, protect us from the humiliation of comparisons, juggle with history, and you may call yourselves the wisest of the wise'?—Is

[1] *Fifty Suggestions*, XXVIII (p. 487).
[2] Crépet suggests that this probably came from the *Siècle*.
[3] See *Some Words with a Mummy*.

it not matter for amazement that so simple an idea as the following should not flash across every brain: the idea that Progress (in so far as it exists) perfects pain in proportion as it refines pleasure, and that, if the skin of the peoples of the earth continues to become ever more and more delicate, they are clearly pursuing no more than an *Italiam fugientem*,[1] a victory every minute lost, a progress forever denying itself?

But these illusions are by no means so innocent; they spring from a soil of perversity and falsehood—meteorites of the marshland—which drive to scorn those souls that are enamoured of the eternal fire, like Edgar Poe, and exasperate obscure intelligences, like Jean-Jacques, in whom a wounded and rebellious sensibility does duty for philosophy. That the latter was in the right against the 'depraved animal' is unarguable; but the depraved animal may in its turn legitimately criticize him for invoking simple Nature. Nature can produce only monsters, and the whole question turns on agreeing on the definition of the word 'savages'. No philosopher would dare put forward as models those unhappy, cankerous hordes, at the mercy of the elements, a prey to wild beasts, as incapable of manufacturing arms as of conceiving the idea of a supreme spiritual power. But if you will compare modern man, civilized man, with primitive man, or rather a nation called civilized with a nation called primitive—in other words, with a nation lacking all the ingenious inventions which dispense the individual of heroism—who will not agree that the whole honour lies on the side of the savage? By his nature, by necessity even, he is encyclopedic, while civilized man finds himself confined within the infinitely narrow limits of his speciality. Civilized man has invented the doctrine of Progress to console himself for his surrender and decay; while primitive man, a feared and respected husband, a warrior obliged to personal valour, a poet in those melancholy moments when the declining sun bids him sing the past of his ancestors, comes closer to the fringes of the Ideal. What deficiency shall we dare hold against him? He has his priest, his magician, his doctor. But why stop there? He has also his dandy, that supreme incarnation of the idea of Beauty transported into the sphere of material life, the dictator of form and ruler of manners. His clothes, his adornments, his arms, his calumet bear witness to an inventive faculty which has long since deserted us. Shall we compare our lazy eyes and deafened ears to those eyes which can pierce the mist, those ears which could hear the grass

[1] Virgil, *Aeneid*, v, 629.

growing? And primitive woman, with her simple, childlike soul, an obedient, affectionate animal, surrendering herself without reserve, in the knowledge that she is no more than one half of a destiny—are we to declare her the inferior of the American woman whom M. Bellegarigue (the editor of the *Moniteur de l'Epicerie*!) fancied he was praising when he called her the ideal of the kept woman?[1] That very woman whose morals too positive inspired of Poe—gallant as he was, and respectful of beauty—the following sad lines: 'The frightfully long money-pouches, like "the Cucumber called the Gigantic", which have come in vogue among our belles, are *not* of Parisian origin, as many suppose, but are strictly indigenous here. The fact is, such a fashion would be quite out of place in Paris, where it is money *only* that women keep in a purse. The purse of an American lady, however, must be large enough to carry both the money and the soul of its owner!'[2]—Turning to religion, I shall not speak of Vitzilipoutzli[3] as lightly as did Alfred de Musset; I am not ashamed to admit that I far prefer the cult of Teutates[4] to that of Mammon, and the priest who offers up to the cruel extorter of human sacrifice victims who die *honourably*, victims who *take it upon themselves* to die,[5] seems to me an altogether gentle and humane being in comparison with the financier who immolates whole populations solely for his own personal interest. Now and again these things have already been caught sight of, and I remember once finding in an article by M. Barbey d'Aurevilly a cry of philosophical melancholy which neatly sums up all that I would wish to say on the subject: 'Civilized peoples, you who never stop throwing stones at the savages, soon you will cease to deserve even the name of idolaters!'

A society of this kind—I have said it before, and cannot resist repeating it—was hardly made for poets. What even the most democratic of Frenchmen understands by the word 'State' would find no place in

[1] This was in his book, *Les Femmes d'Amérique*, published in 1853, and two years later discovered and violently attacked by Barbey d'Aurevilly (*Le Pays*, 26 January 1855).
[2] *Fifty Suggestions*, xv (pp. 482–3).
[3] The Aztec god of War. See Crépet's note for the obscure source in a manuscript by Alfred de Musset.
[4] A Gaulish god.
[5] This idea is closely connected with Baudelaire's opinions concerning the death-penalty, which derive from De Maistre; see, for example, *Mon coeur mis à nu*, XXI: 'Théorie du sacrifice. Légitimation de la peine de mort. Le sacrifice n'est complet que par le *sponte sua* de la victime.'

the mind of an American. For any citizen of the Old World a political State has a centre of activity which is its sun and its brain, ancient and glorious memories, long poetic and military annals, an aristocracy to which poverty, daughter of revolutions, can only add a paradoxical lustre; but *that!* that rabble of buyers and sellers, that nameless thing, that headless monster, that convict deported beyond the seas, a State?!—Very well, I allow it, on condition that a vast tavern, thronged with customers conducting their business-deals round filthy tables, amid a racket of vile language, can be likened to a *Salon*, to what we used once to call a Salon, a Republic of the Mind with Beauty its President!

It will always be difficult to pursue at once nobly and fruitfully the profession of man of letters without laying oneself open to the slander and calumny of the impotent, the envy of the rich—that envy which is their punishment!—and the vengeance of bourgeois mediocrity. But what is difficult enough in a benevolent monarchy or a regular republic becomes well-nigh impossible in a kind of nightmare chaos in which everyone is a police-constable of opinion and keeps order on behalf of his own vices—or of his virtues, it is all one; in which a poet or a novelist of a slave-owning state is a detestable writer in the eyes of an abolitionist critic; in which it is impossible to say which is the greater scandal—the Bohemianism of the cynical or the impenetrable carapace of pious hypocrisy. To tie up and burn negroes whose sole crime is to have felt their black cheeks pricking with the red blush of honour; to brandish a revolver in a theatre-pit; to establish polygamy in those Elysiums of the West which the Savages (this word looks like an act of injustice) have not yet soiled with their shameful Utopias; to adorn the walls, doubtless so as to enshrine the principle of freedom unlimited, with posters promising a 'cure for the nine-months' sickness';—such are a few of the salient characteristics, some of the moral illustrations of the noble land of Franklin, the inventer of the ethics of the shop-counter, the hero of an age dedicated to materialism. It is well to persist in calling attention to these marvels of brutishness, at a time when Americomania has become almost a genteel passion, to such a point that an Archbishop has found it possible to keep a straight face while promising that Providence would shortly call us to share this transatlantic ideal!

III

A SOCIAL environment of this kind is bound to beget corresponding literary errors. It was against these errors that Poe reacted as often as he could, and with all his strength. We should not be surprised therefore that American writers, while recognizing his singular powers as poet and story-writer, should always have striven to invalidate his worth as a critic. In a land where the idea of utility, which is the most hostile of all to the idea of beauty, outweighs and dominates everything, the perfect critic will be the most *honourable*—in other words, the critic whose desires and tendencies will most approximate to those of his public, the critic who, confusing mental capacities and literary genres, will assign to all an unique aim, the critic who will look in a volume of poetry for the means of perfecting the moral being. Naturally he will become all the less concerned with the real, positive beauties of the poetry; he will be all the less shocked by imperfections and even faults in the execution. Edgar Poe, on the other hand, divided the world of the mind into *Pure Intellect*, *Taste* and the *Moral Sense*, and he applied his criticism in accordance as the object of his analysis belonged to one or other of these three divisions.[1] He was sensitive before all else to the perfection of the plan and the correctness of the execution; he would dismantle literary works like defective pieces of machinery—defective, that is, in relation to their professed aim—carefully noting any errors of construction; and when he moved on to the detail of the work, to its plastic expression, in a word, to its style, he would mercilessly strip bare faults of prosody, grammatical imperfections and all that mass of dead wood which, with writers who are not also artists, vitiates the best intentions and distorts the noblest conceptions.

For Poe the Imagination is the Queen of the Faculties;[2] but by this word he understood something greater than what is understood by the generality of readers. Imagination is distinct from Fancy; no more is it Sensibility, though it would be hard to conceive of an imaginative man who was not also sensitive. The Imagination is an almost divine faculty

[1] See *The Poetic Principle* (p. 202).

[2] This idea was to be returned to and developed in the *Salon of 1859*. The distinction Imagination/Fancy came to Baudelaire from Poe (cf. *The Poetic Principle*, p. 211), who had it himself from Coleridge. On 'Imagination' see also *Marginalia*, XCII (p. 393), and Gilman pp. 128 ff.

which perceives at once, quite without resort to philosophic methods, the intimate and secret connections between things, *correspondences*[1] and analogies. The honours and the functions which our poet bestows upon this capacity give it such a status (at least, when one has properly grasped his thought) that a scholar without imagination appears now as a false scholar, or at least as an incomplete one.

Among the territories of literature in which the imagination can obtain the most interesting results, can harvest not perhaps the richest, the most precious treasures (these belong to poetry), but the most manifold and the most various, there is one for which Poe showed a particular fondness: the Tale. The Tale has one great advantage over the large-scale novel; its very brevity contributes to the intensity of its effect. The reading of a tale, which can be accomplished in a single breath, as one might say, leaves a far more powerful imprint in the mind than a reading which is frequently broken up and interrupted by the hurly-burly of business and the care of worldly affairs. This unity of impression and *totality* of effect is an immense advantage which can give to this kind of composition an altogether special superiority, so that it is possible to say that a tale which is too short (which is undoubtedly a fault) is still more praiseworthy than one which is too long. If an artist is skilful, he will never seek to adapt his ideas to his incidents, but having conceived, at his leisure, an effect to produce, he will invent incidents and combine events which are most fitted to bring about the desired effect. If the first sentence is not written with a view to preparing this final impression, the work will be abortive from the very beginning. Throughout the whole composition not a single word must be allowed to intrude which is not also an intention, which does not aim, directly or indirectly, at completing the premeditated design.

There is one point at which the Tale has an advantage even over the Poem. Rhythm is necessary to the development of the idea of Beauty, which is the greatest and noblest aim of a poem. Now the artifices of rhythm are an insurmountable obstacle to that precise development of thought and expression which has as its object the Truth. For Truth can often be the aim of a Tale, and reasoning the best tool for the construction of a perfect tale. That is the reason why this kind of composition, which is not situated on such a lofty eminence as pure poetry,

[1] A favourite conception of Baudelaire's, familiar (if not necessarily fully intelligible) to all scholars of his work.

can produce results more varied and more easily appreciable for the generality of readers. Moreover the author of a tale has at his disposal a multitude of tones and shades of language—the argumentative, the sarcastic, the humorous, for example—which poetry renounces and which are, like dissonances, outrages to the idea of pure poetry. And this is also why an author who, in writing a tale, pursues the simple aim of Beauty, is only working at a great disadvantage, deprived as he is of his most useful instrument, Rhythm. I know that in all literatures attempts have been made, and often happy ones, to create purely poetic tales; Poe himself has produced some very fine ones.[1] But these efforts and struggles only serve to draw attention to the power of the true means adapted to its corresponding aims, and I should be inclined to believe that with certain authors, chosen from among the greatest, these heroic endeavours may have originated in a sense of despair.

IV

'*Genus irritabile vatum!*' 'That poets (using the word comprehensively, as including artists in general) are a *genus irritabile* is well understood, but the *why* seems not to be commonly seen. An artist *is* an artist only by dint of his exquisite sense of Beauty, a sense affording him rapturous enjoyment, but at the same time implying or involving an equally exquisite sense of Deformity, of disproportion. Thus a wrong—an injustice—done a poet who is really a poet, excites him to a degree which to ordinary apprehension appears disproportionate with the wrong. Poets *see* injustice, *never* where it does not exist, but very often where the unpoetical see no injustice whatever. Thus the poetical irritability has no reference to 'temper' in the vulgar sense, but merely to a more than usual clear-sightedness in respect to wrong, this clear-sightedness being nothing more than a corollary from the vivid perception of right—of justice—of proportion—in a word, of *τὸ καλόν*. But one thing is clear, that a man who is *not* "irritable" (to the ordinary apprehension) is *no poet*.'[2]

So speaks the poet himself, drawing up an excellent and irrefutable apologia for the whole of his race. This sensitivity Poe carried over into his literary affairs, and the extreme importance that he attached to matters of poetry led him often to adopt a tone in which, in the

[1] See, for example, *Shadow—A Parable*, *Silence—A Fable* and *The Island of the Fay*.

[2] *Fifty Suggestions*, XXII (p. 484).

opinion of the weak, an element of superiority made itself too much felt. I think that I have already observed that several of the prejudices that he had to combat, several of the false and vulgar opinions which beset him, have long since begun to infect the French press. It will therefore be not without point to give a summary account of some of his most important views relating to poetic composition. The parallelism of the error will make their application quite easy.

First of all I should say that having allotted his portion to the natural poet, to the quality of *innateness*, Poe went on to allot another to science, work and analysis, which may well seem extravagant to the proud who are not also learned. Not only did he go to great trouble to force to his will the fugitive demon of happy moments, to recall at his pleasure those exquisite sensations, those spiritual yearnings, those states of poetic well-being which are so rare and so precious that they might really be regarded as acts of grace external to man, as visitations; he has also subjected his inspiration to method and to a most rigorous analysis. The choice of means! To this he returns without ceasing; with a learned eloquence he insists on the appropriation of means to effect, on the use of rhyme, on the perfection of the refrain, in the adaptation of rhythm to sentiment. He used to declare that anyone who cannot grasp the intangible is no poet; that he alone is a poet who is master of his memory, lord of words and dictionary of his own feelings which is always open for consultation. Everything for the *dénouement!* he never tires of repeating. Even a sonnet needs a plan, and construction—the armature, so to speak—is the most important guarantee of the mysterious life of works of the spirit.

Turning naturally to his article, *The Poetic Principle*,[1] I find at the very outset a vigorous protest against what might be called, in the realm of poetry, the heresy of length and size—the absurd value attached to *large* poems. 'A long poem does not exist. I maintain that the phrase "a long poem" is simply a flat contradiction in terms.' In fact a poem deserves its title only inasmuch as it excites and enraptures[2] the soul, and the positive value of a poem is in exact ratio to this excitement and rapture. But,

[1] A great deal of this part of Baudelaire's study is composed of reminiscences—sometimes word-for-word, sometimes modified—of Poe; no attempt has been made here to track them all down.

[2] Poe has 'excites by *elevating* the soul' (p. 197), Baudelaire 'autant qu'il excite, qu'il *enlève* l'âme' (my italics). Is this an example of Baudelaire's faulty knowledge of English—or of an intentional 'improvement' of his original?

through a psychical necessity, all excitements are fugitive and transient. That strange state, where the reader's soul has been, so to speak, forcibly abducted, will certainly not be sustained for the length of a poem that, by its nature, outlasts the enthusiasm of which human nature is capable.

Here the epic poem stands clearly condemned. For a work of these dimensions can only be considered as poetic insofar as we lose sight of that vital requisite of all works of Art, Unity;—I do not refer to unity of conception, but rather to unity of Impression, to totality of effect, as I said before when I compared the Tale with the Novel. The epic poem thus appears to us, aesthetically speaking, as a paradox. It is possible that the ancients produced sequences of lyric poems, later sewn together by compilers into epics; but any *epic intention* is clearly the result of an imperfect sense of Art. The day of these artistic anomalies is over, and it is even very doubtful whether any long poem can ever have been truly popular, in the full force of the term.

It must be added that a poem which is too brief, a poem which provides insufficient *pabulum* for the excitement created, and which is unequal to the reader's natural appetite, is also very imperfect. However brilliant and intense may be its effect, it will not be lasting; the memory does not retain it; it will be like a seal which, placed too lightly and hurriedly upon the wax, has had no time to impress its image thereon.

But[1] there is yet another heresy which, thanks to hypocrisy and to the dullness and vulgarity of minds, is much more to be feared and has far greater chances of lasting—an error which dies harder : I refer to the heresy of *The Didactic*,[2] which includes as inevitable corollaries the heresies of *Passion*, *Truth* and *the Moral*. A whole host of people imagine that the aim of poetry is some kind of instruction—that it ought now to fortify the conscience, now to perfect manners, now to *demonstrate* some aspect of utility. Poe claims that his own countrymen have especially supported this peculiar idea—but alas, it is unnecessary to go as far as Boston to find it. Here too it besets us, every day launching its

[1] The following paragraphs, down to 'supernatural realms of Poetry' were later quoted by Baudelaire in his essay on Gautier (*l'Art romantique*, ed. Crépet, pp. 157 ff.). The fact that whole sentences are translated from Poe (without acknowledgement) would make the later quotation only the more disingenuous, were it not that Baudelaire's ability to 'assimilate' the work of others is one of his well-known characteristics. The borrowings from De Quincey in the *Paradis artificiels* are a case in point.

[2] *The Poetic Principle* (p. 201).

33. *Edgar Allan Poe*. From a daguerreotype.

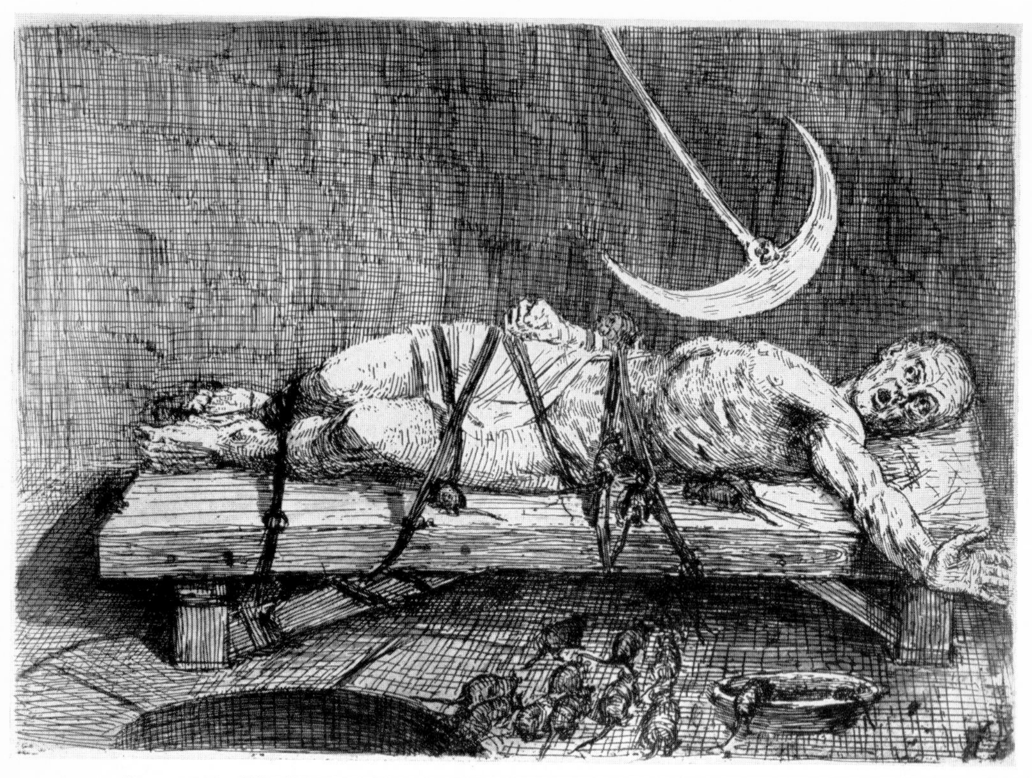

34. LEGROS: *The Pit and the Pendulum.* Etching touched with wash. London, Victoria and Albert Museum.

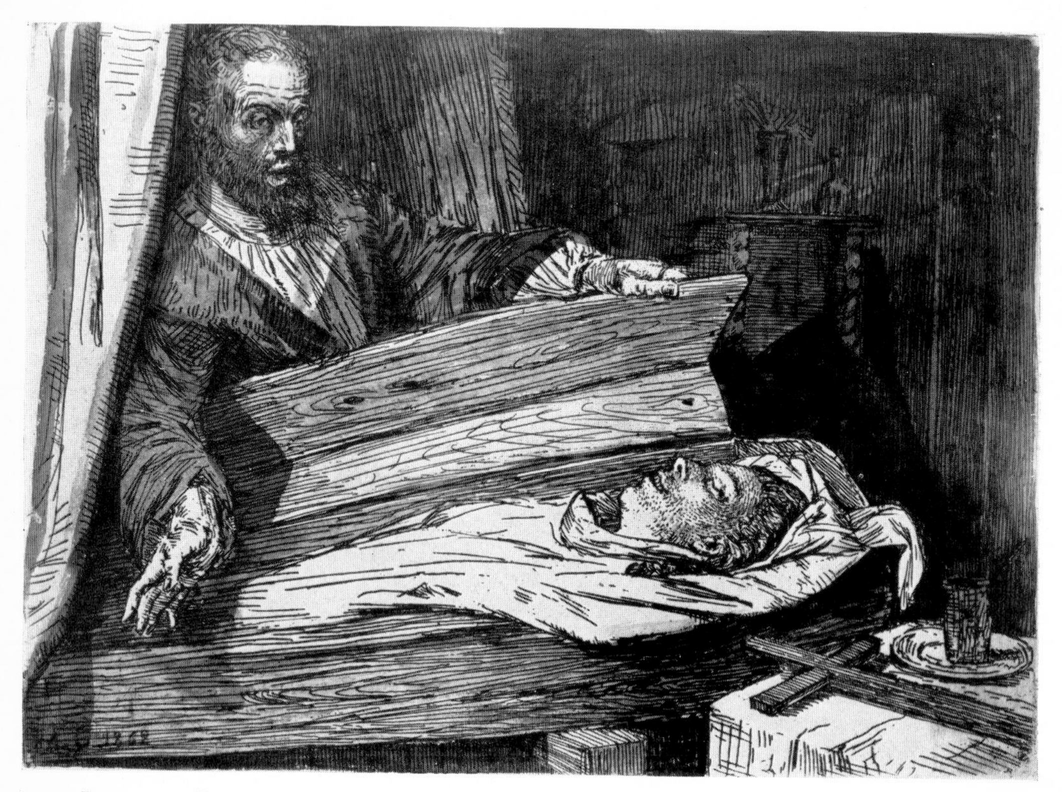

35. LEGROS: *Berenice.* Etching touched with wash. London, Victoria and Albert Museum.

brutal assaults upon true poetry. But we have only to descend into ourselves, to look into our own souls and recapture our memories of enthusiasm to see that Poetry has no other aim or object but herself; she can have no other, and no poem will be as great, as noble, as supremely worthy of the name as one that has been written for the sole pleasure of writing a poem.

I am not attempting to say that poetry does *not* ennoble morals—please understand me aright—or that its final result is not to lift man up above the level of vulgar interests; that would be a palpable absurdity. I am simply saying that if a poet pursues a moral aim, he will have weakened his poetic powers and it would not be rash to wager that the result will be a bad work. On pain of death or decay, poetry cannot transform herself into a branch of science or ethics; her object is not Truth, but only Herself. The modes of demonstration of Truth are other and elsewhere. Truth has nothing to do with Song. Everything that goes to make up the charm, the grace, the irresistible fascination of a Song would only take away from Truth her authority and power. Cool, calm and unimpassioned, the demonstrative mood rejects the gems and flowers of the Muse; it is thus the absolute opposite of the poetic mood.

Pure Intellect has as its goal the Truth, Taste informs us of the Beautiful, while the Moral Sense teaches us Duty. It is true that the middle term has intimate relations with either extreme, and from the Moral Sense is separated by so faint a difference that Aristotle has not hesitated to place certain of its delicate operations among the virtues themselves. Thus, what especially offends the Man of Taste in the spectacle of Vice is its deformity, its disproportion. Vice does injury to Justice and Truth, and revolts the Intellect and the Conscience; but as a dissonance, an outrage to harmony, it will wound more particularly certain poetic minds; and I see no reason to suppose that it will seem shocking to regard any breach of Morality, of Moral Beauty, as a kind of fault against universal rhythm and prosody.

It is this admirable and immortal instinct for Beauty that makes us consider the Earth and its shows as a glimpse, a *correspondence* of Heaven. The unquenchable thirst for all that lies beyond, and which life reveals, is the liveliest proof of our immortality. It is at once by means of and *through* poetry, by means of and *through* music, that the soul gets an inkling of the glories that lie beyond the grave; and when an exquisite poem melts us into tears, those tears are not the proof of an excess of pleasure, but rather evidence of a certain petulant, impatient sorrow—of a nervous postulation—of a nature exiled amid the imperfect, and eager to seize immediately, on this very earth, upon a revealed paradise.

Thus the Poetic Principle lies, strictly and simply, in human aspiration towards a supernal Beauty, and the manifestation of that principle is in an enthusiasm, an excitement of the soul—an enthusiasm entirely independent of Passion, which is the intoxication of the heart, and of Truth, which is the grazing-ground of reason. For Passion is natural—too natural to fail to introduce an offensive, discordant note into the domain of pure beauty, too familiar and violent to fail to shock those pure Desires, graceful Melancholies and noble Despairs which dwell in the supernatural realms of Poetry.

This extraordinary loftiness, this exquisite delicacy, this accent of immortality which Poe demands of the Muse, far from rendering him less attentive to the practical details of execution, have driven him ceaselessly to whet his practical genius. Many readers—and particularly those who are acquainted with his strange poem, *The Raven*—would be horrified were I to analyse the article in which, with seeming artlessness, but with a touch of impertinence which I cannot blame, our poet has minutely explained the method of construction which he adopted, the adjustment of the rhythm, the choice of a refrain—the briefest possible and the most susceptible of varied applications, and at the same time the most expressive of melancholy and despair, adorned with the most sonorous of all rhymes, 'nevermore'—the choice of a bird capable of imitating the human voice, but of a bird, the raven, stamped in the popular imagination with an ill-omened and fatal character—the choice of the most poetic of all tones, the melancholic—and of the most poetic sentiment, love of a dead woman, etc., etc.—He decides not to place the hero of his poem in poor surroundings, for poverty is trivial and contrary to the idea of Beauty; rather his melancholy should have for setting a 'richly and poetically furnished chamber'. In several of Poe's Tales the reader will find curious symptoms of this immoderate taste for beautiful forms, particularly when they have some element of strangeness—for richly appointed settings and Oriental luxury.

I said above that this article struck me as touched with a hint of impertinence. The partisans of inspiration will not however fail to go further and find it a blasphemy and a profanation; nevertheless I believe that it was for them that the article was specially written. Just as certain writers make a show of abandon, taking aim at a masterpiece with their eyes closed, filled with confidence in the midst of a chaos, waiting for the characters thrown up to the ceiling to fall back to the floor in the form of a poem; so Edgar Poe—one of the most *inspired* men that I know of—made a show of *concealing* spontaneity and *simulating* composure and deliberation. 'I think I may boast,' says he with an engaging pride which I cannot find in bad taste, 'that no one point in my composition is referable either to accident or intuition—that the work proceeded step by step to its completion with the precision and rigid consequence of a mathematical problem'. Only the lovers of pure chance, the fatalists of inspiration and the fanatics of blank verse could possibly find these *minutiae* strange. So far as Art is concerned, there are no such things as *minutiae*.

While on the subject of blank verse, I would add that Poe attached an extreme importance to rhyme, and that, in the analysis that he made of the mathematical and musical pleasure which the mind obtains from this device, he brought as much care, as much subtlety, as he did to all subjects relating to the craft of poetry. Just as he showed that the refrain is susceptible of infinitely varied applications, so also he sought to rejuvenate, to redouble our pleasure in rhyme by adding an unexpected ingredient, *strangeness*, which is as it were the indispensable condiment of all Beauty. He often makes a happy use of repetitions of one or several lines, relentless reiterations of sentences which echo the obsessions of melancholy or an *idée fixe*—of the refrain pure and simple, but led up to in various different ways—of the variant-refrain, which suggests indolence and distraction—of double and triple rhymes, and also of a kind of rhyme which introduces into modern poetry, but with greater precision and purpose, the surprises of Leonine verse.

It is clear that the merit of all these devices can only be proved in their practical application; and while the translation of poems so calculated and so concentrated may be an attractive dream, it can hardly be more than just a dream.[1] Poe wrote little poetry, though sometimes he would complain that he could not devote not just more, but *all* of his time and energies to this type of work which he regarded as the noblest of all. But his poetry is always powerfully effective. It is not the fiery outpouring of Byron, nor the soft, harmonious, well-bred melancholy of

[1] Nevertheless it had originally been Baudelaire's intention to place at the end of the *Nouvelles histoires extraordinaires* 'one or two samples of poetry'.

Tennyson, for whom he had, by the way, a well-nigh fraternal admiration. It is something deep and glistening like a dream, something mysterious and perfect like a crystal. I take it that there is no need for me to add that American critics have often denigrated it; quite recently in an American Biographical Dictionary I came across an article in which it was arraigned for its strangeness—in which the fear was expressed that this 'well turned-out Muse' might set up a school in the glorious country of Utilitarianism, and it was regretted finally that Poe had not applied his gifts to the expression of moral truths, instead of wasting them in pursuit of an eccentric ideal and pouring out in his verse a mysterious but, alas, a sensual rapture.

We all know these patriotic champions; the censure which bad critics mete out to good poets is the same in all countries. As I read that article I seemed to myself to be reading a translation of one of those countless indictments drawn up by Parisian critics against those of our own poets who are most in love with perfection. Our own preferences are easy to guess, and every soul that is wedded to pure poetry will understand my meaning when I say that among our antipoetic race Victor Hugo himself would be less admired if he were perfect, and that the only way in which he could gain acceptance for his lyric genius was by rudely and violently introducing into his poetry what Edgar Poe regarded as the capital modern heresy—*the Didactic*.

RICHARD WAGNER AND TANNHÄUSER IN PARIS

I

I PROPOSE, with the reader's permission, to go back some thirteen months, to the beginning of the affair; and further I must beg to be allowed in the course of this appreciation to make frequent use of the first person singular. That notorious 'I', which is often so justly accused of impertinence, nevertheless implies a great modesty; it imprisons the writer within the strictest bonds of sincerity. By restricting his task, it makes it easier. Finally, it is hardly necessary to be a consummate judge of probabilities to convince oneself that this sincerity will find friends among unprejudiced readers; there is clearly a reasonable chance that, in describing no more than his own impressions, the candid critic will describe also those of certain unknown sympathizers.

Thirteen months ago, then, there was a great uproar in Paris. A German composer who had lived long among us[1] without our knowledge, poor, unknown, existing by means of wretched tasks, but a man whom for fifteen years now the German public had been acclaiming as a genius—this man was returning to the city which had witnessed his youthful struggles, to submit his works to our judgement. Until then Paris had heard but little of Wagner, though we knew vaguely that on the far side of the Rhine the question of a reform in opera was being hotly debated and that Liszt had espoused the reformer's opinions with enthusiasm. M. Fétis had launched a kind of indictment against him, and any reader who is sufficiently interested to thumb through the back numbers of the *Revue et Gazette musicale de Paris*[2] will be able to satisfy himself once again that those writers who boast of professing the wisest and most classical opinions make little pretence either of wisdom or of moderation, to say nothing of common politeness, when they come to criticize opinions which are opposed to theirs. M. Fétis's articles are hardly more than a depressing diatribe; if, however, the old dilettante's

[1] From 1839 to 1842.

[2] 6, 13, 20, 27 June, 25 July and 8 August 1852.

exasperation went to establish anything, it was the importance of the works that he was condemning to ridicule and anathema. Besides, for thirteen months, during which time public interest has in no wise abated, Richard Wagner has had to endure many other insults. Several years ago on his return from a visit to Germany where he had been much moved by a performance of *Tannhäuser*, Théophile Gautier had written an article in the *Moniteur*,[1] in which he set down his impressions with that plastic firmness which gives such an irresistible charm to all his writings. But these various documents, appearing as they did at lengthy intervals, had made but little impression on the public mind.

As soon as the posters announced that Richard Wagner was proposing to offer us some extracts from his works at the Salle des Italiens,[2] a curious thing happened, a thing that we have noticed before and which proves the instinctive, irresistible need of the French to take sides on every matter before having either deliberated or examined. Some prophesied marvels, others set about an extravagant denigration of works that they had not heard. This grotesque situation still obtains today, and it would surely be true to say that never was an unknown topic so hotly argued. In short, Wagner's concerts proclaimed themselves as a veritable battle of the doctrines, as one of those solemn crises of art, one of those free-for-alls into which critics, artists and the public are in the habit of hurling indiscriminately all their passions: happy crises which denote health and richness in the intellectual life of a nation and which we had practically forgotten about since the great days of Victor Hugo. I take the following lines from M. Berlioz's article of 9 February 1860:[3] 'The vestibule of the Théâtre Italien was a strange sight on the evening of the first concert. It was nothing but a mêlée of passions, shouts and arguments which seemed always on the point of degenerating into acts of physical violence.' If it had not been for the presence of the sovereign, the same scandal might have repeated itself several days ago at the Opera,[4] above all with a *truer* public. At the end of one of the public dress-rehearsals, I remember seeing one of our

[1] 29 September 1857. The performance of *Tannhäuser* was given at Wiesbaden.

[2] The concerts were given on the 25 January and 1 and 8 February 1860.

[3] In the *Journal des Débats*: reprinted in *A travers champs* (1862). For an account of the article see Newman, vol. III, pp. 26–8.

[4] The first performance of *Tannhäuser* took place on the 13 March 1861. It was followed by two others, after which Wagner withdrew the work.

established Paris critics ostentatiously planting himself in front of the box-office, fronting the crowd so as almost to bar their exit, and setting about laughing like a maniac, like one of those poor wretches in asylums who are called *agités*. This poor man, in the belief that his face was familiar to everyone present, seemed to be saying, 'Just watch me laughing, me, the great S. . . .[1] And take very good care to suit your verdict to mine.' In the article to which I alluded a moment ago, M. Berlioz—who nevertheless showed much less warmth than one might have expected of him—added, 'The amount of nonsense, foolishness and even downright dishonesty that was uttered at that time was really fantastic and proves only too clearly that with us, at least, when it is a question of appreciating a type of music different from the common run, passion and prejudice alone take the floor and prevent good sense and good taste from speaking.'

Wagner had shown great daring; the programme of his concert contained neither instrumental solos, nor songs, nor any of those exhibitions so dear to a public which dotes on virtuosos and their *tours de force*. Nothing but concerted numbers, choral or symphonic. The struggle was a violent one, it is true; but the public, being thrown back upon itself, took fire at certain of those irresistible passages in which it found the thought more clearly expressed, and Wagner's music triumphed by its own strength. The *Tannhäuser* overture, the solemn march from the second act, the *Lohengrin* overture in particular, and the Bridal Procession and Chorus were magnificently received.[2] Much no doubt remained obscure, but impartial critics contented themselves with saying, 'Since these compositions were written for the stage, we must wait and see; whatever has been insufficiently defined will become clear in production.' Meanwhile it had been established that as a symphonist, as an artist using the thousand combinations of sound to translate the tumults of the human soul, Richard Wagner was able to scale the loftiest peaks, he was unquestionably as great as the greatest.

I have often heard it said that music cannot pride itself on being able to translate all or anything with precision, as can painting or writing.

[1] Paul Scudo. He was a convinced anti-Wagnerite; see particularly his articles in the *Revue des Deux-Mondes*, March and April 1860. It is perhaps poetically just that he should die insane in 1864.

[2] It seems curious that Baudelaire should not mention the *Tristan* prelude, which was also included in the programme.

This is true up to a point, but it is not entirely so. Music translates in its own way and using means which are proper to it. In music, just as in painting and even in the written word, which is nevertheless the most positive of the arts, there is always a lacuna which is filled in by the listener's imagination.

It is doubtless considerations of this kind that have led Wagner to consider the dramatic art, which is the marriage, the *coincidence* of several arts, as the art *par excellence*, the most synthetic and the most perfect. Now if we dispense for a moment with the aid of stage-production, of decor, of the embodiment of the imagined characters in living actors, and even of the sung word, it still remains unarguable that the more eloquent the music, the swifter and truer is its power of suggestion and the more chances there are that sensitive minds will conceive ideas in harmony with those that inspired the artist. Let me take an immediate example, the famous *Lohengrin* overture, of which M. Berlioz has written a magnificent eulogy in technical terms; here however, I will content myself with examining its worth with reference to the ideas that it suggests.

The programme, sold at the time at the Théâtre Italien, reads as follows:

> 'From the very first bars the soul of the pious wanderer who is awaiting the holy vessel *plunges into an infinity of space*. Little by little there forms before his eyes a strange vision which takes a body and a face. The vision becomes clearer, and the *miraculous host of angels* passes before him, bearing the holy cup in their midst. The sacred procession draws nearer; the heart of the elect of God gradually stirs; it swells, it expands; ineffable yearnings awaken within him; *he yields to a growing feeling of bliss* as the *radiant vision* comes ever closer, and when at last the Holy Grail itself appears in the midst of the sacred procession, *he is swallowed up in an ecstasy of adoration, as if the whole world had suddenly disappeared.*
>
> 'Meanwhile the Holy Grail pours its blessings upon the saint in prayer, consecrating him its knight. Then the *burning flames gradually mitigate their brilliance;* in holy joy, the angelic host, smiling upon the earth that they are leaving, returns to the heavenly heights. They have left the Holy Grail in the care of pure men, *into whose hearts the divine essence has flowed*, and the majestic company vanishes *into the infinities of space* in the same way that it first appeared.'

The reader will shortly understand why I have italicized certain passages. In the meantime let us take up Liszt's book[1] and open it at the page on which the imagination of the famous pianist (who is also an artist and a philosopher) interprets the same passage in its own way:

'The prelude contains and reveals that *mystical element* which is always present and always latent in the work. . . . To teach us the untellable power of this secret, Wagner shows us first of all the *ineffable beauty of the sanctuary*, the dwelling-place of a God who avenges the oppressed and asks no more than *faith and love* from his followers. He introduces us to the Holy Grail; we are made to see glimmering before our eyes the temple of incorruptible wood, with its sweet-smelling walls, its doors of *gold*, its joists of *asbestos*, its columns of *opal*, its partitions of *cymophane*, and its splendid porticoes, which may only be approached by those whose hearts are uplifted and whose hands pure. He is very careful not to present it to us in all its awe-inspiring reality, but, as though to spare our feeble senses, he shows it first of all reflected in *some azure wave* or mirrored by *some iridescent cloud*.

'At the beginning it is a *vast, slumbering lake* of melody, a *vaporous, extending ether*, on which the holy picture may take form before our profane eyes: this is a passage given exclusively to the violins, divided into eight different desks, which, after several bars of harmonious chords, continue in the highest part of their register. The motive is then taken up by the mellowest of the wind instruments; the horns and the bassoons join in to prepare for the entrance of the trumpets and the trombones which repeat the melody for the fourth time *with a dazzling burst of colour*, as if at this unique moment the holy edifice had *blazed forth* before our *blinded eyes*, in *all its radiant and luminous magnificence*. But the vivid sparkle which has been gradually raised to this *intensity of solar effulgence* dies away swiftly, like a *celestial glimmer*. The *diaphanous vapour* of the clouds closes in once more, the vision dissolves little by little amid the same *iridescent* incense in which it first appeared, and the piece concludes with a repetition of the first six bars, only *more ethereal still*. The *ideally mystical* quality which characterizes it is conveyed not least by the *pianissimo* which is always preserved by

[1] *Lohengrin et Tannhäuser*, 1851, pp. 48–50.

the orchestra and which is barely interrupted by the brief moment in which the *brass bursts forth* with the marvellous phrases of the prelude's single motive. Such is the image which stirs our senses at a first hearing of this sublime adagio.'

May I now be permitted to describe, to convey in words the inevitable translation made by my own imagination of the same piece when I heard it for the first time, with my eyes closed, feeling, as it were, lifted from the earth? I would certainly not venture to speak smugly of my own reveries if they were not in fact relevant to those that we have already considered. The reader will already have understood the drift of our argument, which is to demonstrate that true music evokes analogous ideas in different brains. However it would be by no means absurd at this point to argue *a priori*; for what would be truly surprising would be to find that sound *could not* suggest colour, that colours *could not* evoke the idea of a melody, and that sound and colour were *unsuitable* for the translation of ideas, seeing that things have always found their expression through a system of reciprocal analogy ever since the day when God uttered the world like a complex and indivisible statement.

La nature est un temple où de vivants piliers
Laissent parfois sortir de confuses paroles;
L'homme y passe à travers des forêts de symboles
Qui l'observent avec des regards familiers.

Comme de longs échos qui de loin se confondent
Dans une ténébreuse et profonde unité,
Vaste comme la nuit et comme la clarté,
Les parfums, les couleurs et les sons se répondent.[1]

Let me continue. I remember that from the very first bars I suffered one of those happy impressions that almost all imaginative men have known, through dreams, in sleep. I felt myself released from the *bonds of gravity*, and I rediscovered in memory that extraordinary *thrill of*

[1] The first two stanzas of the poem *Correspondances*, from the *Fleurs du mal*. The following is a literal translation:

Nature is a temple in which living pillars sometimes let slip confused words; there man passes through forests of symbols that watch him with familiar glances.

Like long-drawn echoes mingled from afar in a deep and shadowy unity, vast as the night and the brightness of day, scents, colours and sounds answer one another.

pleasure which dwells in *high places* (be it noted in passing that I was as yet ignorant of the programme quoted a moment ago). Next I found myself imagining the delicious state of a man in the grip of a profound reverie, in an absolute solitude, a solitude with an *immense horizon* and a *wide diffusion of light; an immensity with no other decor but itself.* Soon I experienced the sensation of a *brightness* more vivid, an *intensity of light* growing so swiftly that not all the nuances provided by the dictionary would be sufficient to express *this ever-renewing increase of incandescence and heat.* Then I came to the full conception of the idea of a soul moving about in a luminous medium, of an ecstasy *composed of knowledge and joy*, hovering high above the natural world.

It would be easy enough to note the differences in these three interpretations. Wagner prescribes *a host of angels bringing a holy vessel;* Liszt sees *a monument of miraculous beauty*, reflected in a vaporous mirage. My own reverie is much less adorned with material objects; it is vaguer and more abstract. But the important thing here is to concentrate on the resemblances. Even if they had been few, they would still constitute a sufficient proof; fortunately however they are numerous and striking to excess. In all three interpretations we find a sensation of *spiritual and physical bliss;* of *isolation;* of the contemplation of *something infinitely great and infinitely beautiful;* of an *intensity of light* which rejoices *the eyes and the soul until they swoon;* and finally a sensation of *space reaching to the furthest conceivable limits.*

No musician excels as Wagner does in *painting* space and depth, both material and spiritual. It is an observation that several critics, and those among the best, have been constrained to make on several occasions. He possesses the art of translating, by means of the subtlest shades, all that is excessive, immense and ambitious in spiritual and natural man. One seems sometimes, when listening to this fiery and peremptory music, to recapture the dizzy perceptions of an opium-dream, painted upon a backcloth of darkness.

From that very moment, at the first concert, I was possessed by a desire to enter into a deeper understanding of these extraordinary works. I had—or at least it seemed to me that I had—undergone a spiritual operation, a revelation. My thrill of pleasure had been so powerful and terrible that I could not prevent myself from ceaselessly wanting to return to it. The experience that I had had doubtless contained much of what Weber and Beethoven had already taught me, but there was also something new which I was incapable of defining, and this incapacity caused me a rage and a curiosity mingled with a strange delight. For several days—for a long time—I continually asked myself, 'Where can I go this evening to hear some of Wagner's music?' Those of my friends that owned pianos were more than once my victims.[1] Soon, as always happens with every novelty, selections from Wagner's music echoed through the *casinos* which throw open their doors each evening to a crowd in search of trivial pleasures. There the volcanic splendour of this music fell upon the air like thunder in a bawdy-house. The news spread quickly, so that we were often treated to the comic spectacle of grave, fastidious men rubbing shoulders with the vulgar herd, so as to enjoy, in default of anything better, the Grand March from *Tannhäuser* or the majestic Bridal Procession from *Lohengrin*.

Nevertheless frequent repetitions of the same melodic phrases in different extracts taken from the same opera seemed to imply mysterious intentions and a method which were all unknown to me. I resolved to make myself master of the why and the wherefore, and to transform my pleasure into knowledge, until a stage-production should come to provide me with a perfect explanation. I cross-questioned both friends and enemies. I gnawed at M. Fétis's abominable, indigestible pamphlet. I read Liszt's book, and finally, in default of *Art and Revolution* and *The Art-Work of the Future*, which had neither of them been translated, I got hold of Wagner's own book, *Opera and Drama*, in an English translation.

II

THE French continued to indulge their love of jesting, and popular journalism carried on unremittingly with its professional pranks. As Wagner had never tired of repeating that (dramatic) music ought to *speak* the sentiment, to match the sentiment with the same precision as the word, but obviously in a different way, by which I mean that it ought to express the vague and indefinite part of the sentiment which the word, by its very positiveness, is incapable of rendering (in all of which there was nothing that could not be accepted by any sensible man), a crowd of people, under the persuasion of the newspaper humourists, imagined that the master was claiming for music the power

[1] Particularly Mme Meurice and Villiers de l'Isle Adam.

to express the positive form of things; in other words, that he was inverting the roles and the functions. It would be as profitless as it would be boring to enumerate all the taunts and gibes which resulted from this false premiss, and which, powered now by ill-will and now by ignorance, had the consequence of misleading public opinion in advance. But in Paris, more than anywhere else, there is no means of stopping a pen which fancies itself amusing. As a result of the general interest which was thus concentrated upon Wagner, we had a spate of articles and brochures which introduced us to his life, his weary struggles and all his sufferings. Among these documents which today are so well known, I would refer only to those which seem to me more likely to elucidate and to define the nature and the distinctive character of the master. The man who wrote, 'Whoever did not receive at birth the fairies' gift of a sense of dissatisfaction, will never achieve the discovery of the new',[1] was bound to find the conflicts of life more painful than anyone else. It is in this gift for suffering, which is common to all artists but which is all the greater as their instinct for the beautiful and the exact is more pronounced, that I find the explanation of Wagner's revolutionary opinions. Embittered by so many miscalculations, disappointed by so many dreams, there arrived the inevitable moment when, as a result of an error excusable in a sensitive and excessively nervous mind, he came to postulate an ideal complicity between bad music and bad government. Possessed by a supreme desire to see the ideal in art finally dominating the conventional routines, he found it in him (and this is an essentially human illusion) to hope that revolutions in the sphere of politics would favour the cause of revolution in art. Wagner's success has itself given the lie to his hopes and expectations; for in France it required a *despot's* order to have the work of a revolutionary performed. In the same way we in Paris have already seen the evolution of Romanticism favoured by the monarchy, while liberals and republicans alike remained obstinately wedded to the routine of that literature called classical.

From the notes that he himself has given us about his youth, I see that while still a child he lived in the bosom of the theatre, haunted the green-rooms and wrote plays. The music of Weber, and later that of Beethoven,

[1] *Die Operndichtungen nebst Mitteilungen an seine Freunde als Vorwort*, 1852. Fétis had already used this quotation in one of his articles, and it was probably from there that Baudelaire took it.

acted upon his mind with an irresistible force, and soon, with an accumulation of years and study, he found it impossible not to think in a double manner, poetically and musically; not to catch sight of each idea in two simultaneous forms, one of the two arts coming into play at the point where the frontiers of the other were marked out. The dramatic instinct, which occupied such an important place among his faculties, was bound to incite him to revolt against all the frivolities, platitudes and absurdities of the conventional opera-libretto. Thus the Providence which presides over artistic revolutions was gradually bringing to solution in a young German brain the problem which had so much exercised the eighteenth century. Anyone who has carefully read the *Letter on Music* which serves as preface to *Four Opera-poems translated into French prose*[1] can be in no doubt at all on this point. The names of Gluck and Méhul are constantly being mentioned with a glowing sympathy. With all due deference to M. Fétis, whose one and only desire is to establish for all time the predominance of music in lyric drama, the opinions of minds such as Gluck, Diderot, Voltaire and Goethe are not to be lightly brushed aside. If the two last went back later on their chosen theories, with them it was no more than an act of discouragement and despair. As I turned the pages of the *Letter on Music*, I seemed by some phenomenon of mnemonic echo to be hearing again various passages of Diderot, in which he declares that true dramatic music can be nothing else but the sigh or the cry of passion, set to notes and rhythms. The same scientific, poetic, and artistic problems ceaselessly recur through the ages, and Wagner makes no claim to be an inventor, but simply the vindicator of an old idea which will doubtless be more than once in the future alternately vanquished and victorious. In truth all these questions are extremely simple, and it is not a little surprising to find in revolt against the *music of the future*[2] (to make use of an expression as inexact as it is accepted) those very people whom we have so often heard complaining of the tortures inflicted on any rational mind by the ordinary run of opera-libretto.

In this same *Letter on Music*, in which the author gives a very brief and lucid analysis of his three earlier books, *Art and Revolution*, *The*

[1] Published in Paris in 1861.

[2] This well-known phrase was coined by a German journalist, Professor Bischoff of Cologne, as a result of a misunderstanding of Wagner's *Art-Work of the Future*. Wagner protested against it in his published *Letter to Berlioz*, part of which is quoted below. Nevertheless it stuck, just as the term 'Impressionist', also coined by a journalist, was to stick.

Art-Work of the Future and *Opera and Drama*, we find an exceptionally keen preoccupation with the Greek theatre, which is altogether natural, inevitable even, in a composer-playwright who had to turn to the past to find a warrant for his disgust with the present, no less than positive suggestions which would be helpful in the establishment of the new conditions of lyric drama. In his letter to Berlioz[1] he was already saying, more than a year ago:—

> 'I asked myself what were the conditions required to enable art to inspire an inviolable respect in the public; and to avoid venturing too far afield in my examination of this question, I decided to seek my point of departure in ancient Greece. There I immediately found the art-work *par excellence*, the drama, in which, however profound an idea may be, it can yet manifest itself with the greatest degree of clarity and in the most universally intelligible way. We have every right to be astonished today that thirty thousand Greeks were capable of following performances of the tragedies of Aeschylus with unflagging interest; but if we inquire into the means whereby results of this kind were obtained, we will find that it was by an alliance of all the arts uniting in a common object, which was the creation of the most perfect, the only true art-work. This led me to study the reciprocal connections between the various branches of art, and after having grasped the relation which exists between the *plastic* and the *mimetic*, I proceeded to examine that which is to be found between music and poetry; my examination resulted in a sudden burst of light which entirely dissipated the obscurity which until then had troubled me.
>
> 'I recognized in fact that it was precisely at the point at which one of these arts reached impassable frontiers that the sphere of action of the other started, with the most rigorous exactitude; and that in consequence, by the intimate union of these two arts it was possible to express what neither of them could express in isolation; and conversely that any attempt to render by means of the resources of one of them what could only be rendered by the two together was doomed to lead at first to obscurity and confusion, and then to the degeneration and corruption of each art individually.'

[1] *Journal des Débats*, 22 February 1860. This was in answer to Berlioz's less than cordial review of the concerts. See Newman, vol. III, pp. 28–9.

In the preface to his last book[1] he returns to the same topic in the following terms:

> 'A few, rare artistic creations had provided me with a solid basis on which to establish my musical and dramatic ideal; now history in its turn was offering me a model and a type of the ideal relations of theatre and public life such as I conceived them. This model I found in the theatre of ancient Athens; there the theatre only opened its precincts to certain solemn ceremonials during which a religious festival was performed, to the accompaniment of the enjoyments of art. The most distinguished men of the state played a direct part in these rites, either as poets or directors; to the eyes of the population assembled from the city and the countryside they seemed like priests, and this same population was filled with so high an expectation of the sublimity of the works that were about to be played before it, that the profoundest poems, those of an Aeschylus and a Sophocles, could be put before the people and assured of a perfect hearing.'

This absolute, despotic taste for a dramatic ideal in which everything, from a piece of declamation so meticulously noted and underlined by the music that it is impossible for the singer to depart from it in a single syllable—a veritable arabesque of sound traced by passion—down to the most scrupulous niceties in matters of decor and production, in which every detail must ceaselessly contribute to the total effect—it is this, I say, that has moulded Wagner's destiny. With him it was like a continual postulation. Ever since the day when he broke away from the old routines of libretto and courageously disowned his *Rienzi*,[2] a youthful opera which had had the honour of a great success, he has marched on, without deviating by an inch, towards that peremptory ideal. Thus I was in no sense surprised to find in such of his works as have been translated, and particularly in *Tannhäuser*, *Lohengrin* and *The Flying Dutchman*, an excellent method of construction and a sense of order and structural division that recalls the architecture of the antique tragedies. But the phenomena and the ideas which occur periodically through the ages always, at each resurrection, assume the complementary character of the variant and the circumstances. The radiant Venus of antiquity, the foam-born Aphrodite, has not passed unscathed through the dreadful

[1] I.e. the *Letter on Music*. [2] 1842.

36. *Richard Wagner*. From a photograph by Nadar.

37. *Tannhäuser: the décor for Act I, Scene 2*, designed by Desplechin for the Paris Opéra. Wood-engraving.

shades of the Middle Ages. Her dwelling is no longer Olympus, nor the shores of a perfumed archipelago. She has retired into the depths of a cavern, magnificent, it is true, but illumined by fires very different from those of benign Apollo. In going underground, Venus has moved a step towards Hell, and doubtless, on certain abominable feast-days, she goes regularly to pay homage to the Archfiend, Prince of the Flesh and Sovereign of Sin. In the same way Wagner's poems, while revealing a sincere taste for classical beauty, and a perfect understanding of it, are also strongly imbued with the Romantic spirit. If they make one think of the grandeur of Sophocles and Aeschylus, at the same time they force the mind back to the Mysteries of the most plastically Catholic epoch. They are like those superb visions which the Middle Ages displayed on the walls of its churches or wove into its magnificent tapestries. Their general appearance is decisively legendary: *Tannhäuser*, *Lohengrin* and *The Flying Dutchman*—each one is a legend. Moreover it is not only an inclination natural to every poetic mind that has led Wagner towards this apparent speciality; it is a formal principle derived from a study of the most favourable conditions of lyric drama.

He has himself taken care to elucidate the matter in his books. All subjects are not in fact equally suited to provide a vast drama, imbued with a character of universality. It would clearly be courting disaster to attempt to translate an exquisite and perfect genre-picture into a fresco. Where else but in the universal heart of man and in the history of that heart will the dramatic poet find pictures which are universally intelligible? To have complete freedom to construct the ideal drama, it will be wise to eliminate all those difficulties which could arise out of technical, political, or even too positively historical details. Let the master speak for himself:

> 'The only picture of human life which may be called poetic is that in which those motives which have meaning for the abstract intelligence alone give way to the purely human impulses which govern the heart. This tendency (in its reference to the invention of the poetic subject) is the sovereign law which presides over poetic form and representation. . . . Rhythmic arrangement and the almost musical ornament of rhyme are means available to the poet to endow his lines and phrases with a power which charms as though by magic and bends the feeling to its will. Essential to the poet, this tendency leads him to the very limits of his art, to the

point where the domain of music begins; and consequently the poet's most complete work should be that which, in its final consummation, would be perfect music.

'From that point I found myself inexorably led to postulate *Myth* as the ideal subject-matter for the poet. Myth is the primitive and anonymous poetry of the people, and throughout history we find if being returned to and ceaselessly recast by the great poets of cultivated epochs. In Myth, in fact, human relations strip themselves almost entirely of their conventional form which is intelligible only to abstract reason; instead they show the truly human and eternally comprehensible element of life, and they show it in that concrete form, a form exclusive of all imitation, which confers upon all true myths that individual character which is recognisable at the very first glance.'[1]

Later on he takes up the same theme in the following words:

'I said a final farewell to the domain of history and established myself in that of legend. . . . All the detail required for the description and representation of historical fact and its accidents, all the detail demanded, for its perfect comprehension, by a special and remote period of history, detail which contemporary writers of plays and historical novels accumulate, for this very reason, in such a circumstantial manner, I was free to leave on one side. . . . To whatever epoch or nation it may belong, legend has the advantage of exclusively comprising the purely human elements of that epoch and that nation, and of presenting them in a very striking original form which is consequently intelligible at a first glance. A ballad or a popular song is sufficient to give one an instantaneous picture of this distinctive character in the most definitive and striking outline. . . . The character of the scene and the tone of the legend together contribute to throw the mind into that *dream-state* which soon carries it onward to full *illumination*, when it discovers a new concatenation of the phenomena of the world which the eyes could not perceive in the ordinary state of waking. . . .'

It would of course be surprising if Wagner did not have an admirable understanding of the sacred and divine nature of Myth, being at once both poet and critic. Indeed I have heard many people deducing from

[1] From the *Letter on Music*, as is the next quotation also.

the very range of his faculties, and from his high critical intelligence, a reason for mistrust concerning his musical genius, and this seems to me to be a suitable opportunity to refute a very common error whose principal root is perhaps that ugliest of human emotions, Envy. 'A man so given to reasoning about his art cannot spontaneously produce fine works,' say some, who would thus strip genius of its rationality and assign to it a function purely instinctive and, so to speak, vegetable. There are others who prefer to regard Wagner as a theorist who would never have written operas save to confirm, *a posteriori*, the truth of his own theories. Not only is this completely false, since, as we know, the master began quite young by producing poetic and musical essays of a different nature, and has only arrived by degrees at his own ideal of lyric drama; it is in fact absolutely impossible. To find a critic turning into a poet would be an entirely new event in the history of the arts, a reversal of all the psychical laws, a monstrosity; on the other hand, all great poets naturally and fatally become critics. I pity those poets who are guided by instinct alone: I regard them as incomplete. In the spiritual life of the former a crisis inevitably occurs when they feel the need to reason about their art, to discover the obscure laws in virtue of which they have created, and to extract from this study a set of precepts whose divine aim is infallibility in poetic creation. It would be unthinkable for a critic to become a poet; and it is impossible for a poet not to contain within him a critic. Therefore the reader will not be surprised at my regarding the poet as the best of all critics. Those who rebuke the composer Wagner for having written books on the philosophy of his art, and who derive from this the suspicion that his music is not a natural, spontaneous growth, should equally deny the ability of Leonardo, Hogarth and Reynolds to paint good pictures, simply because they too deduced and analysed the principles of their art. Who speaks more eloquently about painting than our own great Delacroix? Diderot, Goethe, Shakespeare—as many creators as admirable critics. Poetry exists and asserts itself first, and then gives birth to the study of the rules. Such is the undisputed history of the human *modus operandi*. Now since each man is the diminutive of everyman, and since the history of an individual brain represents in microcosm the history of the universal brain, it would be just and natural to suppose (quite apart from existing proofs) that the gradual development of Wagner's thoughts has been analogous to the *modus operandi* of humanity.

III

Tannhäuser represents the struggle between the two principles that have chosen the human heart for their chief battlefield; in other words, the struggle between flesh and spirit, Heaven and Hell, Satan and God. And this duality is established at the very outset, and with incomparable skill, by the Overture. How much has not already been written about this piece of music? It is nevertheless to be presumed that it will continue to provide matter for many a thesis and eloquent commentary; for it is the nature of true art-works to be inexhaustible mines of suggestion. The Overture, then, sums up the dramatic thought in two motifs, the religious and the sensual which, to have recourse to Liszt's expression, 'are placed here like two mathematical terms which find their equation in the finale'. The Pilgrims' Chorus appears first, with the authority of the supreme law, as though to mark at the outset the true direction of life, the goal of the universal pilgrimage, which is God. But as the intimate sense of God is soon drowned in every consciousness by the lusts of the flesh, the motif which represents holiness is gradually overwhelmed by the sighs of the senses. The true, terrible and universal Venus is already looming up in every imagination. But I must warn anyone who has not yet heard this marvellous overture to beware of envisaging at this point a chorus of everyday lovers whiling away their time in shady bowers, or the accents of an ecstatic band hurling their challenge at God in the cultivated language of Horace. This is quite a different matter, at once more true and more sinister. Languors, fevered and agonized delights, ceaseless returns towards an ecstasy of pleasure which promises to quench, but never does quench, thirst; frenzied palpitations of heart and senses, imperious orders of the flesh, the whole onomatopœic dictionary of Love is to be heard here. Finally the religious theme little by little resumes its sway, slowly, by degrees, overwhelming the other at last in a peaceful victory, as glorious as that of the irresistible being over his sickly and anarchic adversary, of St. Michael over Lucifer.

At the beginning of this study I drew attention to the power with which Wagner, in the *Lohengrin* overture, had expressed the ardours of mysticism, the appetitions of the spirit towards the incommunicable Deity. In the *Tannhäuser* overture, in the struggle of the two contrary principles, he has shown himself no less subtle or powerful. Where, I ask, can the master have discovered this frenzied song of the flesh, this absolute knowledge of the diabolic part of man? From the very first bars the nerves quiver in unison with the melody; no fleshly body that remembers itself but starts to tremble. Every healthy brain carries within it two infinites, Heaven and Hell, and in any image of one of these it immediately recognizes a half of itself. The satanic titillations of a vague sensuality are soon succeeded by impulsive movement, swoonings, cries of victory, moans of gratitude, and then howls of ferocity, the reproachful cries of the victims and the impious hosannas of their sacrificers, as if savagery must always find a place in the drama of love and the enjoyment of the flesh must always lead, by some ineluctable Satanic logic, to the ecstatic delights of crime. When the religious theme makes its invasion athwart this anarchy of evil, coming gradually to re-establish order and to resume the ascendancy, when it takes its stand once more in all its massive beauty above that chaos of agonizing ecstasies, the entire soul feels as it were refreshed, in a bliss of redemption: an ineffable feeling which will be repeated at the beginning of the second scene, when Tannhäuser, having escaped from Venus's grotto, will find himself once again amid the realities of life, between the holy sound of natal bells,[1] the herdsman's rustic song, the pilgrim's hymn and the cross planted by the road, a symbol of all those crosses which must be carried on every road. In this latter case there is a power of contrast which acts irresistibly on the mind and makes one think of the broad, free manner of Shakespeare. A moment ago we were in the depths of the earth (Venus's dwelling, as we have already observed, being in the neighbourhood of Hell), breathing a perfumed but stifling atmosphere, lit by a rosy light which came not from the sun; we were not unlike the knight Tannhäuser himself, who, surfeited with exhausting joys, *yearns for pain!*—a sublime cry which any official critic would admire in Corneille, but which no one perhaps will be prepared to notice in Wagner. At last we are put back on earth; we breathe in its fresh air, we accept its joys with thankfulness, its pains with humility. Poor humanity is returned to its homeland.

A moment ago, while attempting to describe the sensual part of the overture, I asked the reader to turn his thoughts away from commonplace

[1] It is not clear what Baudelaire means by 'cloches natales': at this point in the opera Wagner calls only for sheep-bells.

hymns of love, such as a sprightly gallant might conceive them; for in fact there is nothing trivial here; rather it is the overflowing of a vigorous nature, pouring into Evil all the energies which should rightly go to the cultivation of Good; it is love unbridled, immense, chaotic, raised to the level of a counter-religion, a Satanic religion. Thus in his musical translation the composer has avoided that vulgarity which only too often accompanies the painting of the most *popular*—I was about to say plebeian—emotion, and for this he has found it sufficient to paint the excess in desire and energy, and the indomitable, immoderate ambition of a sensitive soul which has taken the wrong turning. Likewise in his plastic representation of the idea, he has happily said farewell to that wearisome crowd of victims, those endless Elviras. The pure idea, incarnate in the unique figure of Venus, speaks very much more clearly and eloquently. It is no ordinary rake, *leaping from beauty to beauty*, that we see here, but man, general, universal man, living morganatically with the absolute ideal of sensual love, the Queen of all the she-devils, faunesses and satyresses which have been banished underground since the death of the great god Pan—in a word, with indestructible and irresistible Venus herself.

A hand more practised than mine in the analysis of operatic works will be offering the reader in these very columns a complete technical account of this strange and misunderstood masterpiece;* my task is to confine myself to more general views which, sketchy though they may be, are none the less useful. Besides is it not preferable, for certain people, to judge of the beauty of a landscape by placing themselves on an eminence, rather than by successively traversing all the paths with which it is quilted?

I am anxious only to point out, to the great glory of Wagner, that in spite of the very proper importance that he gives to the dramatic poem, the *Tannhäuser* overture, no less than that of *Lohengrin*, is perfectly intelligible even to one who may be ignorant of the libretto; and secondly that this overture contains not only the seminal idea, the psychological quality which constitutes the drama, but also the principal themes, in a

* The first part of this study appeared in the *Revue européenne*, whose music critic is M. Perrin, former Director of the Opéra Comique and well-known for his Wagnerian sympathies (C.B., note in the booklet). In fact Perrin's article (15 March 1861) was barely half a page long. The year before he had however come out warmly in favour of Wagner.

sharply emphatic form, which are destined to depict the general sentiments expressed in the main body of the work—as is shown by the relentless returns of the diabolically sensual theme and of the religious motif, or Pilgrims' Chorus, every time that the action demands it. As for the Grand March in the second act, it has long since won the plaudits of the most obstinate critics, and we may apply to it the same praise as to the two overtures of which I have spoken; namely that it expresses in the most visual, highly-coloured and descriptive manner what it sets out to express. For who, when listening to those accents so rich and so proud, that stately, elegantly-measured rhythm, those regal fanfares, could imagine anything else but a piece of feudal pageantry, a solemn procession of heroes, in dazzling clothes, all of them tall in stature, iron of will and simple of faith, as magnificent in their pleasures as they are terrible in their warfare?

And what shall we say of Tannhäuser's description of his journey to Rome, in which the literary beauty is so admirably completed and supported by the vocal line that the two elements are no longer anything but an inseparable unity? Some took fright at the length of this episode, and yet the narration contains, as has been seen, an irresistible dramatic power. The sinner's sadness, his despondency during his hard journey, his joyfulness at the sight of the supreme pontiff who has power to absolve sins, his despair when he is shown the irreparable nature of his crime, and finally that almost unspeakable emotion, so terrible it is, of joy in the midst of damnation; all is said, expressed, and translated by the words and the music in so positive a manner that it is almost impossible to conceive of any other way in which it could be done. We understand now full well that a disaster of this kind can only be undone by a miracle, and we pardon the unfortunate knight for seeking once more the mysterious path which leads to the grotto, to recover at least the blessings of Hell beside his devilish spouse.

The plot of *Lohengrin*, like that of *Tannhäuser*, is stamped with the sacred, mysterious and yet universally intelligible character of legend. A young princess, accused of an abominable crime, the murder of her brother, has no means of proving her innocence. Her case will be settled by the judgement of God. There is no knight present to champion her cause; but she puts her trust in a strange vision; an unknown warrior has come to visit her in a dream. This is the knight who will undertake her defence. As it turns out, at the critical moment, just as everyone is pronouncing her guilty, a bark approaches the river-bank, drawn by a swan harnessed by a golden chain. Lohengrin, knight of the Holy Grail, protector of the innocent, defender of the weak, has heard her supplication in the depths of that wondrous fastness, shrine of the divine cup, twice consecrated, by the Last Supper and by the blood of Our Lord, which Joseph of Arimathea gathered therein as it streamed from His wound. Lohengrin, son of Parsifal, steps out of the bark, clad in silver armour, his helmet on his head, his buckler on his shoulder, a little golden trumpet at his side, leaning on his sword. 'If I win the victory for thee,' says Lohengrin to Elsa, 'wilt thou have me for thy husband? . . . Elsa, if thou wilt have me called thy spouse . . . thou must make me a promise: never question me, never seek to know from what regions I come, nor what is my name and my nature.' And Elsa replies, 'Never, Sir, wilt thou hear this question from my lips.' And as Lohengrin solemnly repeats the formula of the promise, Elsa cries, 'My sword and my buckler, my angel, my saviour! O thou who firmly believest in my innocence, could any doubt be more criminal than to fail to have faith in thee? As thou defendest me in my distress, I shall likewise faithfully keep the solemn charge which thou imposest upon me.' And Lohengrin, clasping her in his arms, cries out, 'Elsa, I love thee.' In all this there is a beauty of dialogue such as is often to be found in Wagner's dramas, all soaked as it is in primitive magic, all ennobled by ideal feeling, a beauty whose solemnity in no wise diminishes its natural grace.

Elsa's innocence is proclaimed by Lohengrin's victory; Frederick and Ortrud the witch, two wicked characters intent on Elsa's condemnation, contrive to arouse her feminine curiosity and to mar her joy by doubt, and then provoke her to the point when she breaks her oath and demands that her husband reveal his origin. Doubt has killed faith, and in vanishing, faith takes away happiness with it. Lohengrin punishes Frederick by death for a trap which he had set for him, and in the presence of the king and the assembled warriors and people he at last declares his true origin: '. . . Whoever is chosen to serve the Grail is in that instant clothed with a supernatural power; even he whom It sends into faraway lands, charged with the mission of defending the rights of virtue, is not stripped of his sacred potency so long as his quality of Knight of the Grail remains unknown; but such is the nature of this virtue that, once unveiled, it straightway flees from profane eyes; that is the reason why you must not allow yourselves to form any doubts concerning Its knight; once he is recognized, he must straightway leave you. Hark now how I reward the forbidden question! I was sent to you by the Grail; my father, Parsifal, wears Its crown; I, Its knight, am named Lohengrin.' The swan reappears at the water's edge to take the knight back to his miraculous country. The witch, in the infatuation of her spite, reveals that the swan is none other than Elsa's brother, imprisoned by her in a magic spell. Lohengrin climbs into the bark after addressing a fervent prayer to the Grail. A dove takes the place of the swan, and Godfrey, Duke of Brabant, reappears. The knight has returned to Montsalvat. Elsa, the doubter, she who wanted to know, to examine, to verify, has lost her happiness. The ideal has fled away.

The reader can hardly fail to have noticed a striking analogy in this legend with the ancient myth of Psyche, who in the same way was victim of a devilish curiosity, and, being unwilling to respect the secret of her divine spouse, sacrificed all her happiness by probing the mystery. Elsa hearkens to Ortrud, as Eve to the serpent. The eternal Eve falls into the eternal trap. Can it be that the nations and races of mankind transmit their fables to one another, just as individual men bequeath amongst them inheritances, patrimonies and scientific secrets? It would be tempting to believe it, so striking is the moral analogy which marks the myths and legends which blossom forth in different parts of the world. But this explanation is too simple to be for long attractive to a philosophic mind. An allegory created by a people cannot be compared to those seeds which one husbandman will fraternally hand over to another who wishes to acclimatize them in his country. Nothing eternal and universal needs to be acclimatized. The moral analogy of which I was speaking is like the divine trademark of all popular fables. Call it, if you like, the sign of a single origin, the proof of an undeniable kinship; but only on condition that you seek this origin in the absolute principle and the common origin of all beings. Such and such a myth may be regarded as akin to another, in the same way as the negro is called the white man's brother. In certain cases I deny neither the fraternity nor the blood-relationship; I think only that in many another case the mind might well be led into error by surface-resemblances, or even by the moral analogy, and that, to resume our vegetable metaphor, myth is a tree which grows everywhere, in every climate, under every sun, spontaneously and without artificial culture. The religions and the poetry of the four corners of the globe provide us with superabundant proofs in this matter. As sin is everywhere, so is redemption and so is myth. There is nothing more cosmopolitan than the Eternal. I must ask you to pardon this digression which opened out before me with an irresistible attraction. I return now to the author of *Lohengrin.*

It would seem that Wagner has a very special love for feudal pageantry, Homeric assemblages in which are concentrated accumulations of vital force, eager crowds from which, as though from a reservoir of human electricity, the heroic style gushes forth with a natural impetuosity. The wedding Music and Bridal Chorus in *Lohengrin* are a worthy pendant to the introduction of the guests at the Wartburg in *Tannhäuser*, being perhaps even more majestic and powerful. So unerring however is the master's taste and his attention to nuance that there is no question here of the unruly behaviour which in similar circumstances would characterize a crowd of yokels. Even at its climax of violence and tumult, the music never goes beyond the transport of people who are accustomed to the rules of etiquette; for this is a court at play, and its liveliest ecstasies still keep within the rhythm of decorum. The boisterous joy of the crowd alternates with the epithalamium, which is soft, tender and solemn; the gale of public rejoicing contrasts over and over again with the modest and loving hymn which celebrates the union of Elsa and Lohengrin.

I have already spoken of certain melodic phrases whose relentless reappearances in different passages from the same work had keenly intrigued my ear at the first concert given by Wagner at the Salle des Italiens. We have observed how, in *Tannhäuser*, at each recurrence of the two principal themes, the religious motif and the hymn of the flesh, the audience's attention was quickened and its state of mind transformed into one in keeping with the new situation. In *Lohengrin* this mnemonic method is applied much more systematically. Each character is so to speak heraldically blazoned by the theme which represents his moral nature and the role which he is called to play in the fable. At this point I will humbly call upon Liszt, whose book (*Lohengrin et Tannhäuser*) I take the opportunity of recommending to all who love the profundities and refinements of art, and who, in spite of the somewhat eccentric language which he affects—a kind of personal idiom made up of extracts from several different tongues—brings an infinite charm to his translation of the full range of the master's rhetoric:

'The spectator who is prepared and resigned not to look for *any of those detached numbers which, fed in as they are, one after another, upon the thread of some intrigue, make up the substance of our usual operas*—the spectator thus prepared, I say, will be in a position to find an uncommon interest in following through the space of three acts the deeply-pondered, astonishingly skilful and poetically intelligent combination with which Wagner, *by means of several leading phrases*, has tied *a melodic knot* which constitutes his whole drama. The twists and turns made by these phrases as they wind and interlace around the words of the poem have an effect which is to the utmost degree moving. But if, after having been impressed and struck by all this at a performance, the listener should still wish to have a better appreciation of what had made such a lively effect upon him and to study the printed score of this work of so novel a kind, he will remain astonished at the wealth of nuance and implication which it contains and which could not be immediately grasped. But where are the dramas and epics by great poets which do not require lengthy study before one can become master of their full meaning?

'Using a method which he applies in an entirely original manner, Wagner succeeds in extending the empire and the territorial rights of music. Not content with the power which she wields over the heart by awakening there the whole range of human feelings, he makes it possible for her to prompt our ideas, to address herself to our thought, to appeal to our reflective powers; he endows her with a moral and intellectual sense. . . . He portrays melodically the individual natures of his characters and of their principal emotions, and these melodies appear, *in the vocal line or the accompaniment*, each time that the relevant emotions and sentiments come into play. This systematic tenacity of purpose is combined with an art of organization which, by the acuteness of the psychological, poetical and philosophic insights of which it gives proof, would offer something of the highest interest to those too for whom quavers and semiquavers are no more than dead letters or pure hieroglyphs. By forcing our memory and our power of meditation to so constant an exercise, if in no other way, Wagner snatches the action of music from the domain of vague emotionalism, and adds to its charms some of the pleasures of the mind. By using a method far more complicated than the facile delights produced by *a string of songs, seldom related to one another*, he demands an unusual degree of attention from the public; but at the same time he is preparing more perfect emotional experiences for those who are capable of appreciating them. His melodies are as it were personifications of ideas; their recurrence announces that of the sentiments which the words uttered do not indicate at all explicitly; it is on them that Wagner relies to reveal to us all the secrets of the heart. There are phrases—that, for example, in the first scene of the second act—which run through the opera like a poisonous snake, winding around its victims and fleeing before their holy champions; there are others, like that of the prelude, which return but seldom, at moments of supreme and divine revelation. Every situation or character of any importance is musically expressed by a melody which becomes its constant symbol. Now as these melodies are of a rare beauty, we can safely say to those whose study of a score is confined to a consideration of the interrelations of quavers and semi-quavers, that even were the music of this opera to be shorn of its noble text, it would still remain a creation of the highest order.'

Without the poetry, in fact, Wagner's music would still be a poetic work, endowed as it is with all the qualities which go to make a well-constructed poem; it explains itself, to such a degree are all its elements harmoniously wedded, mutually adapted, and (if I may be allowed to commit a barbarism in order to express the superlative of a quality) skilfully *concatenated.*

The Flying Dutchman is the immensely popular story of that Wandering Jew of the Ocean for whom, however, a succouring angel has obtained a condition of redemption: *If, when he goes ashore once every seven years, the sea-captain can ever find a faithful wife, he will be saved.* Once when trying to round a dangerous cape and each time being driven back by the storm, the hapless one had cried out, 'I shall force this impassable barrier, let me struggle for all eternity.' Eternity accepted the bold seaman's challenge. Since that moment the fated vessel had been seen here and there, off different shores, charging the storm with the desperation of a warrior seeking death; but always the storm spared her and even the pirate fled before her face, making the sign of the cross. The Dutchman's first words after his ship has reached the mooring are sinister and solemn:

'The time is up; seven years have once more passed! The sea spews me on land with disgust. . . . Ah! proud Ocean, a few days and thou shalt feel my weight once more! . . . Nowhere a grave! nowhere Death! such is my terrible doom. . . . Day of Judgement, Day Supreme, when wilt thou dawn upon my night? . . .' Alongside the dreadful vessel a Norwegian has dropped anchor; the two captains strike up an acquaintance, and the Dutchman asks the Norwegian 'to afford him the shelter of his house for a few days . . . to give him a new home'. He offers him untold riches at which his eyes dazzle, and finally he curtly asks, 'Hast thou a daughter? . . . Let her be my wife! I shall never reach my homeland. What then is the object of my amassing riches? Be persuaded, agree to this union, and take all my treasures.' 'I have a daughter,' replies the Norwegian, 'fair, faithful unto death, and full of love and devotion for me.' 'Let her continue to keep this pious love for her father, let her keep faith with him; she will be no less faithful to her spouse.' 'Thou givest me jewels, pearls beyond price; but a faithful wife is the most precious jewel of all.' 'Dost thou give me this jewel? And shall I see thy daughter this very day?'

In the Norwegian's room a group of young girls are talking about the Flying Dutchman, and his daughter Senta, victim of a fatal obsession, her eyes ever fixed upon a mysterious portrait, sings a ballad which recounts the seaman's doom: 'Have you met with the ship with the blood-red sails and the black mast? On board the captain, his face pale as death, watches without respite, without rest. He flies and flees, without end, without respite, without rest. One day however this man can find deliverance, if he discover a woman on earth to be faithful to him unto death. . . . Pray Heaven that soon a woman may keep faith with him!—In the teeth of the wind, mid a raging storm, he tried once to round a cape; in his mad bravado he blasphemed: "In all eternity I shall not yield!" Satan heard him, and took him at his word. And now his doom is to wander the oceans, without respite, without rest! . . . But so that the hapless one may still find deliverance on earth, an angel of God proclaims to him whence salvation may yet come! Pray Heaven that soon a woman will keep faith with him!—Every seventh year he drops anchor and goes on shore to seek a wife. Every seven years he has wooed, and never yet found a faithful woman. . . . Hoist sail! weigh anchor! false love, false vows! Look lively there! to sea! without respite, without rest!' And suddenly, coming out of a kind of trance, Senta cries out as though inspired: 'May it be my lot to deliver thee by my faithfulness! Would to God that His holy angel could show me to thee! It is through *me* that thou shalt win thy salvation!' The girl's mind is magnetically drawn to misfortune; her true betrothed is the doomed sea-captain whom love alone can redeem.

At last the Dutchman appears, led in by Senta's father; there is no doubt that he is the man in the portrait, the legendary face hanging on the wall. When, like the terrible Melmoth[1] moved by the fate of his victim, Immalee, the Dutchman tries hard to turn her from a devotion too perilous, when, in an access of pity, the poor damned soul pushes away from him the instrument of his salvation, when, wishing to leave her in the happiness of her family and of commonplace love, he rushes back on board his ship, she resists, bent on following him: 'I know thee well! I know thy fate! I knew thee the first moment that I saw thee!' And he, in the hope of terrifying her, cries out: 'Ask the seas the world over, ask the mariner who has ploughed the ocean in all directions; he knows this ship, the dread of godfearing men; they call me the *Flying Dutchman*.' Pursuing the departing vessel with her love and her cries, she answers: 'Glory to thy delivering angel! Glory to its charge! Look and see if I am faithful unto death!' And she leaps into the sea. The ship founders. Two airy forms rise up out of the waves; it is the Dutchman and Senta, transfigured.

To love the wretched for his wretchedness is too noble a thought to occur elsewhere but in a simple heart, and it is certainly a very beautiful idea to have made the redemption of a damned soul depend upon the passionate imagination of a young girl. The entire drama is firmly treated, in a direct manner; each situation is openly attacked; and the character of Senta bears within it a supernatural and fantastic grandeur which both enchants and terrifies. The extreme simplicity of the poem serves only to intensify its effect. Everything is in place, everything well ordered and correctly proportioned. The Overture, which we heard at the concert at the Théâtre Italien, is as deep and gloomy as the ocean, the winds and the darkness themselves.

I am obliged to keep this study within reasonable limits, but I think that I have said enough (today, at least) to indicate Wagner's ideas and dramatic form to an unprejudiced reader. Apart from *Rienzi*, *The*

[1] The reference is to Maturin's *Melmoth the Wanderer* (1820); Baudelaire was much taken with this novel; see p. 153.

Flying Dutchman, *Tannhäuser* and *Lohengrin*, he is the composer of *Tristan and Isolde*, and four other operas which form a tetralogy, based on the Nieblung saga, without taking into account his numerous critical works. Such are the achievements of this man, whose personality and idealistic ambitions have for so long kept our newspaper-public amused, and whom glib humourists have made their daily butt for more than a year.

IV

IT IS always possible to shut one's eye for a moment to the systematic element which every great artist, with a will of his own, inevitably introduces into his works; it remains then to seek and define by what special, personal quality he distinguishes himself from the others. A man truly worthy of the great name of artist must possess something essentially *sui generis*, thanks to which he is *himself* and no one else. From this point of view artists may be compared to different flavours in the realm of cooking, and the receipt-book of human metaphors is not perhaps vast enough to provide the approximate definition of all known and all *possible* artists. We have, I think, already distinguished two men in Richard Wagner, the man of order and the man of passion. It is the man of passion, the man of feeling with whom we are concerned here. Even the slightest of his pieces bears so indelibly the brand of his personality that our search for his principal quality should not be very hard to accomplish. One point had struck me keenly from the very outset; it is that the artist had put as much power and developed as much energy in the sensual and orgiastic part of the *Tannhäuser* overture as in the representation of mysticism which characterizes the *Lohengrin* prelude. Each contains the same strivings, the same titanic scaling of the heights, no less than the same refinements and the same subtlety. What then seems to me to be the chief and unforgettable mark of this master's music is its nervous intensity, its violence in passion and in purpose. In the blandest or the most strident accents it expresses all the deepest-hidden secrets of the human heart. It is true that an ideal ambition presides over all of Wagner's compositions; but if in choice of subject and dramatic method he comes near to antiquity, in his passionate energy of expression he is at the moment the truest representative of modernity. Truth to tell, all the knowledge, all the efforts, all the permutations and combinations of this rich mind are no more than the very humble and zealous slaves of this overmastering passion. Whatever subject he may be treating, the result is a superlative solemnity of accent. By means of this passion a strange superhuman quality is added to everything; by means of this passion he understands everything and makes everything understandable. Whatever is implied by the words 'purpose', 'desire', 'concentration', 'nervous intensity' or 'explosion' is felt, and makes itself felt, in his works. I do not think that I am deluding myself or anyone else when I assert that I see here the principal characteristics of that phenomenon which we call *genius*; or at least that we find the same characteristics in our analysis of all that up to now we have legitimately called by that name. As far as art is concerned I admit that I am no enemy of extravagance; moderation has never seemed to me to be a sign of a robust artistic nature. I love those excessive states of physical vigour, those floods of intellectual energy which write themselves on works of art like flaming lava on the slopes of a volcano, and which, in ordinary life, often mark that delicious phase which follows after a great moral or physical crisis.

To turn to the reforms which the master is seeking to introduce into the application of music to the stage, one may ask what it will lead to. In this it is impossible to offer any exact prophecy. In a vague and general sense one can join the psalmist in saying that sooner or later those who have been brought down will be raised up, and that those who have been raised up will be humbled; but nothing more than what is equally applicable to the common run of all human affairs. We have seen many things which were formerly declared absurd only to be later adopted as models by the multitude. Who today has forgotten the spirited resistance encountered initially by the plays of Victor Hugo or the paintings of Eugène Delacroix? Besides, as we have already pointed out, the difference of opinion which now divides the public was an already forgotten difference, suddenly to be revived, and that it was in the past that Wagner himself had discovered the first elements of the foundation on which to establish his ideal. What cannot be gainsaid is that his doctrine constitutes a ready-made rallying-point for all those men of intelligence who have long grown weary of the imperfections of the Opera; and it is hardly surprising that men of letters should have been in the forefront in showing sympathy for a musician who glories in being a poet and a dramatist. It was the same thing when the writers of the eighteenth century acclaimed the works of Gluck; and I cannot help noticing that the very people who show most distaste for the works of Wagner show also a decided antipathy to his predecessor.

Finally the success or the failure of *Tannhäuser* can prove absolutely nothing; nor even can it have any bearing on the favourable or unfavourable chances for the future. Even supposing it to have been an execrable work, *Tannhäuser* could have stormed the heights; supposing it perfect, it could still provoke disgust. In point of fact the question of operatic reform is by no means settled; the battle will go on; even if it dies down, it will start again. Recently I heard someone say that if Wagner obtained a brilliant success with his opera, it would be a purely individual accident, and his method would have no further influence on the destiny and development of the lyric drama. I think that my study of the past, by which I mean the eternal, authorizes me to predict the exact opposite, namely that a complete setback in no way demolishes the possibility of new ventures in the same direction, and that in the not so far distant future we may well expect to see not only new composers, but even some for long accredited, taking more or less profit from the ideas put forth by Wagner, and advancing happily through the breach opened by him. What history-book has ever shown us a great cause lost in a single round?

18th March 1861

A FEW WORDS MORE

'It has been put to the test! The *Music of the Future* is dead and buried!', is the joyful cry of all the cliques and the cabals. 'It has been put to the test!', echo the morons of the press. And all our boulevard wits take them up in chorus, with a great show of innocence: 'It has been put to the test!'

Something has indeed been put to the test, but it is a test which will be repeated many thousands of times yet before the end of the world. What has been proved is first of all that no great and serious work can take up its abode in the human memory, nor its place in history, without lively dispute; next, that ten stubborn and self-opinionated men, equipped with shrill whistles and catcalls, can disconcert the actors, override the goodwill of the public, and even with their cacophonous protests cut through the enormous voice of an orchestra, be it equal in power to that of the ocean itself. Finally a most interesting evil has been confirmed, which is that a system of booking which allows people to subscribe for their seats by the year creates a kind of aristocracy which, at a given moment, and for one or other motive or interest, can exclude the vast public from all participation in passing judgement on a work. If we were to adopt this same system at other theatres, at the Comédie Française for example, we should soon see the same dangers and the same scandals arising there too. A restricted society will be in a position to deprive the vast metropolitan public of its right to appraise a work whose judgement belongs to all.[1]

Those who think that they have seen the last of Wagner have congratulated themselves far too soon; let them be assured of that. My urgent advice to them is to celebrate somewhat less vocally a triumph which is hardly among the more honourable, and even to arm themselves with a little resignation for the future. In truth they are showing but scant understanding of the see-saw of human affairs, the ebb and flow of human passions. They seem ignorant also of the stubborn patience with which Providence habitually endows those whom she invests with a function to perform. Already the reaction has set in; it sprang into being the very day when a coalition of ill-will, stupidity, red-tape and envy attempted to bury the work. The immensity of this injustice touched a thousand hearts, and today expressions of sympathy are to be heard on all sides.

To those people who live away from Paris and are fascinated and intimidated by this monstrous conglomeration of men and stones, the unparalleled treatment of *Tannhäuser* must seem like an insoluble enigma. It is easy enough to explain it by the unhappy coincidence of several different causes, of which some have nothing to do with art. Let us at once acknowledge the principal, dominant reason; Wagner's opera is a *serious work*, demanding sustained attention; it is hardly necessary to point out how much this fact must tell against its chances in a country where the chief reason for the success of classical tragedy lay in the opportunities which it offered for distraction. In Italy people eat sorbets and dance can-cans in the intervals of the performance in which the dictates of fashion do not include applause; in France we

[1] For a full account of the first Paris performances of *Tannhäuser*, see Newman, vol. III, chap. 5.

play cards. 'How impertinent of you to want to force me to give your work my continuous attention,' cries the recalcitrant ticket-holder, 'when all I ask of you is to provide me with an after-dinner pleasure, not an occasion to use my intelligence.' To this root-cause we must add others which today are familiar to everyone, in Paris at least. The imperial edict, which has done so much honour to the prince and for which he deserves our sincerest thanks (which I think I can say without being accused of obsequiousness), loosed upon the artist a pack of envious curs, including many of those gaping boobies who always fancy that they are exercising their independence when they yap in unison. This decree, which had just restored certain liberties to the press and to speech, opened the flood-gates to a natural and long-restrained turbulence which fell like a mad beast upon the first passer-by. This proved to be *Tannhäuser*, sanctioned by the chief of state and under the open patronage of the wife of a foreign ambassador.[1] What a splendid opportunity! For several hours an entire French audience amused itself at this woman's discomfiture; and what is less well known, Mme Wagner herself was insulted during one of the performances. A prodigious triumph!

A more than inadequate production, directed by an ex-vaudevillist[2] (can you imagine *Les Burgraves* produced by M. Clairville?[3]); a flabby and inaccurate performance on the part of the orchestra;[4] a German tenor[5] on whom our chief hopes had been set, and who addresses himself to the task of singing out of tune with a lamentable assiduity; a slumbering Venus,[6] dressed in a bundle of white rags, who no more seemed to have come down from Olympus than to have been born of the iridescent imagination of a medieval artist; all the seats booked,

[1] This was Princess Pauline Metternich, wife of the Austrian ambassador. Nadar tells us that one day not long after the publication of Baudelaire's booklet, he found himself next to her at a dinner-party. He took the opportunity of praising his friend's work, and the Princess expressed a lively interest. Next day he sent her a copy, and nothing was heard until many weeks later the book was returned with a polite note of thanks—uncut. Baudelaire has the following note in *Mon coeur mis à nu*: 'Madame de Metternich, although a Princess, forgot to reply to me concerning what I said about her and Wagner. Nineteenth-century manners.'

[2] Eugène Cormon.

[3] *Les Burgraves*, Hugo's last play and one of his greatest theatrical disasters, was produced in 1843. The Clairvilles, father and son, were actors and *vaudevillistes*. The father was Director of the Théâtre du Luxembourg; the son wrote more than six hundred pieces—*vaudevilles*, etc.

[4] Conducted by P. L. P. Dietsch.

[5] Albert Niemann.

[6] Fortunata Tedesco.

for two performances, by a crowd of people if not hostile, at least indifferent to any kind of ideal aspiration—all these factors must be taken into account. Mlle Sax[1] and Morelli[2] alone—and this is the natural moment to thank them—braved the storm. It would not be enough just to praise their gifts; we must also extol their gallantry. They stood their ground against the rout; without a moment's flinching, they kept their faith with the composer. With his admirable Italian flexibility, Morelli humbly adapted himself to the style and taste of his author, and those who have had the good fortune to study his work over a period say that this amenability stood him in good stead, and that he has never appeared to better advantage than in the part of Wolfram. But what are we to say of M. Niemann and his faintings and swoonings and fits of childish ill-temper—we who have been present at theatrical storms in which men such as Frédérick and Rouvière (and even Bignon, without the buttress of fame) openly braved the public's error, playing only the more spiritedly as it showed itself the more unjust, and constantly standing solidly by their author?

Finally not a little was added to the general confusion by the matter of the ballet, which after several months' argument had become a matter of life or death. 'An opera without a ballet? Unheard of!' cried the voice of conformity. 'What sort of opera is that?' asked the supporters of mistresses. 'Beware!' cried the Minister[3] himself in alarm to the author. As a kind of consolation a short-skirted Prussian army was caused to manoeuvre about the stage with the mechanical gestures of a military academy. Misled by the sight of all those legs and by the general badness of the production, a section of the public declared that it was a wretched ballet, set to music which was not appropriate for dancing. To which the voice of good sense replied, 'It is *not* a ballet; but what it should have been is a bacchanal, an orgy, as is made clear by the music, and such as the Porte St. Martin, the Ambigu, the Odéon, and even lesser theatres have occasionally been capable of giving us—something quite beyond the imaginative powers of the Opéra, which is incapable of anything at all.'[4] Likewise it was no literary reason, but simply the

[1] In the part of Elisabeth. [2] In the part of Wolfram. [3] Count Walewski.

[4] The fact that the ballet, or bacchanal, took place at the beginning of the first act of the opera told markedly against its success with the 'supporters of mistresses' who were unaccustomed to appearing in the audience (or to allowing their property to appear on the stage) until later in the evening. The ballet-master was the great Marius Petipa. See Newman, vol. III, pp. 77–9.

incompetence of the stage-staff that necessitated the cutting of a whole scene (Venus's later reappearance).[1]

That those gentlemen who can afford the luxury of a mistress from among the dancers of the Opéra should be anxious for the talents and beauty of their property to be as often as possible on show, is evidence of an almost fatherly feeling which will be readily intelligible and pardonable by all; but that these same gentlemen, without a moment's thought for the public interest or the pleasures of others, should stand in the way of a work which displeases them, simply because it does not satisfy the demands of their protégées, is an intolerable thing. By all means keep your harem and devoutly preserve its traditions; but let us be allowed to have a theatre in which those who do not think as you do will be able to find other pleasures, better adapted to their taste. Thus we shall be rid of you, and you of us; and each will be happy.[2]

It had been hoped to snatch the victim from the jaws of these mad dogs by offering it to the public on a Sunday, which is the day when the regular subscribers and the Jockey Club willingly abandon the house to the multitude which takes advantage at once of the unoccupied seats and of their own free time. But they reasoned, and correctly reasoned, in some such way as this: 'If we let *Tannhäuser* succeed today, the management will make it a sufficient excuse to saddle us with it for thirty more performances.' And they returned to the attack, armed to the teeth—with murderous instruments fabricated in advance. The public, the entire public, struggled for two acts, and its generosity, backed by indignation, caused it to applaud not only the irresistibly beautiful passages, but even those which surprised and disconcerted it, either because they were obscured by a muddy execution or because they demanded an impossible degree of peaceful concentration for their proper understanding. But these storms of rage or enthusiasm led to a reaction no less violent, if much less exhausting for the opponents. For in the hope that the cabal would be grateful for its forbearance, the public quietened down, wanting above all else a chance to get to know and to judge. But the handful of cat-callers *courageously* persevered,

[1] This was done after the first performance. It was not so much the incompetence of the stage-staff as the impatience of the audience that was responsible. See Newman, vol. III, p. 117.

[2] During the next few months there were several projects—all of them abortive—for staging *Tannhäuser* at other theatres. Baudelaire himself had ambitions to be a theatre-director, and he may well have hoped to realize them now.

without motive and without interruption; the admirable narration of Tannhäuser's journey to Rome was not heard (was it even sung? I do not know), and the whole of the third act was drowned in the tumult.

In the press there was no resistance, no protest,[1] except for that of M. Franck Marie in *La Patrie*.[2] M. Berlioz contrived to avoid voicing his opinion, which was an act of negative courage; let us at least be grateful to him for not having added to the universal tide of abuse. And then an immense whirlwind of imitation swept up every pen and caused every tongue to rave, like that strange spiritual force which incites crowds to alternate miracles of gallantry and dastardliness; collective courage and collective cowardice; Gallic enthusiasm and French panic. And *Tannhäuser* had not even been heard.

And now on all sides we hear nothing but complaints and recriminations; everyone would like to see Wagner's work performed, and everyone cries tyranny. But the management has bowed its head before a small clique of intriguers, and money paid for advance bookings is already being refunded. The result is an unheard-of spectacle—if indeed anything can be more scandalous than the spectacle that we have already described; we see today a defeated management which in spite of the enthusiastic backing of the public is prepared to abandon performances which would have been most profitable to it.

It seems moreover that this type of accident is spreading, and that the public is no longer regarded as supreme judge in theatrical matters. At the very moment at which I am writing, I learn that a fine play,[3] admirable in construction and excellent in style, is to be taken off at the end of a few days at another theatre where it was put on with brilliant success, and that in spite of the efforts of a certain impotent group of people, formerly called the 'educated class', which today in intelligence and fineness of taste is inferior to the public of a seaport. The author must really have been out of his mind to be able to imagine that his audience would take fire at something so impalpable, so aeriform as *honour*! The very most that they can rise to is to *bury* it!

[1] As Crépet points out in his note, there is real exaggeration here, which was criticized at the time in the musical press. Among those who did in fact protest was Champfleury, who had already published, after the concerts, a booklet by which Wagner was much moved.

[2] 24 March 1861.

[3] Auguste Vacquerie's *Les Funérailles de l'honneur*, at the Porte Saint-Martin. One of the principal roles was taken by Philibert Rouvière, whom Baudelaire much admired.

But what are the deep, underlying reasons for this proscription? Would a success have interfered with the director's future projects? Have some inscrutable official considerations coerced his good will and done violence to his interests? Or alternatively are we to believe something quite monstrous, which is that a director can make believe that he is looking for good works to put on, in order to further his career, but that once having attained his object, he will return to his true taste, which is that of the halfwits, and is evidently the most profitable? What is even more difficult to explain is the feebleness of the critics (some of them poets too), who have been clasping their chief enemy to their bosoms, and if occasionally, in an access of momentary valour, they have censured his commercialism, nevertheless persist over and over again in encouraging his business activities with every kind of flattery.

Throughout all this pandemonium, and the lamentable buffoonery of the newspapers, at which I blushed like a sensitive man at an indecency committed in his presence, a cruel idea continued to obsess me. Although I have always been careful to stifle at birth that exaggerated sentiment of patriotism whose fumes can cloud the brain, I remember that occasionally on distant shores, in hotel dining-rooms peopled with the most varied human elements, I have suffered bitterly at the sound of voices disparaging France—whether justly or unjustly is immaterial. All the filial feeling which until then I had philosophically held in check came bursting forth. When some years ago a deplorable Academician[1] took it into his head to include in his inaugural discourse an appreciation of the genius of Shakespeare, whom he familiarly called 'old *Williams*' or 'good old *Williams*'—(as an appreciation it was worthy of a doorkeeper at the Comédie Française)—I shuddered as I felt the damage which this illiterate pedant was going to do my country. And sure enough, for the next few days the entire English press made fun of us, in the most distressing way.[2] To hear them talk, French men of letters did not

[1] François Ponsard, the popular playwright for whom Baudelaire elsewhere expressed great contempt. His inaugural discourse was pronounced in December 1856.

[2] *The Illustrated London News*, 13 December 1856, contained a front-page article entitled 'Shakespeare and Literature in France'. The following extracts will show its tone: 'Dumas the younger reigns supreme as the exponent of French literature, with its "Demi-mondes", its "Filles de marbre" and its "Ladies with Camellias"; and for poets the Empire has nothing better or worthier to offer to France and to the world than—M. Ponsard!' 'M. Ponsard, who speaks of Shakespeare as the "divine Williams" . . . finds little to admire in our great bard. "He is old—he is obsolete—*ce bonhomme* Shakespeare." He is not only "a divine Williams", but he is "*ce vieux Billy*".'

even know how to spell Shakespeare's name correctly; of his genius they had not an inkling, and oafish France knew but two authors, Ponsard and Dumas the younger, the 'favourite poets of the new Empire', as the *Illustrated London News* put it. Please note that here political hatred was joining forces with outraged literary patriotism.

Likewise during the scandalous behaviour occasioned by Wagner's opera, I found myself asking, 'What is Europe going to think of us? what will they say of Paris in Germany? A handful of rowdies is disgracing us collectively!' But no, this shall not be. I think, I know, I am willing to swear that among writers, artists, and even the fashionable world there is still a fair number of individuals with good manners and a sense of justice, whose minds are always liberally open to any novelties that are offered to them. Germany would do wrong to think that Paris is solely inhabited by urchins who blow their noses on their fingers with the express intention of wiping them on the back of the first great man to pass by. Such a supposition would not be entirely fair. On all sides, as I have said, a reaction is setting in; the most unexpected expressions of sympathy have come to encourage the composer to persevere in his destiny. If things go on in this way, it is to be presumed that many a sorrow will shortly find consolation, and that *Tannhäuser* will reappear[1]—but in a place where the regular opera-goers will not be interested in following it.

In a word, the idea has been launched, the breach has been forced; that is the important thing. More than one French composer will be ready to avail himself of the life-giving ideas put forth by Wagner. Only a short time after *Tannhäuser's* first public performance, the edict of the Emperor (to whom we owe it that we heard the work at all) came to give great encouragement to our national spirit—a logical, order-loving spirit, which will readily take up once more its natural train of development. Under the Republic and the First Empire music rose to a height which, in the place of poor, depressed literature, made it one of the glories of the times. What was the motive of the head of the Second Empire? Was it no more than curiosity to hear the work of a man about whom our neighbours were speaking, or was it a more patriotic, a more comprehensive idea? Whatever the truth, his curiosity, even if it was no more, will prove to have been of profit to us all.

8 April 1861

[1] But not, as it happened, until 1895.

ON THE ESSENCE OF LAUGHTER

AND, IN GENERAL,

ON THE COMIC IN THE PLASTIC ARTS

I HAVE no intention of writing a treatise on caricature: I simply want to acquaint the reader with certain reflections which have often occurred to me on the subject of this singular genre. These reflections had become a kind of obsession for me, and I wanted to get them off my chest. Nevertheless I have made every effort to impose some order, and thus to make their digestion more easy. This, then, is purely an artist's and a philosopher's article. No doubt a general history of caricature in its references to all the facts by which humanity has been stirred—facts political and religious, weighty or frivolous; facts relative to the disposition of the nation or to fashion—would be a glorious and important work. The task still remains to be done, for the essays which have been published up to the present are hardly more than raw materials. But I thought that this task should be divided. It is clear that a work on caricature, understood in this way, would be a history of facts, an immense gallery of anecdote. In caricature, far more than in the other branches of art, there are two sorts of works which are to be prized and commended for different and almost contrary reasons. One kind have value only by reason of the *fact* which they represent. No doubt they have a right to the attention of the historian, the archaeologist, and even the philosopher; they deserve to take their place in the national archives, in the biographical registers of human thought. Like the flysheets of journalism, they are swept out of sight by the same tireless breeze which supplies us with fresh ones. But the others—and it is with these that I want to concern myself especially—contain a mysterious, lasting, eternal element, which recommends them to the attention of artists. What a curious thing, and one truly worthy of attention, is the introduction of this indefinable element of beauty, even in works which are intended to represent his proper ugliness—both moral and physical—to man! And what is no less mysterious is that this lamentable spectacle excites in him an undying and incorrigible mirth. Here, then, is the true subject of my article.

A doubt assails me. Should I reply with a formal demonstration to the kind of preliminary question which no doubt will be raised by certain spiteful pundits of solemnity—charlatans of gravity, pedantic corpses which have emerged from the icy vaults of the *Institut* and have come again to the land of the living, like a band of miserly ghosts, to snatch a few coppers from the obliging administration? First of all, they would ask, is Caricature a genre? No, their cronies would reply, Caricature is not a genre. I have heard similar heresies ringing in my ears at academicians' dinners. It was these fine fellows who let the comedy of *Robert Macaire*[1] slip past them without noticing any of its great moral and literary symptoms. If they had been contemporaries of Rabelais, they would have treated him as a base and uncouth buffoon. In truth, then, have we got to show that nothing at all that issues from man is frivolous in the eyes of a philosopher? Surely, at the very least, there will be that obscure and mysterious element which no philosophy has so far analysed to its depths?

We are going to concern ourselves, then, with the essence of laughter and with the component elements of caricature. Later, perhaps, we shall examine some of the most remarkable works produced in this genre.

II

The Sage laughs not save in fear and trembling. From what authority-laden lips, from what completely orthodox pen, did this strange and striking maxim fall?[2] Does it come to us from the Philosopher-King of Judea? Or should we attribute it to Joseph de Maistre,[3] that soldier quickened with the Holy Spirit? I have a vague memory of having read it in one of his books, but given as a quotation, no doubt. Such severity of thought and style suits well with the majestic saintliness of Bossuet; but the elliptical turn of the thought and its quintessential refinement would lead me rather to attribute the honour to Bourdaloue, the relentless Christian psychologist. This singular maxim has kept recurring to my mind ever since I first conceived the idea of my article, and I wanted to get rid of it at the very start.

[1] The character of Robert Macaire (in the play *L'Auberge des Adrets*) had been created by the actor Frédérick Lemaître, in the 1820s. Later (see p. 178 below) Daumier developed the character in a famous series of caricatures.

[2] Lavater's remark 'Le Sage sourit souvent et rit rarement' (*Souvenirs pour des voyageurs chéris*) has been suggested by G. T. Clapton; see Gilman p. 237, n. 32.

[3] On Baudelaire's debt to Joseph de Maistre, see Gilman pp. 63–6.

But come, let us analyse this curious proposition—

The Sage, that is to say he who is quickened with the spirit of Our Lord, he who has the divine formulary at his finger tips, does not abandon himself to laughter save in fear and trembling. The Sage trembles at the thought of having laughed; the Sage fears laughter, just as he fears the lustful shows of this world. He stops short on the brink of laughter, as on the brink of temptation. There is, then, according to the Sage, a certain secret contradiction between his special nature as Sage and the primordial nature of laughter. In fact, to do no more than touch in passing upon memories which are more than solemn, I would point out—and this perfectly corroborates the officially Christian character of the maxim—that the Sage *par excellence*, the Word Incarnate, never laughed.[1] In the eyes of One who has all knowledge and all power, the comic does not exist. And yet the Word Incarnate knew anger; He even knew tears.

Let us make a note of this, then. In the first place, here is an author—a Christian, without doubt—who considers it as a certain fact that the Sage takes a very good look before allowing himself to laugh, as though some residue of uneasiness and anxiety must still be left him. And secondly, the comic vanishes altogether from the point of view of absolute knowledge and power. Now, if we inverted the two propositions, it would result that laughter is generally the apanage of madmen, and that it always implies more or less of ignorance and weakness. I have no wish, however, to embark recklessly upon a theological ocean, for which I should without doubt be insufficiently equipped with compass or sails; I am content just to indicate these singular horizons to the reader —to point them out to him with my finger.

If you are prepared, then, to take the point of view of the orthodox mind, it is certain that human laughter is intimately linked with the accident of an ancient Fall, of a debasement both physical and moral. Laughter and grief are expressed by the organs in which the command and the knowledge of good and evil reside—I mean the eyes and the mouth. In the earthly paradise—whether one supposes it as past or to come, a memory or a prophecy, in the sense of the theologians or of the socialists—in the earthly paradise, that is to say in the surroundings in which it seemed to man that all created things were good, joy did not

[1] This suggests a line in a poem by Baudelaire's friend Gustave le Vavasseur, published in 1843: *Dieux joyeux, je vous hais. Jésus n'a jamais ri.* See also Gilman p. 237, n. 32.

find its dwelling in laughter. As no trouble afflicted him, man's countenance was simple and smooth, and the laughter which now shakes the nations never distorted the features of his face. Laughter and tears cannot make their appearance in the paradise of delights. They are both equally the children of woe, and they came because the body of enfeebled man lacked the strength to restrain them.* From the point of view of my Christian philosopher, the laugh on his lips is a sign of just as great a misery as the tears in his eyes. The Being who sought to multiply his own image has in no wise put the teeth of the lion into the mouth of man—yet man rends with his laughter; nor all the seductive cunning of the serpent into his eyes—yet he beguiles with his tears. Observe also that it is with his tears that man washes the afflictions of man, and that it is with his laughter that sometimes he soothes and charms his heart; for the phenomena engendered by the Fall will become the means of redemption.

May I be permitted a poetic hypothesis in order to help me prove the accuracy of these assertions, which otherwise many people may find tainted with the *a priori* of mysticism? Since the comic is a damnable element, and one of diabolic origin, let us try to imagine before us a soul absolutely pristine and fresh, so to speak, from the hands of Nature. For our example let us take the great and typical figure of Virginie,[1] who perfectly symbolizes absolute purity and naïveté. Virginie arrives in Paris still bathed in sea-mists and gilded by the tropic sun, her eyes full of great primitive images of waves, mountains and forests. Here she falls into the midst of a turbulent, overflowing and mephitic civilization, all imbued as she is with the pure and rich scents of the East. She is linked to humanity both by her birth and her love, by her mother and her lover, her Paul, who is as angelic as she and whose sex knows no distinction from hers, so to speak, in the unquenched ardours of a love which is unaware of itself. God she has known in the church of *Les Pamplemousses*—a modest and mean little church, and in the vastness of the indescribable tropic sky and the immortal music of the forests and the torrents. Certainly Virginie is a noble intelligence; but a few images and a few memories suffice her, just as a few books suffice the Sage.

* Philippe de Chennevières (C.B.), an early friend of Baudelaire's. He wrote a number of books, and had a distinguished career in the official world of art. The exact source of this idea has not been traced among his works.

[1] From Bernardin de Saint-Pierre's *Paul et Virginie*.

Now one day by chance, in all innocence, at the Palais-Royal, at a glazier's window, on a table, in a public place, Virginie's eye falls upon—a caricature! a caricature all very tempting for us, full-blown with gall and spite, just such as a shrewd and bored civilization knows how to make them. Let us suppose some broad buffoonery of the prize-ring, some British enormity, full of clotted blood and spiced with a monstrous 'Goddam!' or two: or, if this is more to the taste of your curious imagination, let us suppose before the eye of our virginal Virginie some charming and enticing morsel of lubricity, a Gavarni of her times, and one of the best—some insulting satire against the follies of the court, some plastic diatribe against the Parc-aux-Cerfs,[1] the vile activities of a great favourite, or the nocturnal escapades of the proverbial *Autrichienne*.[2] Caricature is a double thing; it is both drawing and idea—the drawing violent, the idea caustic and veiled. And a network of such elements distresses a simple mind which is accustomed to understand by intuition things as simple as itself. Virginie has glimpsed; now she gazes. Why? She is gazing at the unknown. Nevertheless she hardly understands either what it means or what it is for. And yet, do you observe that sudden folding of the wings, that shudder of a soul that veils herself and wants to draw back? The angel has sensed that there is offence in it. And in truth, I tell you, whether she has understood it or not, she will be left with some strange element of uneasiness—something which resembles fear. No doubt, if Virginie remains in Paris and knowledge comes to her, laughter will come too: we shall see why. But for the moment, in our capacity as analysts and critics who would certainly not dare to assert that our intelligence is superior to that of Virginie, let us simply record the fear and the suffering of the immaculate angel brought face to face with caricature.

III

IF YOU wished to demonstrate that the comic is one of the clearest tokens of the Satanic in man, one of the numerous pips contained in the symbolic apple, it would be enough to draw attention to the unanimous agreement of physiologists of laughter on the primary ground of this monstrous phenomenon. Nevertheless their discovery is not very profound and hardly goes very far. Laughter, they say, comes from

[1] Louis XV's private brothel at Versailles.

[2] Marie Antoinette.

superiority. I should not be surprised if, on making this discovery, the physiologist had burst out laughing himself at the thought of his own superiority. Therefore he should have said: Laughter comes from the idea of one's *own* superiority. A Satanic idea, if there ever was one! And what pride and delusion! For it is a notorious fact that all madmen in asylums have an excessively overdeveloped idea of their own superiority: I hardly know of any who suffer from the madness of humility. Note, too, that laughter is one of the most frequent and numerous expressions of madness. And now, see how everything falls into place. When Virginie, once fallen, has declined by one degree in purity, the idea of her own superiority will begin to dawn upon her; she will be more learned from the point of view of the world; and she will laugh.

I said that laughter contained a symptom of failing; and, in fact, what more striking token of debility could you demand than a nervous convulsion, an involuntary spasm comparable to a sneeze and prompted by the sight of someone else's misfortune? This misfortune is almost always a *mental* failing. And can you imagine a phenomenon more deplorable than one failing taking delight in another? But there is worse to follow. The misfortune is sometimes of a very much lower kind—a failure in the physical order. To take one of the most commonplace examples in life, what is there so delightful in the sight of a man falling on the ice or in the street, or stumbling at the end of a pavement, that the countenance of his brother in Christ should contract in such an intemperate manner, and the muscles of his face should suddenly leap into life like a timepiece at midday or a clockwork toy? The poor devil has disfigured himself, at the very least; he may even have broken an essential member. Nevertheless the laugh has gone forth, sudden and irrepressible. It is certain that if you care to explore this situation, you will find a certain unconscious pride at the core of the laugher's thought. That is the point of departure. 'Look at me! *I* am not falling', he seems to say. 'Look at me! *I* am walking upright. *I* would never be so silly as to fail to see a gap in the pavement or a cobblestone blocking the way.'

The Romantic school, or, to put it better, the Satanic school, which is one of its subdivisions, had a proper understanding of this primordial law of laughter; or at least, if they did not all understand it, all, even in their grossest extravagances and exaggerations, sensed it and applied it exactly. All the miscreants of melodrama, accursed, damned and fatally marked with a grin which runs from ear to ear, are in the pure orthodoxy of laughter. Furthermore they are almost all the grand-children, legitimate or illegitimate, of the renowned wanderer Melmoth,[1] that great satanic creation of the Reverend Maturin. What could be greater, what more mighty, relative to poor humanity, than the pale, bored figure of Melmoth? And yet he has a weak and contemptible side to him, which faces against God and against the light. See, therefore, how he laughs; see how he laughs, as he ceaselessly compares himself to the caterpillars of humanity, he so strong, he so intelligent, he for whom a part of the conditional laws of mankind, both physical and intellectual, no longer exist! And this laughter is the perpetual explosion of his rage and his suffering. It is—you must understand—the necessary resultant of his contradictory double nature, which is infinitely great in relation to man, and infinitely vile and base in relation to absolute Truth and Justice. Melmoth is a living contradiction. He has parted company with the fundamental conditions of life; his bodily organs can no longer sustain his thought. And that is why his laughter freezes and wrings his entrails. It is a laugh which never sleeps, like a malady which continues on its way and completes a destined course. And thus the laughter of Melmoth, which is the highest expression of pride, is for ever performing its function as it lacerates and scorches the lips of the laugher for whose sins there can be no remission.[2]

IV

AND NOW let us recapitulate a little and establish more clearly our principal propositions, which amount to a sort of theory of laughter. Laughter is satanic: it is thus profoundly human. It is the consequence in man of the idea of his own superiority. And since laughter is essentially human, it is, in fact, essentially contradictory; that is to say that it is at

[1] *Melmoth the Wanderer* (1820) was the masterpiece of its author, the Rev. C. R. Maturin (1782–1824). It was one of the most influential of all the novels of horror, and Baudelaire's great admiration for it was revealed in his desire to make a new French translation, on the grounds that the existing translation was inadequate. See G. T. Clapton, 'Balzac, Baudelaire and Maturin,' *French Quarterly*, June and Sept. 1930; see also Mario Praz, *The Romantic Agony* (O.U.P., 2nd edn., 1951) pp. 116–8.

[2] 'A mirth which is not gaiety is often the mask which hides the convulsed and distorted features of agony—and laughter, which never yet was the expression of rapture, has often been the only intelligible language of madness and misery. Ecstasy only smiles—despair laughs . . .' *Melmoth* (2nd edn., 1824), vol. III, p. 302.

once a token of an infinite grandeur and an infinite misery—the latter in relation to the absolute Being of whom man has an inkling, the former in relation to the beasts. It is from the perpetual collision of these two infinites that laughter is struck. The comic and the capacity for laughter are situated in the laugher and by no means in the object of his mirth. The man who trips would be the last to laugh at his own fall, unless he happened to be a philosopher, one who had acquired by habit a power of rapid self-division and thus of assisting as a disinterested spectator at the phenomena of his own ego. But such cases are rare. The most comic animals are the most serious—monkeys, for example, and parrots. For that matter, if man were to be banished from creation, there would be no such thing as the comic, for the animals do not hold themselves superior to the vegetables, nor the vegetables to the minerals. While it is a sign of superiority in relation to brute creation (and under this heading I include the numerous pariahs of the *mind*), laughter is a sign of inferiority in relation to the wise, who, through the contemplative innocence of their minds, approach a childlike state. Comparing mankind with man, as we have a right to do, we see that primitive nations, in the same way as Virginie, have no conception of caricature and have no comedy (Holy Books never laugh, to whatever nations they may belong), but that as they advance little by little in the direction of the cloudy peaks of the intellect, or as they pore over the gloomy braziers of metaphysics, the nations of the world begin to laugh diabolically with the laughter of Melmoth; and finally we see that if, in these selfsame ultra-civilized nations, some mind is driven by superior ambition to pass beyond the limits of worldly pride and to make a bold leap towards pure poetry, then the resulting poetry, as limpid and profound as Nature herself, will be as void of laughter as is the soul of the Sage.

As the comic is a sign of superiority, or of a belief in one's own superiority, it is natural to hold that, before they can achieve the absolute purification promised by certain mystical prophets, the nations of the world will see a multiplication of comic themes in proportion as their superiority increases. But the comic changes its nature, too. In this way the angelic and the diabolic elements function in parallel. As humanity uplifts itself, it wins for evil, and for the understanding of evil, a power proportionate to that which it has won for good. And this is why I find nothing surprising in the fact that we, who are the children of a better law than the religious laws of antiquity—we, the favoured disciples of

Jesus—should possess a greater number of comic elements than pagan antiquity. For this very thing is a condition of our general intellectual power. I am quite prepared for sworn dissenters to cite the classic tale of the philosopher who died of laughing when he saw a donkey eating figs, or even the comedies of Aristophanes and those of Plautus. I would reply that, quite apart from the fact that these periods were essentially civilized, and there had already been a considerable shrinkage of belief, their type of the comic is still not quite the same as ours. It even has a touch of barbarity about it, and we can really only adopt it by a backward effort of mind, the result of which is called *pastiche*. As for the grotesque figures which antiquity has bequeathed us—the masks, the bronze figurines, the Hercules (all muscles), the little Priapi, with tongue curled in air and pointed ears (all cranium and phallus); and as for those prodigious phalluses on which the white daughters of Romulus innocently ride astride, those monstrous engines of generation, equipped with wings and bells—I believe that these things are all full of deep seriousness.[1] Venus, Pan and Hercules were in no sense figures of fun. It was not until after the coming of Christ, and with the aid of Plato and Seneca, that men began to laugh at them. I believe that the ancients were full of respect for drum-majors and for doers of mighty deeds of all kinds, and that none of those extravagant fetishes which I instanced a moment ago were anything other than tokens of adoration, or, at all events, symbols of power; in no sense were they intentionally comic emanations of the fancy. Indian and Chinese idols are unaware that they are ridiculous; it is in us, Christians, that their comicality resides.

V

IT WOULD be a mistake to suppose that we have got rid of every difficulty. The mind that is least accustomed to these aesthetic subtleties would very quickly be able to counter me with the insidious objection that there are *different varieties of laughter*. It is not always a disaster, a failing or an inferiority in which we take our delight. Many sights which provoke our laughter are perfectly innocent; not only the amusements of childhood, but even many of the things that tickle the palate of artists have nothing to do with the spirit of Satan.

[1] Curious readers will find examples reproduced in Fuchs, *Geschichte der erotischen Kunst*, 1908, vol. I, book 2, 'Das Altertum'.

There is certainly some semblance of truth in that. But first of all we ought to make a proper distinction between laughter and joy. Joy exists in itself, but it has various manifestations. Sometimes it is almost invisible; at others, it expresses itself in tears. Laughter is only an expression, a symptom, a diagnostic. Symptom of what? That is the question. Joy is a unity. Laughter is the expression of a double, or contradictory, feeling; and that is the reason why a convulsion occurs. And so the laughter of children, which I hold for a vain objection, is altogether different, even as a physical expression, even as a form, from the laughter of a man who attends a play, or who looks at a caricature, or from the terrible laughter of Melmoth—of Melmoth, the outcast of society, wandering somewhere between the last boundaries of the territory of mankind and the frontiers of the higher life; of Melmoth, who always believes himself to be on the point of freedom from his infernal pact, and longs without ceasing to barter that superhuman power, which is his disaster, for the pure conscience of a simpleton, which is his envy. For the laughter of children is like the blossoming of a flower. It is the joy of receiving, the joy of breathing, the joy of contemplating, of living, of growing. It is a vegetable joy. And so, in general, it is more like a smile—something analogous to the wagging of a dog's tail, or the purring of a cat. And if there still remains some distinction between the laughter of children and such expressions of animal contentment, I think that we should hold that this is because their laughter is not entirely exempt from ambition, as is only proper to little scraps of men—that is, to budding Satans.

But there is one case where the question is more complicated. It is the laughter of man—but a true and violent laughter—at the sight of an object which is neither a sign of weakness nor of disaster among his fellows. It is easy to guess that I am referring to the laughter caused by the grotesque. Fabulous creations, beings whose authority and *raison d'être* cannot be drawn from the code of common sense, often provoke in us an insane and excessive mirth, which expresses itself in interminable paroxysms and swoons. It is clear that a distinction must be made, and that here we have a higher degree of the phenomenon. From the artistic point of view, the comic is an imitation: the grotesque a creation. The comic is an imitation mixed with a certain creative faculty, that is to say with an artistic *ideality*. Now human pride, which always takes the upper hand and is the natural cause of laughter in the case of the comic, turns out to be the natural cause of laughter in the case of the grotesque too, for this is a creation mixed with a certain imitative faculty—imitative that is, of elements pre-existing in nature. I mean that in this case laughter is still the expression of an idea of superiority—no longer now of man over man, but of man over nature. Do not retort that this idea is too subtle; that would be no sufficient reason for rejecting it. The difficulty is to find another plausible explanation. If this one seems far-fetched and just a little hard to accept, that is because the laughter caused by the grotesque has about it something profound, primitive and axiomatic, which is much closer to the innocent life and to absolute joy than is the laughter caused by the comic in man's behaviour. Setting aside the question of utility, there is the same difference between these two sorts of laughter as there is between the *implicated* school of writing and the school of art for art's sake. Thus the grotesque dominates the comic from a proportionate height.

From now onwards I shall call the grotesque 'the absolute comic', in antithesis to the ordinary comic, which I shall call 'the significative comic'. The latter is a clearer language, and one easier for the man in the street to understand, and above all easier to analyse, its element being visibly *double*—art and the moral idea. But the absolute comic, which comes much closer to nature, emerges as a *unity* which calls for the intuition to grasp it. There is but one criterion of the grotesque, and that is laughter—immediate laughter. Whereas with the significative comic it is quite permissible to laugh a moment late—that is no argument against its validity; it all depends upon one's quickness of analysis.

I have called it 'the absolute comic'. Nevertheless we should be on our guard. From the point of view of the definitive absolute, all that remains is *joy*. The comic can only be absolute in relation to fallen humanity, and it is in this way that I am understanding it.

VI

IN ITS triple-distilled essence the absolute comic turns out to be the prerogative of those superior artists whose minds are sufficiently open to receive any absolute ideas at all. Thus, the man who until now has been the most sensitive to these ideas, and who set a good part of them in action in his purely aesthetic, as well as his creative work, is Theodore

Hoffmann.[1] He always made a proper distinction between the ordinary comic and the type which he called 'the innocent comic'. The learned theories which he had put forth didactically, or thrown out in the form of inspired conversations or critical dialogues, he often sought to boil down into creative works; and it is from these very works that I shall shortly draw my most striking examples when I come to give a series of applications of the above-stated principles, and to pin a sample under each categorical heading.

Furthermore, within the absolute and significative types of the comic we find species, sub-species and families. The division can take place on different grounds. First of all it can be established according to a pure philosophic law, as I was making a start to do: and then according to the law of artistic creation. The first is brought about by the primary separation of the absolute from the significative comic; the second is based upon the kind of special capacities possessed by each artist. And finally it is also possible to establish a classification of varieties of the comic with regard to climates and various national aptitudes. It should be observed that each term of each classification can be completed and given a *nuance* by the adjunction of a term from one of the others, just as the law of grammar teaches us to modify a noun by an adjective. Thus, any German or English artist is more or less naturally equipped for the absolute comic, and at the same time he is more or less of an idealizer. I wish now to try and give selected examples of the absolute and significative comic, and briefly to characterize the comic spirit proper to one or two eminently artistic nations, before coming on to the section in which I want to discuss and analyse at greater length the talent of those men who have made it their study and their whole existence.

If you exaggerate and push the consequences of the significative comic to their furthest limits, you reach the *savage* variety, just as the synonymous expression of the innocent variety, pushed one degree further, is the *absolute* comic.

In France, the land of lucid thought and demonstration, where the natural and direct aim of art is utility, we generally find the significative type. In this genre Molière is our best expression. But since at the root of our character there is an aversion for all extremes, and since one of the

[1] On Hoffmann, and on the particular stories which Baudelaire cites in this section, see H. W. Hewett-Thayer's *Hoffmann, Author of the Tales* (Princeton and O.U.P., 1948).

symptoms of every emotion, every science and every art in France is an avoidance of the excessive, the absolute and the profound, there is consequently but little of the savage variety to be found in this country; in the same way our grotesque seldom rises to the absolute.

Rabelais, who is the great French master of the grotesque, preserves an element of utility and reason in the very midst of his most prodigious fantasies. He is directly symbolic. His comedy nearly always possesses the transparence of an allegory. In French caricature, in the *plastic* expression of the comic, we shall find this dominant spirit. It must be admitted that the enormous poetic good humour which is required for the true grotesque is found but rarely among us in level and continuous doses. At long intervals we see the vein reappear; but it is not an essentially national one. In this context I should mention certain interludes of Molière, which are unfortunately too little read or acted—those of the *Malade Imaginaire* and the *Bourgeois Gentilhomme*, for example; and the carnivalesque figures of Callot. As for the essentially French comedy in the *Contes* of Voltaire, its *raison d'être* is always based upon the idea of superiority; it is entirely significative.

Germany, sunk in her dreams, will afford us excellent specimens of the absolute comic. There all is weighty, profound and excessive. To find true comic savagery, however, you have to cross the Channel and visit the foggy realms of spleen. Happy, noisy, carefree Italy abounds in the innocent variety. It was at the very heart of Italy, at the hub of the southern carnival, in the midst of the turbulent Corso, that Theodore Hoffmann discerningly placed his eccentric drama, *The Princess Brambilla*. The Spaniards are very well endowed in this matter. They are quick to arrive at the cruel stage, and their most grotesque fantasies often contain a dark element.

It will be a long time before I forget the first English pantomime that I saw played. It was some years ago, at the *Théâtre des Variétés*. Doubtless only a few people will remember it, for very few seem to have taken to this kind of theatrical diversion, and those poor English mimes had a sad reception from us. The French public does not much like to be taken out of its element. Its taste is not very cosmopolitan, and changes of horizon upset its vision. Speaking for myself, however, I was excessively struck by their way of understanding the comic.[1] It was said—chiefly by

[1] It has not proved possible to identify this pantomime beyond doubt, but, according to information kindly supplied by the Bibliothèque de l'Arsénal, it seems more than

the indulgent, in order to explain their lack of success—that these were vulgar, mediocre artists—understudies. But that was not the point. They were English; that was the important thing.

It seemed to me that the distinctive mark of this type of the comic was *violence*. I propose to prove it with a few samples from my memories.

First of all, Pierrot was not the figure to which the late-lamented Deburau had accustomed us—that figure pale as the moon, mysterious as silence, supple and mute as the serpent, long and straight as a gibbet—that artificial man activated by eccentric springs. The English Pierrot swept upon us like a hurricane, fell down like a sack of coals, and when he laughed his laughter made the auditorium quake; his laugh was like a joyful clap of thunder. He was a short, fat man, and to increase his imposingness he wore a be-ribboned costume which encompassed his jubilant person as birds are encompassed with their down and feathers, or angoras with their fur. Upon his floured face he had stuck, crudely and without transition or gradation, two enormous patches of pure red. A feigned prolongation of the lips, by means of two bands of carmine, brought it about that when he laughed his mouth seemed to run from ear to ear.

As for his moral nature, it was basically the same as that of the Pierrot whom we all know—heedlessness and indifference, and consequently the gratification of every kind of greedy and rapacious whim, now at the expense of Harlequin, now of Cassandre or Léandre. The only difference was that where Deburau would just have moistened the tip of his finger with his tongue, he stuck both fists and both feet into his mouth.

likely that it was a production entitled 'Arlequin, pantomime anglaise en 3 actes et 11 tableaux,' performed at the Théâtre des Variétés from the 4th until the 13th August, 1842. The newspaper *Le Corsair* (4th August) gives the following cast:—Arlequin: Howell.—Clown: Matthews (presumably the well-known clown, Tom Matthews).—Pantalon: Garders.—Colombine: Miss Maria Frood.—Une fée: Anne Plowman—Reine des fées: Emilie Fitzj (?). A review of this pantomime by Gautier, in *La Presse*, 14th August 1842, has several points of agreement with Baudelaire's description. First, Gautier describes the apathy of the audience; secondly, he gives special praise to the clown's costume; finally, he refers to the incident of the clown's stealing his own head and stuffing it into his pocket (though the guillotine is not mentioned). Champfleury quotes the whole passage in his *Souvenirs des Funambules*, 1859, pp. 256–7, and provides evidence for dating the pantomine to the early 1840s when he ironically assigns the fragment to an article by Baudelaire 'sous presse depuis quinze ans seulement'.

And everything else in this singular piece was expressed in the same way, with passionate gusto; it was the dizzy height of hyperbole.

Pierrot walks past a woman who is scrubbing her doorstep; after rifling her pockets, he makes to stuff into his own her sponge, her mop, her bucket, water and all! As for the way in which he endeavoured to express his love to her, anyone who remembers observing the phanerogamous habits of the monkeys in their famous cage at the Jardin des Plantes can imagine it for himself. Perhaps I ought to add that the woman's role was taken by a very long, very thin man, whose outraged modesty emitted shrill screams. It was truly an intoxication of laughter—something both terrible and irresistible.

For some misdeed or other, Pierrot had in the end to be guillotined. Why the guillotine rather than the gallows, in the land of Albion? . . . I do not know; presumably to lead up to what we were to see next. Anyway, there it was, the engine of death, there, set up on the French boards which were markedly surprised at this romantic novelty. After struggling and bellowing like an ox that scents the slaughter-house, at last Pierrot bowed to his fate. His head was severed from his neck—a great red and white head, which rolled noisily to rest in front of the prompter's box, showing the bleeding disk of the neck, the split vertebrae and all the details of a piece of butcher's meat just dressed for the counter. And then, all of a sudden, the decapitated trunk, moved by its irresistible obsession with theft, jumped to its feet, triumphantly 'lifted' its own head as though it was a ham or a bottle of wine, and, with far more circumspection than the great St. Denis, proceeded to stuff it into its pocket!

Set down in pen and ink, all this is pale and chilly. But how could the pen rival the pantomime? The pantomime is the refinement, the quintessence of comedy; it is the pure comic element, purged and concentrated. Therefore, with the English actors' special talent for hyperbole, all these monstrous buffooneries took on a strangely thrilling reality.

Certainly one of the most remarkable things, in the sense of absolute comedy—or if I may call it so, the metaphysics of absolute comedy—was the beginning of this beautiful piece, a prologue imbued with a high aesthetic. The principal characters, Pierrot, Cassandre, Harlequin, Colombine and Léandre are facing the public, gentle and good as gold. They are all but rational beings and do not differ much from the fine fellows in the audience. The miraculous breath which is about to inspire them to such extraordinary antics has not yet touched their brains. A few quips from Pierrot can give no more than a pale idea of what he will be doing shortly. The rivalry between Harlequin and Léandre has just declared itself. A fairy takes Harlequin's side; she is the eternal protectress of mortals who are poor and in love. She promises him her protection, and, to give him immediate proof of it, she waves her wand in the air with a mysterious and authoritative gesture.

At once a dizzy intoxication is abroad; intoxication swims in the air; we breathe intoxication; it is intoxication that fills the lungs and renews the blood in the arteries.

What is this intoxication? It is the absolute comic, and it has taken charge of each one of them. The extraordinary gestures executed by Léandre, Pierrot and Cassandre make it quite clear that they feel themselves forcibly projected into a new existence. They do not seem at all put out. They set about preparing for the great disasters and the tumultuous destiny which awaits them, like a man who spits on his hands and rubs them together before doing some heroic deed. They flourish their arms, like windmills lashed by the tempest. It must be to loosen their joints—and they will certainly need it. All this is carried out to great gusts of laughter, full of a huge contentment. Then they turn to a game of leap-frog, and once their aptitude and their agility have been duly established, there follows a dazzling volley of kicks, punches and slaps which blaze and crash like a battery of artillery. But all of this is done in the best of spirits. Every gesture, every cry, every look seems to be saying: 'The fairy has willed it, and our fate hurls us on—it doesn't worry *me*! Come, let's get started! Let's get down to business!' And then they *do* get down to business, through the whole fantastic work, which, properly speaking, only starts at this point—that is to say, on the frontier of the marvellous.

Under cover of this hysteria, Harlequin and Colombine have danced away in flight, and with an airy foot they proceed to run the gauntlet of their adventures.

And now another example. This one is taken from a singular author—a man of ranging mind, whatever may be said, who unites to the significative mockery of France the mad, sparkling, lighthearted gaiety of the lands of the sun as well as the profound comic spirit of Germany. I am returning once again to Hoffmann.

In the story entitled *Daucus Carota, the King of the Carrots*, or by some translators *The King's Betrothed*, no sight could be more beautiful than the arrival of the great company of the Carrots in the farm-yard of the betrothed maiden's home. Look at all those little scarlet figures, like a regiment of English soldiers, with enormous green plumes on their heads, like carriage-footmen, going through a series of marvellous tricks and capers on their little horses! The whole thing is carried out with astonishing agility. The adroitness and ease with which they fall on their heads is assisted by their heads being bigger and heavier than the rest of their bodies, like those toy soldiers made of elder-pith, which have lead weights in their caps.

The unfortunate young girl, obsessed with dreams of grandeur, is fascinated by this display of military might. But an army on parade is one thing; how different an army in barracks, furbishing its arms, polishing its equipment, or, worse still, ignobly snoring on its dirty, stinking camp-beds! That is the reverse of the medal; the rest was but a magic trick, an apparatus of seduction. But her father, who is a wise man and well versed in sorcery, wants to show her the other side of all this magnificence. Thus, at an hour when the vegetables are sleeping their brutish sleep, never suspecting that any spy could catch them unawares, he lifts the flap of one of the tents of this splendid army. Then it is that the poor dreaming girl sees all this mass of red and green soldiery in its appalling undress, wallowing and snoring in the filthy midden from which it first emerged. In its night-cap all that military magnificence is nothing more than a putrid swamp.

There are many other examples of the absolute comic that I might take from the admirable Hoffmann. Anyone who really wants to understand what I have in mind should read with care *Daucus Carota*, *Peregrinus Tyss*, *The Golden Pot*, and over and above all, *The Princess Brambilla*, which is like a catechism of high aesthetics. What pre-eminently distinguishes Hoffmann is his unintentional—and sometimes very intentional—blending of a certain measure of the significative comic with the most absolute variety. His most supernatural and fugitive comic conceptions, which are often like the visions of a drunken man, have a very conspicuous moral meaning; you might imagine that you had to do with the profoundest type of physiologist or alienist who was amusing himself by clothing his deep wisdom in poetic forms, like a learned man who might speak in parables and allegories.

Take for example, if you will, the character of Giglio Fava, the actor who suffered from a chronic dualism, in *The Princess Brambilla.* This *single* character changes personality from time to time. Under the name of Giglio Fava he swears enmity for the Assyrian prince, Cornelio Chiapperi; but when he is himself the Assyrian prince, he pours forth his deepest and most regal scorn upon his rival for the hand of the Princess—upon a wretched mummer whose name, they say, is Giglio Fava.

I should perhaps add that one of the most distinctive marks of the absolute comic is that it remains unaware of itself. This is evident not only in certain animals, like monkeys, in whose comicality gravity plays an essential part, nor only in certain antique sculptural caricatures of which I have already spoken, but even in those Chinese monstrosities which delight us so much and whose intentions are far less comic than people generally think. A Chinese idol, although it be an object of veneration, looks very little different from a tumble-toy or a pot-bellied chimney-ornament.

And so, to be finished with all these subtleties and all these definitions, let me point out, once more and for the last time, that the dominant idea of superiority is found in the absolute, no less than in the significative comic, as I have already explained (at too great a length, perhaps): further, that in order to enable a comic emanation, explosion, or, as it were, a chemical separation of the comic to come about, there must be two beings face to face with one another: again, that the special abode of the comic is in the laugher, the spectator: and finally, that an exception must nevertheless be made in connection with the 'law of ignorance' for those men who have made a business of developing in themselves their feeling for the comic, and of dispensing it for the amusement of their fellows. This last phenomenon comes into the class of all artistic phenomena which indicate the existence of a permanent dualism in the human being—that is, the power of being oneself and someone else at one and the same time.

And so, to return to my primary definitions and to express myself more clearly, I would say that when Hoffmann gives birth to the absolute comic it is perfectly true that he knows what he is doing; but he also knows that the essence of this type of the comic is that it should appear to be unaware of itself and that it should produce in the spectator, or rather the reader, a joy in his own superiority and in the superiority of man over nature. Artists create the comic; after collecting and studying its elements, they know that such-and-such a being is comic, and that it is so only on condition of its being unaware of its nature, in the same way that, following an inverse law, an artist is only an artist on condition that he is a double man and that there is not one single phenomenon of his double nature of which he is ignorant.

DAUMIER: 'Cholera', from *La Némésis médicale*, Paris 1840. See pp. 176–7.

SOME FRENCH CARICATURISTS

CARLE VERNET–PIGAL–CHARLET–DAUMIER MONNIER–GRANDVILLE–GAVARNI TRIMOLET–TRAVIÈS–JACQUE

HE WAS an astonishing man, was Carle Vernet.[1] His collected works are a whole world, a little *Comédie humaine* of their own; for trivial prints, sketches of the crowd and the street, and caricatures, often constitute the most faithful mirror of life. Often, too, caricatures, like fashion-plates, become more caricatural the more old-fashioned they are. Thus the stiff and ungainly bearing of the figures of those times seems to us oddly unexpected and jarring; and yet the whole of that world is much less intentionally odd than people generally suppose. Such was the fashion, such were its human beings; its men were like its paintings; the world had moulded itself on art. Everyone was stiff and upright; and with his skimpy frock-coat, his riding-boots, and his hair dripping over his brow, each citizen gave the impression of an academic nude which had called in at the old-clothes-shop. But it is not only because they have thoroughly preserved the sculptural imprint and the stylistic pretensions of their period—it is not only from the historical point of view, I mean—that Carle Vernet's caricatures have a great value for us; they also have a positive artistic worth. Each pose and gesture has the accent of truth; each head and physiognomy is endowed with an authentic style for which many of us can vouch when we think of the guests who used to enjoy our fathers' hospitality in the days of our childhood. His fashion-caricatures are superb. I need hardly remind you of that large plate of a gaming-house.[2] Around a vast oval table are gathered players of different types and ages. There is no lack of those indispensable young women whose eyes are greedily fixed upon the odds—those ladies in perpetual

[1] Son of Joseph, and father of Horace Vernet.

[2] It is not however recorded in any of the standard catalogues of Carle Vernet's work, and there is no copy of it at the Bibliothèque Nationale. Crépet suggests that Baudelaire may have had in mind an engraving by Darcis, after Guérain, entitled 'Les Trente-un, ou la Maison de prêt sur nantissement', which is stylistically similar to the work of Carle Vernet, and whose subject-matter agrees with Baudelaire's description.

waiting on the gambler whose luck is in. It is a scene of violent joys and despairs; of fiery young gamblers, burning up their luck; of cold, serious and tenacious gamblers; of old men whose scanty hair betokens the gales of long-departed equinoxes. Admittedly this composition, like everything else from the hand of Carle Vernet and his school, lacks freedom; but in return it has a deep seriousness, a pleasing asperity and a dryness of manner which suits the subject rather well, since gambling is a passion at once violent and restrained.

Pigal was among those who attracted most notice later on. The earliest works of Pigal go back quite a distance, and Carle Vernet lived a very long time. But it is often possible to say that two contemporaries represent two distinct epochs, even if they are quite close together in age. And does not this gentle and amusing caricaturist still grace our annual exhibitions with little pictures whose innocent comicality must seem very feeble to M. Biard? It is character and not age which is the decisive factor. And so Pigal is quite another thing from Carle Vernet. His manner serves as transitional between caricature as conceived by that artist and the more modern caricature of Charlet, for example, of whom I shall have something to say in a moment. Charlet, who belongs to the same generation as Pigal, may be the subject of a similar observation; for the word 'modern' refers to manner and not to date. Pigal's popular scenes are good. I do not mean that their originality is very lively, nor even their drawing very comic, for Pigal is a sober comedian; but the sentiment of his compositions is both just and good. His are commonplace truths, but they are truths for all that. The majority of his pictures are taken direct from nature. The procedure he follows is a simple and a modest one—he observes, he listens, and then he tells what he has seen and heard. In general there is a great simplicity and a certain innocence about all his compositions: they almost always have to do with men of the people, popular sayings, drunkards, family scenes, and in particular they show a spontaneous predilection for elderly types. There is another thing about Pigal, which he shares with many other caricaturists—he is not very good at expressing the quality of youth; it often happens that his young people have a 'made-up' look. His drawing, which generally flows easily, is richer and less *contrived* than Carle Vernet's. Almost the whole of Pigal's merit can thus be summed up under three headings—a habit of sound observation, a good memory, and an adequate sureness of execution: little or no imagination, but a measure of good sense. The carnival gusto and gaiety of the Italians is as foreign to him as the maniac violence of the English. Pigal is an essentially *reasonable* caricaturist.

I am rather at a loss to express my opinion on Charlet in a seemly way. He is a great name, an essentially French name—one of the glories of France. He has delighted, entertained, he is said even to have *moved*, a whole generation of men still living. I have known people who were honestly indignant at not seeing Charlet at the Institut. For them it was as great a scandal as the exclusion of Molière from the Académie. Now I know that to come forward and tell people that they are wrong to have been amused or moved in a certain fashion is rather a shabby part to play: it is truly painful to find oneself at cross-purposes with the universal vote. Nevertheless it is necessary to have the courage to say that Charlet has no place among the eternal spirits—among the cosmopolitan geniuses. This caricaturist is no citizen of the universe; and if you object that a caricaturist can never be quite that, I shall reply that to a certain extent he *can* be. Charlet is a topical artist and an exclusive patriot—two impediments in the way of genius. He has something in common with another famous man whom I do not wish to mention by name, for the time is not yet ripe;* like him he reaped his glory exclusively from France, and above all from the aristocracy of the sword. I submit that this is bad, and denotes a small mind. Again, like that other great man he insulted the clerical party a great deal; this too, I say, is a very bad symptom—these people are unintelligible on the other side of the Channel, on the other side of the Rhine or the Pyrenees. In a minute or two we shall be speaking of the artist proper—that is, of his talent, his execution, his draughtsmanship, his style; we shall settle the matter once and for all. At present it is only his *wit* that I am discussing.

Charlet always paid court to the people. He was a slave, not a free man; do not expect to find a disinterested artist in him. A drawing by Charlet is seldom a truth; it is nearly always a piece of cajolery addressed

* This fragment is taken from a book which I began some years ago, but left unfinished. M. de Béranger was still alive (C.B.). Like Flaubert, Baudelaire focused much of his anti-bourgeois feeling upon the popular poet Béranger. For an opposite, and almost contemporary, English point of view, see Walter Bagehot's essay on Béranger (1857) in his *Literary Studies* (Everyman Edition, vol. II, pp. 233 ff.). Béranger died in 1857.

to the preferred caste. There is no beauty, goodness, nobility, kindness or wit but in the soldier. The million million animalculae that graze upon this planet were created by God and endowed with organs and senses solely to enable them to contemplate the soldier, and the drawings of Charlet, in all their glory. Charlet asserts that the red-coat and the grenadier are the final cause of creation. These things have nothing whatever to do with caricature, I assure you; they are more like panegyrics, or dithyrambs, so strangely perverse is their author's approach to his profession. Admittedly the uncouth blunders which Charlet puts into the mouth of his recruits are turned with a certain charm which does them honour and makes them interesting. This smacks of the *vaudeville*, in which peasants are made to commit the most touching and witty malapropisms. They have hearts as pure as angels', with the wit of an academician (except for the social, or phonetic, *liaisons*). To show the peasant in his true self is an idle fancy of Balzac's: to depict the abominations of man's heart so relentlessly is all very well for a testy and hypochondriac spirit like Hogarth; but to exhibit to the life the vices of the soldier—there's real cruelty for you! it might discourage him! That is the way in which the famous Charlet understood caricature.

It is the same sentiment that guides our biased artist with respect to the clerics. He is not concerned with painting or delineating the moral deformities of the sacristy in an original manner. No, his sole need is to please the soldier-bumpkin; and the soldier-bumpkin used to live on a diet of Jesuits. In the arts, *the only thing that matters is to please*, as the bourgeois say.

Goya, too, attacked the monastic tribe. I imagine that he had no love for monks, for he made them very ugly. But how beautiful they are in all their ugliness! how triumphant in their monkish squalor and crapulence! Here art dominates—art which purifies like fire: there it is servility, which corrupts art. Now compare the artist with the courtier: one gives us superb drawings; the other, a Voltairean sermon.

There has been much talk about Charlet's street-arabs—those angelic little darlings who will one day make such pretty soldiers, who are so fond of retired veterans and who play at war with wooden swords. They are always plump and fresh as rosy apples, all innocence and frankness, with eyes bright and smiling on the world. But what of the 'enfant terrible', what of the great poet's 'pale urchin, with his hoarse voice and skin the colour of an old *sou*'?[1] I am afraid that Charlet has too pure a heart to see such things.

It must be owned, however, that occasionally he had a good idea.—The scene is a forest. Some bandits and their women are sitting eating beside an oak-tree on which a hanged man, already elongated and thin, is loftily taking the air and sniffing the dew, with his nose bent towards the ground and his toes correctly aligned like a dancer's. One of the ruffians points to him with his finger and says, 'Maybe that's how we shall be next Sunday!'[2]

But alas, he has given us few sketches of this kind. And yet, even if the idea is a good one, the drawing is inadequate; there is no well-marked character about the heads. It could be far finer, and is certainly not to be compared with Villon's lines as he supped with his comrades beneath the gallows on the gloomy plain.

Charlet's draughtsmanship hardly ever rises above the 'chic'—it is all loops and ovals. His sentiments he picked up readymade at the vaudeville. He was a thoroughly artificial man who applied himself to imitating the current ideas of his time. He made a tracing, so to speak, of public opinion: he tailored his intelligence to fit the fashion. The public was truly his pattern no less than his patron.

Once however he produced something rather good. This was a series of costumes of the old and the new guard,[3] which is not to be confused with a somewhat similar work published not so long ago—the latter may even be a posthumous work.[4] The figures have the stamp of reality; they must be very lifelike. Their gait, their gestures, the attitudes of their heads are all excellent. Charlet was young then; he did not think of himself as a great man, and his popularity had not yet absolved him from drawing his figures correctly and making them stand firm on their feet. But he always had a tendency towards self-neglect, and he ended by repeating over and over again the same vulgar scribble which the youngest of art-students would be unwilling to acknowledge if he had a scrap of self-respect. It is proper to point out that the work of which I

[1] Le race de Paris, c'est le pâle voyou,
Au corps chétif, au teint jaune comme un vieux sou.
Auguste Barbier, *Iambes*, X. Baudelaire must have quoted from memory.

[2] Charlet, Album lithographique (1832), No. 4 (La Combe 786).

[3] La Combe, 157–86 and 187–201 (1819–21).

[4] La Combe, 209–64 (1845).

38. CHARLET: *Valentin decorated by Marshal Gérard.* Lithograph. London, Victoria and Albert Museum.

39. GAVARNI: *After the Ball.* Lithograph. Paris, Bibliothèque Nationale.

40. PIGAL: '*The other foot, Sir, please.*' Lithograph. London, Victoria and Albert Museum.

41. Daumier: *Robert Macaire—Barrister*. Lithograph. Private Collection.

42. DAUMIER: *Dido and Aeneas*. Lithograph. Private Collection.

43. Traviès: *Liard—The Philosopher Tramp.* Lithograph. London, Victoria and Albert Museum.

44. HOGARTH: *The Reward of Cruelty*. Engraving. London, Victoria and Albert Museum.

45. GOYA: '*Who would have believed it?*' Aquatint. London, Victoria and Albert Museum.

am speaking is of a simple and serious kind, and that it demands none of the qualities which later on were gratuitously accorded to an artist whose sense of the comic was so deficient. But it is *caricaturists* with whom I am concerned here, and if I had followed my design straight through, I should not have introduced Charlet, any more than Pinelli, into my catalogue; but then I should have been accused of grave omissions.

In a word, what was this man but a manufacturer of nationalist nursery rhymes, a licensed purveyor of political catchwords, an idol, in short, whose life is no more proof against mortality than that of any other idol? It will not be long before he knows the full force of oblivion and joins the *great* painter and the *great* poet[1]—his first cousins in ignorance and ineptitude—to slumber in the waste-paper basket of indifference, like this sheet of paper which I have needlessly soiled and which is now only fit for pulping.[2]

But now I want to speak about one of the most important men, I will not say only in caricature, but in the whole of modern art. I want to speak about a man who each morning keeps the populace of our city amused, a man who supplies the daily needs of public gaiety and provides its sustenance. The bourgeois, the business-man, the urchin and the housewife all laugh and pass on their way, as often as not—what base ingratitude!—without even glancing at his name. Until now his fellow-artists have been alone in understanding all the serious qualities in his work, and in recognizing that it is really the proper subject for a study. You will have guessed that I am referring to Daumier.

There was nothing very spectacular about Honoré Daumier's beginnings. He drew because he had to—it was his ineluctable vocation. First of all he placed a few sketches with a little paper edited by William Duckett;[3] then Achille Ricourt, who was a print-dealer at that time, bought some more from him.[4] The revolution of 1830, like all revolutions, occasioned a positive fever of caricature. For caricaturists, those were

[1] Presumably Horace Vernet and Béranger respectively.

[2] Baudelaire's rough handling of Charlet earned him an indignant letter from Colonel de La Combe, whose book on the artist had been published in 1856. Delacroix also was displeased; see p. 63 above.

[3] Presumably *La Silhouette* (1829–31), the first journal of its kind to be published in Paris. In spite of his name, William Duckett was a Frenchman.

[4] Ricourt's shop was near the Louvre, in the rue du Coq. In 1832 he founded *L'Artiste*, to which Baudelaire contributed.

truly halcyon days. In that ruthless war against the government, and particularly against the king, men were all passion, all fire. It is a real curiosity today to look through that vast gallery of historical clowning which went by the name of *La Caricature*[1]—that great series of comic archives to which every artist of any consequence brought his quota. It is a hurly-burly, a farrago, a prodigious satanic comedy, now farcical, now gory, through whose pages all the political élite march past, rigged out in motley and grotesque costumes. Among all those great men of the dawning monarchy, how many are there not whose names are already forgotten! But it is the olympian and pyramidal *Pear*, of litigious memory, that dominates and crowns the whole fantastic epic. You will remember the time when Philipon (who was perpetually at cross-purposes with His Majesty's justice) wanted to prove to the tribunal that nothing was more innocent than that prickly and provoking pear, and how, in the very presence of the court, he drew a series of sketches of which the first exactly reproduced the royal physiognomy, and each successive one, drawing further and further away from the primary image, approached ever closer to the fatal goal—the *pear*! 'There now,' he said: 'What connection can you see between this last sketch and the first?' Similar experiments were made with the head of Christ and that of Apollo, and I believe that it was even possible to refer back one of them to the likeness of a toad. But all this proved absolutely nothing. An obliging analogy had discovered the symbol: from that time onwards the symbol was enough. With this kind of plastic slang, it was possible to say, and to make the people understand, anything one wanted. And so that tyrannical and accursed pear became the focus for the whole pack of patriotic blood-hounds. There is no doubt about it that they went to work with a marvellous ferocity and *esprit de corps*, and however obstinately Justice retorted, it is a matter of enormous surprise to us today, when we turn the pages of these comic archives, that so furious a war should have been able to be kept up for years on end.

A moment ago, I think, I used the words 'a gory farce'; and indeed these drawings are often full of blood and passion. Massacres, imprisonments, arrests, trials, searches and beatings-up by the police—all those episodes of the first years of the government of 1830 keep on recurring. Just judge for yourselves:—

[1] Founded by Charles Philipon (1800–62) in 1830, it lasted until 1835. Daumier contributed to it a great deal, sometimes under the pseudonym Rogelin.

Liberty, a young and beautiful girl, with her Phrygian cap upon her head, is sunk in a perilous sleep. She has hardly a thought for the danger which is threatening her. A *Man* is stealthily advancing upon her, with an evil purpose in his heart. He has the burly shoulders of a market-porter or a bloated landlord. His pear-shaped head is surmounted by a prominent tuft of hair and flanked with extensive side-whiskers. The monster is seen from behind, and the fun of guessing his name must have added no little value to the print. He advances upon the young person, making ready to outrage her.

'*Have you pray'd to-night, Madam?*'—It is Othello-Philippe about to stifle innocent Liberty, for all her cries and resistance!

Or again, along the pavement outside a more than suspicious house quite a young girl is passing; she is wearing her little Phrygian cap with all the innocent coquetry of a grisette, a girl of the people. Monsieur X and Monsieur Y (well-known faces—the most honourable of ministers, for a certainty) are plying a singular trade this time. They are closing in on the poor child, whispering blandishments or indecencies in her ear, and gently pushing her towards a narrow passageway. Behind a door the *Man* can just be made out. His face is almost turned away, but it is he all right! Just look at that tuft of hair and those side-whiskers. He is impatient, he is waiting.

Or here is Liberty arraigned before the Provost's Court or some other Gothic tribunal: this one is a great gallery of contemporary portraits in medieval dress.

And here is Liberty dragged into the torture-chamber. Her delicate ankles are about to be crushed, her stomach to be distended with torrents of water, and every other abomination to be performed upon her. These bare-armed, brawny, torture-hungry athletes are easily recognizable. They are Monsieur X, Monsieur Y, and Monsieur Z—the *bêtes noires* of opinion.*

In every one of these drawings (of which the majority are executed with remarkable conscientiousness and seriousness of purpose) the king

* I no longer have the documents in front of me, and it is possible that one of these last was by Traviès (C.B.). None of these caricatures has been exactly identified. Champfleury (who quotes the passage in his *Histoire de la caricature moderne*, 1865, pp. 227–8) seems to imply that they were by Grandville and Traviès, but *La Caricature* of 27 June 1831 contained a print of Liberté about to receive the sentence of the Cour Prévôtale, by Decamps.

plays the part of an ogre, an assassin, an insatiate Gargantua,[1] and sometimes even worse. But since the February Revolution[2] I have only seen a single caricature whose savagery reminded me of the days of those high political passions; for none of the political appeals displayed in the shop-windows at the time of the great presidential elections offered anything but pale reflections in comparison with the products of the time of which I have just been speaking. The exception occurred shortly after the lamentable massacre at Rouen.[3] In the foreground, on a stretcher, there lies a corpse, riddled with bullets: behind it are assembled all the city bigwigs in uniform, well crimped, well buckled, well turned out, their moustaches *en croc*, and bursting with arrogance; there must surely also be a few bourgeois dandies who are off to mount guard or to take a hand in quelling the riot, with a bunch of violets in the buttonhole of their tunics—in short, the very ideal of the *garde bourgeoise*, as the most celebrated of our demagogues termed it.[4] On his knees before the stretcher, wrapped in his judge's robe, with his mouth open to show his double row of saw-edged teeth like a shark, F.C.[5] is slowly passing his claws over the corpse's flesh and blissfully scratching it.—'Ah! that Norman!' he says. 'He's only shamming dead so as to avoid answering to justice!'

It was with just such a fury that *La Caricature* waged war on the government. And Daumier played an important role in that chronic skirmish. A means had been invented to provide money for the fines which overwhelmed the *Charivari*; this was to publish supplementary drawings, the money from whose sale was appropriated to that purpose.[6] Over the deplorable massacres in the rue Transnonain, Daumier showed his true greatness; his print has become rather rare, for it was confiscated and destroyed.[7] It is not precisely caricature—it is history, reality, both trivial and terrible. In a poor, mean room, the traditional room of the

[1] Daumier's *Gargantua* (*La Caricature*, December 1831) cost him six months in prison.
[2] The 1848 revolution.
[3] This took place at the time of the departmental elections, April 1848; a rising was brutally repressed by General Ordener.
[4] Probably Lafayette. [5] Frank-Carré, a detested local politician.
[6] This was the *Association Mensuelle Lithographique*, which was started in August 1832. On the whole subject, see *Freedom of the Press and 'L'Association Mensuelle': Philipon versus Louis-Philippe*, by E. de T. Bechtel (New York, Grolier Club, 1952).
[7] Published in July 1834 by the *Association Mensuelle* (Delteil 135), it is now one of Daumier's best-known lithographs.

proletarian, with shoddy, essential furniture, lies the corpse of a workman, stripped but for his cotton shirt and cap: he lies on his back, at full length, his legs and arms outspread. There has obviously been a great struggle and tumult in the room, for the chairs are overturned, as are the night-table and the chamber-pot. Beneath the weight of his corpse—between his back and the bare boards—the father is crushing the corpse of his little child. In this cold attic all is silence and death.

It was about the same time that Daumier undertook a satirical portrait gallery of political notabilities. There were two series—one of full-length, the other of bust-portraits: the latter series came later, I think, and only contained members of the upper house.[1] In these works the artist displayed a wonderful understanding of portraiture; whilst exaggerating and burlesquing the original features, he remained so soundly rooted in nature that these specimens might serve as models for all portraitists. Every little meanness of spirit, every absurdity, every quirk of intellect, every vice of the heart can be clearly seen and read in these animalized faces; and at the same time everything is broadly and emphatically drawn. Daumier combined the freedom of an artist with the accuracy of a Lavater. And yet such of his works as date back to that period are very different from what he is doing today. They lack the facility of improvisation, the looseness and lightness of pencil which he acquired later. Sometimes—though rarely—he was a little heavy, but always very finished, conscientious, and strict.

I remember one other very fine drawing which belongs to the same class—*La Liberté de la presse*.[2] Surrounded by his instruments of liberation —his printing-plant—and with his ritual paper-cap pulled down to his ears and his shirt-sleeves rolled up, a typographer's workman is standing four-square and solid on his sturdy legs; he is clenching both his fists and scowling. The man's whole frame is as rough-hewn and muscular as the figures of the great masters. In the background is the inevitable *Philippe* with his policemen. But they dare not come and interfere.

However, our great artist has done a wide diversity of things. What I propose to do is to describe some of his most striking plates, chosen from different genres. Then I shall analyse the philosophic and artistic

[1] In fact the two series were approximately contemporary with one another; the full-length portraits were published in *La Caricature* in 1833–4, and the majority of the bust-portraits in *Le Charivari* in 1833.

[2] Published March 1834 by the *Association Mensuelle* (Delteil 133).

importance of this extraordinary man, and finally, before taking leave of him, I shall give a list of the different series and categories of his work, or at least I shall do the best I can, for at the present moment his *œuvre* is a labyrinth, a forest of trackless abundance.

Le Dernier Bain[1] is a serious and pathetic caricature. Standing on the parapet of a quay and already leaning forward, so that his body forms an acute angle with the base from which it is parting company—like a statue losing its balance—a man is letting himself topple into the river. He must have really made up his mind, for his arms are calmly folded, and a huge paving-stone is attached to his neck with a rope. He has taken his oath not to escape. This is no suicide of a poet who means to be fished out and to get himself talked about. Just look at that shabby, creased frock-coat, with all the bones jutting through! And that seedy cravat, twisted like a snake, and that bony and pointed Adam's apple! Surely nobody would have the heart to grudge this man his underwater escape from the passing show of civilization. In the background, on the other side of the river, a well-fed, contemplative member of the bourgeoisie is devoting himself to the innocent joys of rod and line.

Imagine, now, a very remote corner of some obscure and little-frequented suburb, oppressed beneath a leaden sun. A man of somewhat funereal figure—an undertaker's mute, perhaps, or a doctor—is hob-nobbing and drinking a glass, in a leafless arbour, beneath a trellis of dusty laths, with a hideous skeleton. The hour-glass and the scythe are lying on one side. I forget the title of this plate: but these two self-important creatures are evidently laying some murderous bet, or conducting a learned discussion on mortality.[2]

Daumier has scattered his talent in a thousand different fields. For example, he even produced some wonderful drawings when commissioned to illustrate a baddish medico-poetical publication called *La Némésis médicale*.[3] One of them, which deals with cholera, represents a public square flooded, overwhelmed with light and heat. True to its ironical custom in times of great calamity and political upheaval, the

[1] No. 2 of 'Sentiments et Passions', published in *Le Charivari*, May 1840 (Delteil 800).

[2] Published 26 May 1840 in *Le Charivari*, with the title 'Association en commandite pour l'exploitation de l'humanité'—'Limited Company for the Exploitation of Humanity' (Delteil 796).

[3] Published 1840. These wood-engravings are nos. 111–39 in Arthur Rümann's *Honoré Daumier, sein Holzschnittwerk* (Munich, 1914). The example described by Baudelaire is reproduced above, on p. 165.

sky of Paris is superb; it is quite white and incandescent with heat. The shadows are black and clear-cut. A corpse is lying across a doorway. A woman is hurrying in, stopping up her nose and her mouth as she runs. The square is deserted and like an oven—more desolate, even, than a populous square after a riot. In the background can be seen the silhouettes of two or three little hearses drawn by grotesque old hacks, and in the midst of this forum of desolation a wretched, bewildered dog, starved to the bone, with neither thought nor aim, is sniffing the dusty paving-stones, its tail stuffed between its legs.

The scene now shifts to a prison-yard. A very learned gentleman, with black coat and white cravat—a philanthropist, a redresser of wrongs—is ecstatically seated between two convicts of terrifying aspect—both as stupid as cretins, as ferocious as bull-dogs and as down-at-heel as old boots. One of them is saying that he has murdered his father, ravished his sister, or done some other heroic deed. 'Ah! my friend, what a splendid body of a man you must have been!' cries the savant, in raptures.[1]

These specimens are enough to show how serious Daumier's thought often is, and how spiritedly he attacks his subjects. Look through his works, and you will see parading before your eyes all that a great city contains of living monstrosities, in all their fantastic and thrilling reality. There can be no item of the fearful, the grotesque, the sinister or the farcical in its treasury, but Daumier knows it. The live and starving corpse, the plump and well-filled corpse, the ridiculous troubles of the home, every little stupidity, every little pride, every enthusiasm, every despair of the bourgeois—it is all there. By no one as by Daumier has the bourgeois been known and loved (after the fashion of artists)—the bourgeois, that last vestige of the Middle Ages, that Gothic ruin that dies so hard, that type at once so commonplace and so eccentric. Daumier has lived in intimacy with him, he has spied on him day and night, he has penetrated the mysteries of his bedroom, he has consorted with his wife and his children, he comprehends the form of his nose and the construction of his head, he knows the spirit that animates his house from top to bottom.

To make a complete analysis of Daumier's *œuvre* would be an impossibility; instead I am going to give the titles of his principal series of

[1] No. 12 of the series 'Les Philanthropes du jour,' published in *Le Charivari*, 19 October 1844 (Delteil 1304).

prints, without too much in the way of appreciation and commentary. Every one of them contains marvellous things.

Robert Macaire, *Mœurs conjugales*, *Types parisiens*, *Profils et silhouettes*, *les Baigneurs*, *les Baigneuses*, *les Canotiers parisiens*, *les Bas-bleus*, *Pastorales*, *Histoire ancienne*, *les Bons Bourgeois*, *les Gens de Justice*, *la Journée de M. Coquelet*, *les Philanthropes du jour*, *Actualités*, *Tout ce qu'on voudra*, *les Représentants représentés*. Add the two sets of portraits of which I have already spoken.*

I have two important observations to make about two of these series—*Robert Macaire* and the *Histoire ancienne*. *Robert Macaire*[1] was the decisive starting-point of the caricature of manners. The great political war had died down a little. The stubborn aggressiveness of the law, the attitude of the government which had established its power, and a certain weariness natural to the human spirit had damped its fires a great deal. Something new had to be found. The pamphlet gave way to the comedy. The *Satire Ménippée*[2] surrendered the field to Molière, and the great epic-cycle of Robert Macaire, told in Daumier's dazzling version, succeeded to the rages of revolution and the drawings of allusion. Thenceforth caricature changed its step; it was no longer especially political. It had become the general satire of the people. It entered the realm of the novel.

The *Histoire ancienne*[3] seems to me to be important because it is, so to say, the best paraphrase of the famous line *'Qui nous délivrera des Grecs et des Romains?'*[4] Daumier came down brutally on antiquity—on false antiquity, that is, for no one has a better feeling than he for the grandeurs of antiquity. He snapped his fingers at it. The hot-headed Achilles, the cunning Ulysses, the wise Penelope, Telemachus, that great booby, and the fair Helen, who ruined Troy—they all of them, in fact, appear

* A ceaseless and regular production has rendered this list more than incomplete. Once, with Daumier himself, I tried to make a complete catalogue of his works, but even together we could not manage to do it (C.B.). The catalogue by Delteil, to which reference has been made in notes above, contains almost 4,000 lithographic items.

[1] A hundred plates of this series appeared in *Le Charivari* between August 1836 and November 1838; and a further twenty between October 1840 and September 1842. Daumier developed Robert Macaire into a classic symbol of the rascally impostor; see Champfleury (*op. cit.*) pp. 119 ff.

[2] A political pamphlet written in the form of a dramatic farce in one act, with prologue and epilogue. It was directed against the *Ligue*, and published in 1594.

[3] A series of 50 plates which appeared in *Le Charivari* between December 1841 and January 1843 (Delteil 925–74); see pl. 42.

[4] The first line of a satire by Joseph Berchoux.

before our eyes in a farcical ugliness which is reminiscent of those decrepit old tragic actors whom one sometimes sees taking a pinch of snuff in the wings. It was a very amusing bit of blasphemy, and one which had its usefulness. I remember a lyric poet of my acquaintance[1]—one of the 'pagan school'—being deeply indignant at it. He called it sacrilege, and spoke of the fair Helen as others speak of the Blessed Virgin. But those who have no great respect for Olympus, or for tragedy, were naturally beside themselves with delight.

To conclude, Daumier has pushed his art very far; he has made a serious art of it; he is a *great* caricaturist. To appraise him worthily, it is necessary to analyse him both from the artistic and from the moral point of view. As an artist, what distinguishes Daumier is his sureness of touch. He draws as the great masters draw. His drawing is abundant and easy—it is a sustained improvisation; and yet it never descends to the 'chic'. He has a wonderful, an almost divine memory, which for him takes the place of the model. All his figures stand firm on their feet, and their movement is always true. His gift for observation is so sure that you will not find a single one of his heads which jars with its supporting body. The right nose, the right brow, the right eye, the right foot, the right hand. Here we have the logic of the *savant* transported into a light and fugitive art, which is pitted against the very mobility of life.

As a moralist, Daumier has several affinities with Molière. Like him, he goes straight to the point. The central idea immediately leaps out at you. You have only to look to have understood. The legends which are written at the foot of his drawings have no great value, and could generally be dispensed with.[2] His humour is, so to speak, involuntary. This artist does not search for an idea; it would be truer to say that he just lets it slip out. His caricature has a formidable breadth, but it is quite without bile or rancour. In all his work there is a foundation of decency and simplicity. Often he has gone so far as to refuse to handle certain very fine and violent satirical themes, because, he said, they passed the limits of the comic, and could wound the inner feelings of his fellow-men. And so, whenever he is harrowing or terrible, it is almost without having wished to be so. He has just depicted what he has seen, and this is the result. As he has a very passionate and a very natural love for nature, he would find difficulty in rising to the absolute comic. He

[1] Probably Théodore de Banville. [2] They were mostly invented by Philipon.

even goes out of his way to avoid anything which a French public might not find an object of clear and immediate perception.

A word more. What completes Daumier's remarkable quality and renders him an exceptional artist who belongs to the illustrious family of the masters, is that his drawing is naturally *colourful.* His lithographs and his wood-engravings awake ideas of colour. His pencil contains more than just a black trace suitable for delineating contours. He evokes colour, as he does thought—and that is the sign of a higher art—a sign which all intelligent artists have clearly discerned in his works.

Henri Monnier made much of a stir a few years ago; he had a great success in the bourgeois world and in the world of the studios—which are both sorts of villages. And there are two reasons for this. The first is that, like Julius Caesar, he fulfilled three functions at once—those of actor, writer and caricaturist. The second is that his talent is essentially a bourgeois one. As an actor he was cold and precise: as a writer, captious: and as an artist, he had discovered a method of doing his 'chic' from nature.

He is the exact counterpart of the man of whom we have just been speaking. Instead of instantly seizing upon the whole ensemble of a figure or a subject, Henri Monnier went to work by means of a slow and progressive examination of its details. He has never known great art. Take, for example, Monsieur Prudhomme,[1] that monstrously authentic type. Now Monsieur Prudhomme was never conceived on a large scale. Monnier studied him, the real, living Prudhomme; he studied him from day to day, over a very long period of time. I cannot tell how many cups of coffee Henri Monnier must have swallowed, or how many games of dominoes he must have played, before he arrived at that prodigious result. After studying him, he translated—no, he *traced* him on to his paper. At first sight the finished product strikes one as something extraordinary; but when all of Monsieur Prudhomme had been said, Henri Monnier had nothing left to say. Several of his *Scènes populaires*[2] are pleasant enough—otherwise one would have to deny the cruel and amazing fascination of the daguerreotype; but Monnier is quite unable to create, to idealize, to arrange anything. To return to his drawings, which are the main object of our attention, they are generally cold and hard, and what is so odd is that, in spite of the sharpened precision of

[1] Monnier's best-known creation, a pompous and sententious bourgeois.

[2] Published in 1830.

his pencil, there remains an element of vagueness in his thought. Monnier has a rare gift, but he has no more than one. It is the coldness, the limpidity of a mirror—of a mirror that cannot think, and contents itself with reflecting what passes in front of it.[1]

As for Grandville, he is quite another story. Grandville is a morbidly literary artist, always on the look-out for bastard means of projecting his thought into the domain of the plastic arts; and so we have often seen him employing that old-fashioned device of the 'speaking balloon', attached to the mouths of his characters. A philosopher or a doctor would find material for a very pretty psychological or physiological study in Grandville. He spent his life seeking ideas, and sometimes found them. But as he was an artist by profession and a man of letters by natural inclination, he never succeeded in expressing them properly. Naturally he touched upon several important questions, but he ended by falling between two stools, being neither quite philosopher nor artist. During a large part of his life Grandville was much preoccupied with the general idea of Analogy. He even began that way—with the *Métamorphoses du jour*.[2] But he was never able to draw correct inferences from it; he tossed about hither and thither like a derailed locomotive. With superhuman courage this man devoted his life to refashioning creation. He took it in his hands, wrung it, rearranged it, explained it and annotated it; and Nature was transformed into a fantasmagoria. He turned the world upside down. Did he not, in fact, compose a picture-book called *Le Monde à l'envers?*[3] There are some superficial spirits who are amused by Grandville; for my part, I find him terrifying. For unfortunately it is the artist in whom I am interested, and not his drawings. When I open the door of Grandville's works I feel a certain uneasiness, as though I am entering an apartment where disorder was systematically organized—where preposterous cornices were propped up against the floor, where the pictures showed their faces through an optician's distorting-glass, where all the objects elbowed each other about obliquely, the furniture stood with its feet in the air, and the drawers slid inwards instead of out.

[1] Champfleury (*op. cit.* p. 243) relates how he was once in the company of a 'somewhat testy poet' (no doubt, Baudelaire), when the latter addressed a singular compliment to Monnier. 'Monsieur,' he said, 'I have for long wanted to congratulate you on your excellent *dictionaries*.'

[2] Published in 1829.

[3] Baudelaire is probably referring to Grandville's *Un autre monde* (1844).

Doubtless Grandville produced some good and beautiful things, much assisted by his obstinate and meticulous habits; but he entirely lacked flexibility, and what is more, he was never able to draw a woman. But it is the lunatic side of his talent that makes Grandville important. Before his death he applied his always stubborn will to the noting of his successive dreams and nightmares in a plastic form,[1] with all the precision of a stenographer writing down an orator's speech. Grandville, the artist, wanted—he really wanted—his pencil to explain the law of the Association of Ideas! Grandville is indeed very comic; but he is often so without knowing it.

And now we come to an artist with an odd kind of charm, but who is very much more important. And yet he—Gavarni—started by making engineering drawings; then he went to on fashion-drawings; and he seems to me to have borne for a long time the trace of these things. Nevertheless it is fair to say that Gavarni has always shown progress. He is not entirely a caricaturist, nor even uniquely a visual artist; he is also a man of letters. He touches upon, he evokes. The particular characteristic of his comic gift is a great nicety of observation which sometimes goes as far as tenuity. Like Marivaux, he knows the full force of understatement, which is at once a lure and a flattery for the public intelligence. He writes the legends to his own drawings, and they are sometimes very intricate. Many people prefer Gavarni to Daumier, and there is nothing surprising in that. Gavarni is less of an artist, and therefore he is easier for them to understand. Daumier is a frank and open genius. Take away the text from one of his drawings, and it still remains a thing of beauty and clarity. It is not the same way with Gavarni; he is a double man—with him the legend is superadded to the drawing. In the second place, Gavarni is not essentially a satirist. Often he flatters instead of biting; he encourages, he does not chide. Like all men of letters—being a man of letters himself—he is very slightly tainted with corruption. Thanks to the agreeable hypocrisy of his thought and to the powerful tactics of innuendo, there is nothing he does not dare. At other times, when his bawdry openly declares itself, it dons a graceful garb, it caresses the dogmas of fashion and takes the world into its confidence. How could he fail to be popular? Here is one sample among a thousand. Do you remember that fine, handsome young woman who is giving a disdainful pout as she looks at a young man

[1] Also probably *Un autre monde.*

clasping his hands to her in the attitude of a suppliant? 'One little kiss, I beseech you, my good kind lady, for the love of God!'—'Look in again this evening; your *father* has already had one this morning.' You would really think that the lady must be a portrait. But those rascals of Gavarni's are so engaging that young people will inevitably want to imitate them. Note, besides, that the best part is in the legend, the drawing itself being incapable of saying so many things.

Gavarni created the *Lorette*. She existed, indeed, a little before his time, but he *completed* her. I even believe it was he who invented the word.[1] The Lorette, as has already been observed, is not the same thing as the 'kept women', that feature of the Empire, condemned to live in funereal intimacy with the clinking corpse—a general or a banker—on which she depended. The Lorette is a free agent. She comes and she goes. She keeps open house. She is no one's mistress; she consorts with the artists and the journalists. She does what she can to be witty. I said that Gavarni had completed her; and in fact he is so swept along by his literary imagination that he invents at least as much as he sees, and for that reason he has had a considerable effect upon manners. Paul de Kock[2] created the Grisette, and Gavarni the Lorette; and not a few of those girls have perfected themselves by using her as a mirror, just as the youth of the Latin Quarter succumbed to the influence of his *Students*, and as many people force themselves into the likeness of fashion-plates.

Such as he is, Gavarni is a more than interesting artist, of whom much will endure. It will be absolutely necessary to peruse his works in order to understand the history of the last years of the Monarchy. The Republic put him a little in the shade, according to a cruel but natural law. He emerged with the dawning of peace, and now he vanishes with the storm. The veritable glory and the true mission of Gavarni and Daumier were to complete Balzac, who, moreover, was well aware of this, and reckoned them his auxiliaries and commentators.

Gavarni's chief works are the following sets: *La Boîte aux lettres, les Etudiants, les Lorettes, les Actrices, les Coulisses, les Enfants terribles, Hommes et Femmes de plume*, and a vast series of detached prints.

It remains for me to speak of Trimolet, Traviès and Jacque.—Trimolet's was a melancholy destiny. To see the graceful and childlike drollery which wafts through his compositions, you would hardly

[1] The word was in fact 'invented' by Nestor Roqueplan, the journalist and impresario.

[2] The popular novelist.

suspect that his poor life had been assailed by so many grievous afflictions and gnawing sorrows. He himself etched—for the collection of *Chansons populaires de la France*[1] and for Aubert's *Comic Almanacks*[2]—a number of very beautiful designs, or rather sketches, in which the maddest and most innocent gaiety reigns. Trimolet drew very complicated compositions freely on the plate, without preliminary work—a procedure which results, it must be admitted, in something of a muddle. Obviously this artist had been very much struck by the works of Cruikshank; but for all that, he kept his originality. He is a humorist who deserves a place apart; he has a flavour all his own, a subtle taste which fine palates must find distinct from all others.

One day Trimolet painted a picture.[3] It was well conceived, and the idea was a fine one: on a dark and soaking night one of those old men who look like perambulating ruins, or living bundles of rags, is lying stretched out at the foot of a crumbling wall. He raises his eyes in gratitude towards the starless sky, and cries out, 'I bless Thee, my God, who hast given me this wall for my shelter and this mat for my covering!' Like all the disinherited of the earth, who feel the lash of affliction, this excellent fellow is not hard to please, and for what remains he gladly puts his faith in the All-Powerful. Whatever may be said by the tribe of the optimists, who, according to Désaugiers,[4] have been known to tumble down after drinking (at the risk of crushing to pieces some 'poor man who has had no dinner'), there are geniuses who have passed nights like that! Trimolet is dead; he died at the moment when the dawn was already brightening his horizon and a kindlier fortune seemed to want to smile upon him. His talent was growing; his intellectual machinery was good and actively functioning; but his physical machinery had been gravely impaired and undermined by the storms of the past.

Traviès, too, has had an ill-starred lot. In my opinion, he is an outstanding artist, and one who was not nicely appreciated in his own time. He has produced much, but he lacks sureness. He wants to be amusing, and you can be certain that he will fail. Or else he will make a beautiful discovery—and fail to recognize it. He amends and corrects himself without ceasing; he turns and returns, forever pursuing an intangible ideal. He is the prince of bad luck. His muse is a nymph, but a nymph

[1] Published in three volumes in 1843. Other illustrators collaborated on this work.
[2] 1842 and 1843.
[3] Presumably *La Prière* (Salon 1841).
[4] A prolific writer of *vaudevilles*.

of the suburbs—a little wan and melancholy. But through all his tergiversations you can always follow a subterranean vein of quite noteworthy character and colour. Traviès has a deep feeling for the joys and griefs of the people; he knows the rabble through and through, and may be said to have loved it with a tender sympathy. That is the reason why his *Scènes bachiques*[1] will remain a remarkable work; besides, those tramps of his are generally very lifelike, and all their rags and tatters have that almost indefinable fullness and nobility of a style ready-made, such as nature often provides in her odd moments. We must not forget that Traviès is the creator of *Mayeux*,[2] that true, eccentric character who amused Paris so much. Mayeux is his, just as *Robert Macaire* is Daumier's and *M. Prudhomme* belongs to Monnier. At that already distant time there was in Paris a sort of *physiognomanic* clown called Léclaire, who did the run of the outlying taverns, the drinking clubs and the little theatres. He was a puller of expressive faces, and, sitting between two candles, he used to illuminate his features with all the passions in turn. It was the volume of the *Caractères des passions de M. Lebrun peintre du roi*,[3] all over again. This man was a very melancholy soul—a ridiculous accident more common than one supposes among the eccentric classes—and he was possessed by a mania for friendship. Apart from his studies and his grotesque performances, he spent his time searching for a friend, and when he had had a drink, his eyes would overflow with the tears of solitude. This poor fellow possessed such *objective* power and so great an aptitude for make-up that he could imitate to the very life the hump and wrinkled brow of a hunch-back, no less than his great simian paws and noisy, slobbering utterance. Traviès saw him—it was in the midst of the great patriotic fervours of July—and a radiant idea exploded in his brain. Mayeux was created; and for a long time the turbulent Mayeux spoke, shouted, perorated and gesticulated in the memory of the Parisian people.[4] Since that time it has been assumed that Mayeux really

[1] Published 1839.

[2] The subject of some 160 lithographs published in *La Caricature* and elsewhere. One writer describes him as 'ce fantoche priapique'. Other artists, such as Grandville, also used the character.

[3] Charles Lebrun's *Méthode pour apprendre à dessiner les Passions* was extremely influential throughout the late seventeenth and the entire eighteenth century, and was much translated.

[4] The whole of the above passage dealing with Léclaire is quoted by Champfleury (*op. cit.*, pp. 198–9). Beyond admitting the plausibility of the explanation, as far as it goes, Champfleury does not offer any confirmation.

existed, and it has been thought that Traviès knew and copied him. The same thing has occurred with several other popular creations.

Some time ago Traviès disappeared from the scene—I do not quite know why, for there is today, as always, a healthy growth of comic albums and journals. It is a real misfortune, for he is an acute observer, and in spite of his hesitations and failings, there is a seriousness and a sensitivity about his talent that makes it singularly engaging.

I feel that I should warn collectors of the Mayeux caricatures that the women who, as is well known, played so great a part in the epic history of this gallant and patriotic Ragotin,[1] are not by Traviès; they are by Philipon, who had this exceptionally comic idea, as well as a fascinating way of drawing women. And so it came about that he reserved to himself the pleasant task of doing the women in the Mayeux caricatures of Traviès, and that in this way each drawing came to have a *lining* in a different style—which, however, can hardly be said to *underline* their comic intention.[2]

Jacque, that excellent artist with his multiple intelligence, has also on occasions shown himself an admirable caricaturist. Apart from his paintings and his etchings, in which he has always revealed a solemn poetry, he has also been responsible for some very good grotesque drawings in which the central idea usually tells at first sight. See, for example, his *Militairiana*[3] and his *Malades et Médecins*.[4] He draws richly and with wit, and his caricature, like everything else of his, has the pungency and the immediacy of the poet-observer.

[1] A grotesque character in Scarron's *Roman comique*.

[2] M. Claude Ferment, who has recently been studying Traviès, informs me that he has been able to detect the possible hand of Philipon in only a relatively small number of the Mayeux caricatures.

[3] Published in the *Musée Philipon*.

[4] Published in *Le Charivari*, 1843.

L.-J. Trimolet (1812–43): 'The dead plaintiff.'
From *Physiologie de l'homme de loi*, Paris [1841].

SOME FOREIGN CARICATURISTS

HOGARTH–CRUIKSHANK–GOYA PINELLI–BRUEGHEL

I

AN altogether popular name, not only with artists but also in the polite world: an artist among the most eminent in the sphere of the comic, who fills the memory like a proverb—that is Hogarth. I have often heard it said of Hogarth that he is the death and burial of the comic muse. Well, I have no objection to that. The remark can of course be taken as a witticism, but I am anxious for it to be understood as a tribute; for my part, I find in this ill-intentioned axiom the symptom and the diagnosis of a quite especial merit. Be assured, however, that Hogarth's talent does indeed include in its composition a cold, astringent and funereal ingredient. It wounds and harrows. Brutal and violent, yet always absorbed with the moral meaning of his compositions—a moralist, in fact, before all else—Hogarth, like our Grandville, loads them with allegorical and allusive details whose function, according to him, is to complete and elucidate his thought. For the spectator, however—I was just about to say, for the *reader*—the reverse sometimes happens, so that they may end by retarding and confusing the intelligence.

However, like all very adventurous artists, Hogarth has quite a variety of styles and samples to offer. He does not always adopt so harsh, so literary and so fidgety a manner. Compare, for example, the plates of *Marriage à-la-mode* with *The Rake's Progress*, *Gin Lane*, *The Enrag'd Musician* and the *Distress'd Poet*, and in these latter you will recognize a far greater freedom and spontaneity. Undoubtedly one of the most curious of all is the plate which shows us a corpse stretched out stiff and flat on the dissection-table.[1] On a pulley, or some other piece of tackle attached to the ceiling, the intestines of the dead debauchee are being unwound. How horrible is this most corpse-like of corpses! and what could provide a more singular contrast to it than the surrounding figures of all those British doctors—tall, long, skinny or stout, grotesquely solemn and topped with monstrous periwigs? In one corner there

[1] *The Reward of Cruelty*. See pl. 44.

is a dog gluttonously foraging in a bucket and filching some human remains from it. Hogarth, the death and burial of the comic muse! I would sooner call him the comic muse of death and burial. Hogarth's man-eating dog has always put me in mind of that historical pig which outraged all decency by getting drunk on the blood of the hapless Fualdès, while a barrel-organ provided the dying man with a funeral service.[1]

I declared a moment ago that our studio witticism ought to be taken in the sense of a tribute. And indeed with Hogarth I do find myself renewing acquaintance with that indefinable breath of the sinister, the violent and the ruthless which characterizes almost every product of the land of spleen. *Gin Lane*, for example, quite apart from the innumerable mishaps and the grotesque disasters with which the path of a drunkard's life is strewn, includes some terrible incidents too, which scarce seem comic from our French point of view; these are almost always cases of violent death. But this is not the place to make a detailed analysis of Hogarth's works; numerous appreciations of this unique and punctilious moralist have already been written, and I want to limit myself to establishing the general character which informs the works of each important artist.

While we are on the subject of England it would be unjust not to mention Seymour, whose admirable squibs on shooting and fishing—that two-fold epic of fanaticism—are familiar to all. He was the original inventor of the marvellous allegory of the spider weaving her web between the arm and the line of a fisherman whose composure is absolute.[2]

As with the rest of the English, we find in Seymour a violence, a love of the excessive, and a simple, ultra-brutal and direct manner of stating his subject; when it comes to caricature, the English are extremists. 'Oh! the deep, deep sea!' cries a stout Londoner in blissful contemplation, serenely seated in a rowing boat, a quarter of a league from harbour.[3] I fancy that you can still even make out a few rooftops

[1] Fualdès was assassinated at Rodez in 1817. The barrel-organ was part of the plot, being played in order to drown his cries. The matter became a *cause célèbre*.

[2] The idea was afterwards borrowed by Monnier.

[3] No. 153 in *Sketches by Seymour* (1867), a collection of Seymour's *Humorous Sketches* which had been published separately, at 3d each, between 1834 and 1836. The caption continues: 'Mr. Dobbs singing "Hearts as warm as those above lie under the waters cold." ' Seymour was the illustrator of the first two parts of *The Pickwick Papers*, and thus the creator of the original image of Mr. Pickwick. See p. 220.

in the distance. This imbecile is in such an extreme of ecstasy that he does not notice the two stout legs of his dear wife, projecting above the level of the water and standing straight up, toes in air. It seems that this massive party has allowed herself to tumble head first into that very liquid element whose sight so stirs the thick brain of her spouse. Her legs are all that we can see of the unhappy creature. Soon enough that stalwart nature-lover will be looking round phlegmatically for his wife—and he will not find her.

The special merit of George Cruikshank—setting aside all his other merits, his subtlety of expression, his understanding of the fantastic, etc.—is his inexhaustible abundance in the grotesque. A verve such as his is unimaginable, nor indeed would it be credited if the proofs were not before our very eyes in the form of an immense *œuvre*, a numberless collection of vignettes, a long series of comic albums—in short, of such a quantity of grotesque characters, situations, scenes and physiognomies that the observer's memory quite loses its bearings. The grotesque flows inevitably and incessantly from Cruikshank's etching-needle, like pluperfect rhymes from the pen of a natural poet. The grotesque is his natural habit.

If it was possible to make an unerring analysis of a thing so fugitive and impalpable as *feeling* in art—that indefinable something which always distinguishes one artist from another, however close their kinship may be in appearance—I should say that the essence of Cruikshank's grotesque is an extravagant violence of gesture and movement, and a kind of explosion, so to speak, within the expression. Each one of his little creatures mimes his part in a frenzy and ferment, like a pantomime-actor. The only fault that one might criticize is that he is often more of a wit, more of a *cartoonist*, than an artist; in short, that he is not always an entirely conscientious draughtsman. You might suppose that in the pleasure that he feels in giving way to his prodigious *verve*, the artist forgets to endow his characters with a sufficient vitality. He draws a little too much like those men of letters who amuse themselves scribbling sketches. His fascinating little creatures are not always born to live and breathe. The whole of this diminutive company rushes pell-mell through its thousand capers with indescribable high spirits, but without worrying too much if all their limbs are in their proper places. Only too often they are no more than human hypotheses, which wriggle about as best they can. In a word, such as he is, Cruikshank is an artist endowed with rich comic gifts, and one who will retain his place in every collection. But what is one to say of those modern French plagiarists whose impertinence goes to the length of appropriating not only his subjects and ideas, but even his manner and style? But happily *naïveté* is not a thing to be stolen. Their assumed childishness has not raised their temperature by one degree, and the quality of their draughtsmanship leaves even more to be desired than that of their victim.

II

NEW horizons in the comic have been opened up in Spain by a most extraordinary man.

On the subject of Goya, I must start by referring my readers to Théophile Gautier's excellent article in the *Cabinet de l'Amateur*,[1] which has since been reprinted in a miscellaneous volume. Théophile Gautier is perfectly equipped to understand a nature such as Goya's. Moreover with reference to his technical methods—aquatint and etching mixed, with heightenings of drypoint—the article in question contains all that is required. All I want to do is to add a few words upon that very precious element which Goya introduced into the comic—I want to speak about the *fantastic*. Goya does not fit exactly into any of the special or particular categories; his is neither the absolute nor the purely significative comic, in the French manner. Often of course he plunges down to the savage level, or soars up to the heights of the absolute, but the general aspect under which he sees things is above all fantastic; or rather, the eye which he casts upon things translates them naturally into the language of fantasy. The *Caprichos* are a marvellous work, not only on account of the originality of their conceptions, but also on account of their execution. I like to imagine a man suddenly faced with them—an enthusiast, an amateur, who has no notion of the historical facts alluded to in several of these prints, a simple artistic soul who does not know the first thing about Godoy, or King Charles, or the Queen; but for all that he will experience a sharp shock at the core of his brain, as a result of the artist's original manner, the fullness and sureness of his means, and also of that atmosphere of fantasy in which all his subjects are steeped. I would go further and say that in works which spring from profoundly individual minds there is something analogous to those periodical

[1] Vol. I, 1842, pp. 337 ff.; reprinted in the *Voyage en Espagne*.

or chronic dreams with which our sleep is regularly besieged. That is the mark of the true artist, who always remains firm and indomitable even in those fugitive works—works which are, so to speak, hung upon events—which are called *caricatures*. That, I declare, is the quality which distinguishes *historical* from *artistic* caricaturists—the fugitive from the eternal comic.

Goya is always a great and often a terrifying artist. To the gaiety, the joviality, the typically Spanish satire of the good old days of Cervantes he unites a spirit far more modern, or at least one that has been far more sought after in modern times—I means a love of the ungraspable, a feeling for violent contrasts, for the blank horrors of nature and for human countenances weirdly animalized by circumstances. It is curious to note that this man, who followed after the great destructive and satirical movement of the eighteenth century and to whom Voltaire would have acknowledged his debt for all those monastic caricatures of his—for all those monks yawning or stuffing their stomachs, those bullet-headed cut-throats preparing for matins, those brows as crafty, hypocritical, sharp and evil as profiles of birds of prey (or rather for the idea only of these things, for the great man is to be pitied for not being much of a connoisseur in other artistic matters); it is curious, I say, that this monk-hater should have dwelt so much on witches, sabbaths, scenes of devilry, children roasting on the spit, and Heaven knows what else—on every debauchery of dream, every hyperbole of hallucination, and not least, on all those slim, blond Spanish girls of his, with ancient hags in attendance to wash and make them ready for the Sabbath, perhaps, or it may be for the evening rite of prostitution, which is civilization's own Sabbath! Light and darkness play across all these grotesque horrors; and what a singular kind of playfulness! Two extraordinary plates above all come to mind. The first[1] represents a fantastic landscape, a conglomeration of clouds and boulders. Is it a corner of some unknown and unfrequented Sierra? or a sample of primeval chaos? There, at the heart of that abominable theatre, a life-and-death struggle is taking place between two witches, hanging in mid-air. One is astride the other, belabouring and mastering her. Locked together, these two monsters are spinning through the gloomy void. Every kind of hideousness, every vice and moral filthiness that the human mind can conceive, is written upon these two faces which, according to a frequent custom

[1] *Capricho* No. 62, 'Quien lo creyera!' See pl. 45.

and an inscrutable procedure of the artist's, stand half-way between man and beast.

The second plate[1] shows us a wretched being, a desperate and solitary monad whose one desire is to get out of its tomb. A crowd of mischievous demons, a myriad lilliputian gnomes are bearing down with all their united efforts upon the cover of the half-gaping sepulchre. These watchful guardians of death have banded together against a rebellious soul which is wearing itself out in its impossible struggle. This throbbing nightmare is set amidst all the horror of the vague and the indefinite.

At the end of his career Goya's eyesight weakened to the point at which it is said that his pencils had to be sharpened for him. Yet even at this stage he was able to produce some large and very important lithographs, amongst them a set of bull-fighting scenes,[2] full of rout and rabble, wonderful plates, vast pictures in miniature—new proofs in support of that curious law which presides over the destinies of great artists, and which wills it that, as life and understanding follow opposing principles of development, so they should win on the swings what they lose on the roundabouts, and thus should tread a path of progressive youth and go on renewing and reinvigorating themselves, growing in boldness to the very brink of the grave.

In the foreground of one[3] of these prints, in which a wonderful tumult and hurly-burly prevails, is an enraged bull—one of the spiteful kind that savage the dead. It has just unbreeched the hinder parts of one of the combatants. No more than wounded, the poor wretch is heavily dragging himself along on his knees. The formidable beast has lifted his torn shirt with its horns, thus exposing his buttocks to view; and now, once again, down comes that threatening muzzle—but the audience is scarcely moved by this unseemly episode amid the carnage.

Goya's great merit consists in his having created a credible form of the monstrous. His monsters are born viable, harmonious. No one has ventured further than he in the direction of the *possible* absurd. All those distortions, those bestial faces, those diabolic grimaces of his are impregnated with *humanity*. Even from the special viewpoint of natural

[1] Klingender (*Goya in the Democratic Tradition*, London 1948, p. 221) suggests that Baudelaire is here confusing his recollection of *Capricho* No. 59 ('Y aun no se van!') with Gautier's description of the *Nada* print in the *Desastres de la guerra*. Certainly Baudelaire's description is inaccurate if he has *Capricho* No. 59 in mind.

[2] The four lithographs known as the 'Toros de Burdeos'. [3] *Dibersión de España*.

history it would be hard to condemn them, so great is the analogy and harmony between all the parts of their being. In a word, the line of suture, the point of junction between the real and the fantastic is impossible to grasp; it is a vague frontier which not even the subtlest analyst could trace, such is the extent to which the transcendent and the natural concur in his art.*

III

HOWEVER southern it may be, the climate of Italy is not that of Spain, and the fermentation of the comic in that country does not produce the same results. The pedantry of the Italians—I use that word for want of a better—has found its expression in the caricatures of Leonardo da Vinci and in Pinelli's scenes of contemporary manners. Every artist knows Leonardo's caricatures—they are veritable portraits. Cold and hideous, those caricatures are not lacking in cruelty—it is the comic that they lack; there is no expansiveness, no abandon about them, for the great artist was not amusing himself when he drew them; he made them, rather, in his capacity as savant, geometrician, professor of natural history. He was careful not to omit the least wart, the smallest hair. Perhaps, on the whole, he laid no claim to be doing caricatures. He looked round him for eccentric types of ugliness, and copied them.

Nevertheless the Italian character is not like this as a rule. Its humour is low, but it is open and frank. We can get a just idea of it from Bassano's pictures representing the Venetian carnival.[1] Here we find a gaiety which is bubbling over with sausages, hams and macaroni. Once a year the Italian comic spirit makes its explosion in the Corso, and then it reaches the bounds of frenzy. Everyone is witty, everyone becomes a comic artist; Marseilles or Bordeaux could perhaps provide us with samples of similar temperaments. Just see how well Hoffmann understood the Italian character in his *Princess Brambilla*, and how sensitively it is discussed by the German artists who drink at the Café Greco![2] But the

* Some years ago we possessed several precious paintings by Goya, though they were unhappily relegated to obscure corners of the gallery; they disappeared, however, along with the *Musée Espagnol*. (C.B.)

[1] One such painting, by Leandro Bassano, is in the Kunsthistorisches Museum, Vienna, and it is possible that Baudelaire may have seen a print of it. Even so, the name of Bassano seems an odd one in the present context.

[2] The Café Greco, in the Via Condotti, Rome, had been a favourite resort of artists and writers since the latter part of the eighteenth century.

Italian artists are clowns rather than comics. They lack depth, but they all submit to the sheer intoxication of their national gaiety. Materialistic, as the South generally is, their humour always smacks of the kitchen and the bordello. But all things considered, it is Callot, a French artist, who, by the concentration of wit and the firmness of will proper to our country, has given its finest expression to this species of the comic. It is a Frenchman who has remained the best Italian clown.

A short while ago I spoke of Pinelli, the classic Pinelli, whose glory is now a very diminished one. We would not call him a caricaturist, exactly—he is rather a *snapper-up* of picturesque scenes. I only mention him at all because the days of my youth were burdened by hearing him praised as the type of the *noble caricaturist*. In point of fact, the comic does not enter into his composition at all, save in infinitesimal doses. What we find in all this artist's studies is a constant preoccupation with line and with antique compositions, a systematic aspiration towards style.

But Pinelli—and this has doubtless contributed not a little to his reputation—Pinelli had a life which was much more romantic than his talent. His originality displayed itself much more in his character than in his works. For he was one of the most perfect types of the *artist*, as the good bourgeois imagines him to be—that is, of classic disorder, of inspiration expressing itself in unseemly and violent behaviour. Pinelli possessed all the charlatanism of certain artists: his two enormous dogs which followed him everywhere, like comrades or confidants, his great gnarled stick, his locks in double pigtails framing his cheeks, the tavern, the low company, the deliberate practice of ostentatiously destroying works for which he was not offered a satisfactory price—all these things formed part of his reputation. And Pinelli's household was hardly better ordered than the conduct of its master. Sometimes he returned home to find that his wife and daughter had come to blows, their eyes flashing fire in all the fury and excitability of their race. To Pinelli this was superb: 'Stop!' he shouted to them. 'Don't move! Stay still!' And the drama was transformed into a drawing. It is clear that Pinelli was one of those artists who wander through objective nature in the hope that she will come to the aid of their mental laziness, and who are always ready to *snatch up their brushes*. And thus, in one respect, he may be likened to the unfortunate Léopold Robert, who also claimed to find in, and only in, nature those ready-made subjects which, for more imaginative artists, are only good for notes. And yet Pinelli, no less than

Léopold Robert, always put these subjects—and even the most nationally comic and picturesque of them—through the sieve, through the merciless filter of *taste*.

Has Pinelli been slandered? I do not know; but such is his legend. Now all this seems to me to be a sign of weakness. I wish that someone would invent a neologism, I wish that someone would manufacture a word destined to blast once and for all this species of the 'poncif'—the 'poncif' in conduct and behaviour, which creeps into the life of artists as into their works. And besides I cannot help noticing that history frequently presents us with the contrary, and that those artists who are the most inventive, the most astonishing and the most eccentric in their conceptions are often men whose life is calm and minutely ordered. Several of them have had the most highly-developed domestic virtues. Have you not often noticed that there is nothing more like the perfect bourgeois than the artist of concentrated genius?

IV

FROM the beginning the Flemish and the Dutch have done very fine things, of a really special and indigenous character. Everyone is familiar with the extraordinary, early productions of Brueghel 'the Droll',[1] who is not to be confused with 'Hell' Brueghel,[2] as several writers have done. That he betrays a certain systematization, a certain convention of eccentricity, a method in the bizarre, is in no doubt. But it is also quite certain that this weird talent of his has a loftier origin than in a species of artistic wager. In the fantastic pictures of Brueghel the Droll the full power of hallucination is revealed to us. But what artist could produce such monstrously paradoxical works if he had not been driven from the outset by some unknown force? In art—and this is a thing which is not sufficiently observed—the portion that is left to the human will is much less great than is generally believed. The baroque ideal which Brueghel seems to have pursued shows many affinities with that of Grandville, particularly if you will examine carefully the tendencies which the French artist displayed during the last years of his life: visions of a sick brain, hallucinations of fever, dream's-eye transformations, bizarre associations of ideas, fortuitous and anomalous combinations of forms.

[1] Peter Brueghel, the Elder. [2] Peter Brueghel, the Younger.

The works of Brueghel the Droll can be divided into two classes. The first contains political allegories which are almost undecipherable today; it is in this series that you find houses with eyes instead of windows, windmills with human arms for wings, and a thousand other terrifying compositions in which nature is ceaselessly transformed into a kind of anagram. And yet it is quite often impossible to decide whether this kind of composition belongs to the class of political and allegorical designs, or to the second class, which is patently the more curious. The works in this second class seem to me to contain a special kind of *mystery*, although the present age, which, thanks to its double character of incredulity and ignorance, finds nothing difficult to explain, would doubtless qualify them simply as fantasies and capriccios. The recent researches of a few doctors[1] who have at last glimpsed the need to explain a mass of historical and miraculous facts otherwise than by the means of the Voltairean school (which could nowhere see further than cleverness in charlatanry)—even these researches are very far from disentangling all the secret mysteries of the soul. Now I challenge anyone to explain the diabolic and diverting farrago of Brueghel the Droll otherwise than by a kind of special, Satanic grace. For the words 'special grace' substitute, if you wish, the words 'madness' or 'hallucination'; but the mystery will remain almost as dark. Brueghel's collected works[2] seem to spread a contagion; his absurd capers make one's head swim. How could a human intelligence contain so many marvels and devilries? how could it beget and describe so many terrifying extravagances? I cannot understand it, nor can I positively determine the reason. But often in history, and even in more than one chapter of modern history, do we find proof of the immense power of contagions, of poisoning taking place through the moral atmosphere; and I cannot restrain myself from observing (but without pretension, without pedantry, without positive aim, as of seeking to prove that Brueghel was permitted to see the devil himself in person) that this prodigious efflorescence of monstrosities coincided in the most surprising manner with the notorious and historical *epidemic of witchcraft*.

[1] Baudelaire may be thinking of such doctors as Brierre de Boismont and J. J. Moreau (de Tours), whose *Des Hallucinations* and *Du Hachisch et de l'aliénation mentale* (respectively) had been published in 1845.

[2] Baudelaire must have known Brueghel almost entirely through engravings.

A PHILOSOPHY OF TOYS

MANY years ago—how many? I have quite forgotten; all this goes back into the mists of earliest childhood—I was taken by my mother to visit a certain Madame Panckoucke. Can she have been the mother, or the wife perhaps, or even the sister-in-law of the present Panckoucke?[1] I do not know. I remember that it was in a very peaceful house, one of those town-houses where the corners of the courtyard are green with grass, in a silent street, the rue des Poitevins. This house had the reputation of being very hospitable, and on certain days it would become brilliant with light and noise. I have heard much talk of a masked ball there at which M. Alexandre Dumas, who used then to be referred to as 'the young author of Henri III', made a great effect when he appeared with Mlle Elsa Mercoeur on his arm, dressed as his page.

I remember very clearly that this lady was clad in velvet and fur. At the end of a short time, she said: 'Here we have a little boy whom I would like to give something to—to remember me by.' She took me by the hand and we passed through several rooms; then she opened the door of a chamber where an extraordinary and truly fairylike spectacle met my gaze. The walls were literally invisible, so covered were they with toys. The ceiling had vanished behind an efflorescence of toys which hung from it like marvellous stalactites. On the floor was hardly a narrow catwalk to place one's feet upon. It was a whole world of toys of all kinds, from the most costly to the most trifling, from the simplest to the most complicated.

'This,' said she, 'is the children's treasury. I regularly set aside a small sum of money to add to it, and when a nice little boy comes to see me, I bring him here so that he can take away a souvenir of me. Make your choice.'

With that admirable and luminous alacrity which is typical of children, in whose minds desire, deliberation and action make up, so to speak, but a single faculty—a fact which distinguishes them from degenerate man, with whom, in contrast, deliberation absorbs almost the whole of

[1] She was in fact the mother of Ernest Panckoucke, bookseller and translator, the 'present Panckoucke', and wife of Charles Panckoucke (by this time dead), the well-known translator of Tacitus. She held a literary salon at her house in the rue des Poitevins, and died in 1861.

his time—I seized hold of the most beautiful, the most expensive, the most showy, the newest, the most unusual of the toys. My mother protested against my impertinence and obstinately refused to allow me to take it away with me. She wanted me to be content with an infinitely ordinary object. But I could not agree, and to make everything all right, resigned myself to a fair compromise.

It has often struck me that it would be amusing to know all the 'nice little boys' who have now crossed a good part of life's cruel desert and have for a long time been handling something other than toys, and yet whose carefree childhood once upon a time took away a souvenir from Madame Panckoucke's treasury.

This episode is responsible for my never being able to stop in front of a toyshop and run my eyes over the inextricable muddle of the strange shapes and clashing colours of its contents without thinking of the velvet-and-fur-clad lady who appeared to me as the Toy Fairy.

I have moreover retained a lasting affection and a reasoned admiration for that strange statuary art which, with its lustrous neatness, its blinding flashes of colour, its violence in gesture and decision of contour, represents so well childhood's ideas about beauty. There is an extraordinary gaiety in a great toyshop which makes it preferable to a fine bourgeois apartment. Is not the whole of life to be found there in miniature—and far more highly coloured, sparkling and polished than real life? There we see gardens, theatres, beautiful dresses, eyes pure as diamonds, cheeks ablaze with rouge, charming lace, carriages, stables, cattle-sheds, drunkards, charlatans, bankers, actors, punchinellos like fireworks, kitchens, and whole armies, in perfect discipline, with cavalry and artillery.

All children talk to their toys; the toys become actors in the great drama of life, reduced in size by the *camera obscura* of their little brains. In their games children give evidence of their great capacity for abstraction and their high imaginative power. They play without playthings. I am not referring to those little girls who play at grown-ups, paying social calls, presenting their imaginary children to each other and talking about their dresses. The poor little things are copying their mothers; they are already giving a forecast of their immortal future puerility, and be very sure that none of them will ever become my wife.—But the *diligence!* the eternal drama of the *diligence* played with chairs! the *diligence* itself—a chair; the horses—chairs; the passengers—chairs; the only living actor is the postillion![1] The equipage remains immobile—yet with what scorching speed does it devour those fictive spaces! What simplicity of production! and is there not something here to put to shame the impotent imagination of that blasé public which in the theatre demands a physical and mechanical perfection, and cannot conceive that the plays of Shakespeare can remain beautiful with an apparatus of barbaric simplicity?

And the children who play at war! not in the Tuileries, with real guns and real swords: I mean the solitary child who controls and leads into battle two armies all by himself. The soldiers can be corks, dominoes, draughtsmen, knuckle-bones, the fortifications may be planks, books, etc., the missiles, marbles or anything else you like; there will be dead bodies, peace-treaties, hostages, prisoners, tributes to pay. I have noticed in several children a belief that what constitutes a defeat or a victory in war is the greater or lesser number of dead. Later on, plunged into the maelstrom of universal life and obliged themselves to hit out so as not to be hit, they will learn that a victory is often uncertain, and that it is only a real victory if it is, as it were, the summit of an inclined plane down which the army will thereupon slide with a miraculous speed, or else the first term of an infinitely growing progression.

This ease in gratifying the imagination is evidence of the spirituality of childhood in its artistic conceptions. The toy is the child's earliest initiation to art, or rather for him it is the first concrete example of art, and when mature age comes, the perfected examples will not give his mind the same feelings of warmth, nor the same enthusiasms, nor the same sense of conviction.

But let us go further and analyse that vast universe of childhood; let us consider the barbaric toy, the primitive toy, in which the maker's problem consisted in constructing an image as approximative as possible with elements as simple and as cheap as possible: for example, the card-board punchinello, actuated by a single thread; the blacksmiths hammering at their anvil; the horse and its rider in three pieces, four wooden pins for the legs, the horse's tail forming a whistle, and sometimes the rider wearing a little feather in his cap, which is a great luxury;—these are toys for a penny, a halfpenny, a farthing.—But do you think that these simple images create a lesser reality in the child's mind than those New

[1] See pl. 13.

Year's Day marvels which are a tribute paid by parasitic servility to the wealth of the parents rather than a gift to the poetry of childhood?

Such is the poor child's plaything.[1] When you go out in the morning with the fixed intention of idling away your time on the great thoroughfares, fill your pockets with these little inventions, and all along the wine-shops, under the trees, offer them to the unknown poor children that you meet. You will see their eyes open wide beyond all measure. At first they will not dare accept, they will doubt their good fortune; then their hands will greedily snatch at the gift, and they will scamper off like cats running away to eat afar off the morsel you have given them, having learnt to be distrustful of man. This is certainly a delightful way of passing your time.

On the subject of the plaything of the poor, I once saw something even more simple, but sadder, than the toy for a penny—this was the living toy. By a road, behind the wrought-iron grille of a fine garden, at the far end of which was visible a pretty château, there stood a child, bright and blooming, dressed in those country-clothes which are so full of coquetry. Luxury, freedom from care and the habitual sight of wealth have made these children so pretty that one would hardly think them fashioned of the same clay as the children of the lower orders or of the poor. Beside him on the ground lay a splendid doll, as neat and clean as its master, rich and glittering, wearing a fine dress and covered with feathers and glass beads. But the child had no eyes for his toy; this is what he was looking at: on the other side of the grille, on the road, among the nettles and the thistles, there was another child, dirty, somewhat puny, one of those urchins on whose cheeks a thin trickle of snot winds its slow way through the dust and the grime. Through those symbolic iron bars the poor child was showing his toy to the rich child, who was greedily examining it, as a rare, unknown object. Now this toy which the little brat was teasing, rattling and shaking in a box with bars, was a live rat! To save money his parents had taken the toy from life itself.

I believe that generally children dominate their toys; in other words that their choice is determined by dispositions and desires, vague, if you wish, and by no means formulated, but very real. Nevertheless I would not assert that the contrary does not sometimes happen—I mean that toys do not sometimes dominate children, particularly in a case of

[1] This and the following paragraph were later (1862) used, with minor alterations, to form the prose-poem *Le Joujou du Pauvre*.

literary or artistic predestination. It would hardly be surprising if a child of that kind, to whom his parents chiefly gave toy-theatres so that he could continue by himself the pleasure that he had had from stage-shows and marionettes, should grow used to regarding the theatre as the most delicious form of Beauty.

There is one kind of toy which has tended to multiply for some time, and of which I have neither good nor bad to say. I refer to the scientific toy. The chief defect of these toys is that they are expensive. But they can continue to amuse for a long time and develop in the childish brain a taste for marvellous and unexpected effects. The Stereoscope, which gives a flat image in the round, is one of these. It first appeared several years ago. The Phenakistoscope, which is older, is less well known. Imagine some movement or other, for example a dancer's or a juggler's performance, divided up and decomposed into a certain number of movements; imagine that each one of these movements—as many as twenty, if you wish—is represented by a complete figure of the juggler or dancer, and that these are all printed round the edge of a circular piece of cardboard. Fix this card, as well as a second circular piece cut at equal intervals with twenty little windows, to a pivot at the end of a handle which you hold as one holds a fire-screen in front of the fire. The twenty little figures, representing the decomposed movement of a single figure, are reflected in a mirror placed in front of you. Apply your eye at the level of the little windows and spin the cards rapidly. The speed of rotation transforms the twenty openings into a single circular opening through which you watch twenty dancing figures reflected in the glass—all exactly the same and executing the same movements with a fantastic precision. Each little figure has availed himself of the nineteen others. On the card it spins and its speed makes it invisible; in the mirror, seen through the spinning window, it is motionless, executing on the spot all the movements that are distributed between all twenty figures. The number of pictures that can thus be created is infinite.[1]

[1] Baudelaire's description is a little hard to follow, but he is evidently describing a development of the Fantascope, one of the earliest optical toys, an example of which, dating from *c.* 1833 and 'invented by Professor Plateau', is in the Victoria and Albert Museum. The difference is that in the Fantascope there is only one card, containing both slots and figures. The user rotates the card, looking (from the back) through the coalescing slots at the mirrored reflection of the figures. The Museum's example includes dancing frogs, tortoises and a violoncellist. It is not to be confused with the later Zoetrope, or Wheel of Life.

I would like to say a few words about the manners and customs of children in relation to their toys, and about the ideas of parents on this burning question.—There are some parents who never wish to give them. These are solemn, excessively solemn individuals who have made no study of nature and who generally make all the people around them unhappy. I do not know why I fancy to myself that they reek of Protestantism. They neither know nor allow such poetic ways and means of passing the time. These are the people who would gladly give a sixpenny piece to a poor man on condition that he stuffed himself with bread, but would always refuse him a farthing to have a glass in a tavern. When I think of a certain class of ultra-reasonable and anti-poetic people through whom I have suffered so much, I always feel hatred pinching and worrying at my nerves.

There are other parents who regard toys as objects of mute adoration. There are clothes that at least one is allowed to wear on Sundays; but toys ought to be treated with very much more care! And so no sooner has the family-friend deposited his offering in the child's lap than a savage and parsimonious mother swoops down upon it, locks it in a cupboard, saying, 'It's too beautiful for a child of your age; *you can play with it when you are bigger!*' A friend of mine once confessed to me that he had never been allowed to enjoy his toys.—'And when I began to grow up,' he added, 'I had other things to do.'—Furthermore there are some children who do the same thing for themselves; they do not use their toys, they save them up, put them in order, make libraries and museums of them, very occasionally showing them to their little friends, but taking care to beg them *not to touch*. I would be quick to be on my guard against these *men-children*.

The overriding desire of most children is to get at and *see the soul* of their toys, some at the end of a certain period of use, others *straightaway*. It is on the more or less swift invasion of this desire that depends the length of life of a toy. I do not find it in me to blame this infantile mania; it is a first metaphysical tendency. When this desire has implanted itself in the child's cerebral marrow, it fills his fingers and nails with an extraordinary agility and strength. The child twists and turns his toy, scratches it, shakes it, bumps it against the walls, throws it on the ground. From time to time he makes it re-start its mechanical motions, sometimes in the opposite direction. Its marvellous life comes to a stop. The child, like the people besieging the Tuileries, makes a supreme effort; at last he opens it up, he is the stronger. But *where is the soul?* This is the beginning of melancholy and gloom.

There are others who immediately break the toy which has hardly been put in their hands, hardly examined; so far as these are concerned I must admit that I do not understand the mysterious motive which causes their action. Are they in a superstitious passion against these tiny objects which imitate humanity, or are they perhaps forcing them to undergo a kind of Masonic initiation before introducing them into nursery life?—*Puzzling question!*[1]

[1] These words first appeared in the 1855 version of the article. They are of course taken from Sir Thomas Browne's *Urn Burial* ('What Song the *Syrens* sang, or what name *Achilles* assumed when he hid himself among women, though puzzling Questions, are not beyond all conjecture'). Baudelaire seems, however, to have known it not from the original source but (as Miss Gilman points out, pp. 75–6) from the epigraph to *The Murders in the Rue Morgue*, where the whole sentence is used by Poe. It is significant that Baudelaire's translation of this story first appeared in instalments in February and March 1855, the year of the addition of these words to the text of the present article.

The Anorthoscope, an optical toy, about 1842.
Label from the box-lid.

PHILOSOPHIC ART

WHAT is pure art according to the modern idea? It is the creation of an evocative magic, containing at once the object and the subject, the world external to the artist and the artist himself.

What is Philosophic Art according to the ideas of Chenavard and the German school? It is a plastic art which sets itself up in place of books, by which I mean as a rival to the printing-press in the teaching of history, morals and philosophy.

In fact there have been periods of history in which the role of the plastic arts was to paint the historical archives of a people and its religious beliefs.

But for several centuries now the history of art has been marked by an ever-increasing division of powers, some subjects becoming the special preserve of painting, others of music and others of literature.

Is it by some fatal consequence of decadence that today each art should evince a desire to trespass on the next, so that we have the spectacle of musical scales being introduced into painting, colour into sculpture, plastic devices into literature, and, by other artists—those indeed with whom we are specially concerned today—a sort of encyclopedic philosophy into plastic art itself?

Every good piece of sculpture, painting or music evokes the sentiments and the dreams which it sets out to evoke.

But reasoning and deduction are the province of the printed book.

Thus Philosophic Art is a return towards the picture-making proper to the childhood of the nations, and if it remained strictly faithful to itself, it would feel it its duty to juxtapose as many successive images as are contained in whatever sentence that it might wish to express.

Even so we may reserve the right to doubt whether the hieroglyphic was clearer than the printed sentence.

We thus propose to study Philosophic Art as a kind of monstrous growth in which certain fine talents have chosen to display themselves.

It should be noted moreover that in order to justify its existence, Philosophic Art presupposes an absurdity—I mean the public intelligence in matters of the fine arts.

The more Art strives to be philosophically clear, the more it will degrade itself and revert towards the primitive hieroglyph; on the other hand, the more it divorces itself from the Didactic, the more it will soar aloft into the realms of Beauty pure and disinterested.

As we all know, and as it would be only too easy to guess if we did not, Germany is the country which has sunk deepest into the error of Philosophic Art.

In our examination we shall pass over such well-known examples as Overbeck,[1] who studies the beauty of the past only the better to teach religion, or Cornelius[2] and Kaulbach, who do the same thing in order to teach history and philosophy; let us note moreover that even when he had to deal with a purely picturesque subject, that of a Madhouse,[3] Kaulbach was unable to resist treating it 'categorically'—in an Aristotelian manner, one might almost say—so eternal is the antinomy of the pure poetic mind and the didactic.

Instead, as our first specimen of Philosophic Art, we shall concern ourselves today with a German artist who is much less well-known, but who, in our opinion, was infinitely more gifted from the point of view of pure art; I refer to M. Alfred Rethel,[4] who died insane a short time ago, after having decorated a chapel on the banks of the Rhine,[5] and who is unknown in Paris save for eight wood-cuts, of which the last two figured at the Exposition Universelle.

The first of his 'poems'—an expression that we are obliged to use in speaking of a school which puts the plastic arts on the same footing as the printed word—dates from 1848 and is entitled *The Dance of Death in 1848*.[6]

It is a reactionary poem whose subject is the usurpation of all powers and the fascination exercised upon the people by the fatal goddess of Death.

A detailed description of each of the six plates which go to make up the poem, with an exact translation of the legends in verse which accompany them.—An analysis of M. Rethel's artistic merit—the original element in his work (the genius of epic allegory in the German manner),

[1] Friedrich Overbeck (1789–1869), leader of the 'Nazarenes'; from 1810 he worked in Rome.

[2] Peter Cornelius (1783–1867), chiefly noted for his revival of fresco; from 1824 he was director of the Munich Academy.

[3] See pl. 53.

[4] At one time Baudelaire considered asking Rethel to execute illustrations for the *Fleurs du mal*. He was somewhat improbably known as 'le Delacroix allemand'.

[5] In fact, the Town Hall at Aachen.

[6] See pl. 48.

and the element of plagiarism (imitations of various old masters, Dürer, Holbein, and some not so old); and of the moral value of the poem, its Satanic, Byronic quality, and the feeling of desolation which characterizes it.) What seems to me to be truly original about this poem is the fact that it appeared at a moment when practically the whole of European humanity had rushed headlong, with eyes open, into the follies of revolution.

Two prints which together form an antithesis. One, *The First Onslaught of Cholera upon Paris, at the Bal de l'Opéra.*[1] The bodies of masqueraders stretched out stiff upon the ground, a pierrette with her toes hideously sticking up in the air and her mask slipping off; musicians making their escape with their instruments tucked under their arms; an allegorical, impassive scourge-bearer seated on a bench, and the generally sinister character of the whole composition. The second contrasts with it and represents a type of 'good death'.[2] A virtuous and peaceable man is taken unawares in his sleep; he is depicted in a lofty place, a place which has doubtless been his home for many a long year; it is a room in a bell-tower, commanding a view of the fields and a distant horizon—a place made for peace of mind; the old fellow sleeps in a roughly-made chair, while Death is playing a magical air on his violin.[3] A great sun, bisected by the line of the horizon, shoots on high its geometric rays.—*A fine day is drawing to its close.*

A little bird, perched on the window-sill, is looking into the room; has it come to listen to Death's violin, or is it an allegory of the soul preparing to make its flight?

In interpreting the productions of Philosophic Art, a great attention to detail must be brought to bear; here everything—place, decor, furnishings, accessories (see Hogarth, for example)—everything is allegory, allusion, hieroglyph, rebus.

M. Michelet has attempted a minute analysis of Dürer's *Melancholia*;[4] his interpretation is questionable, however, particularly with reference to the syringe.

Furthermore even at their moment of creation in the mind of the Philosophic artist, these accessories are characterized by a poetic, vague

[1] See pl. 49. [2] See pl. 50.

[3] In fact Death is tolling the bell; in the first plate however Death is playing the violin, using two bones; Baudelaire was evidently writing from memory.

[4] In his *Histoire de France au seizième siècle*, 1855, pp. 86–90.

46. CRUIKSHANK: '*A Skaiting Party.*' Etching.
London, Victoria and Albert Museum.

47. PINELLI: *Roman Carnival*. Water-colour. London, Victoria and Albert Museum.

48. RETHEL: *Dance of Death for the year 1848.* Woodcut. London, Victoria and Albert Museum.

49. RETHEL: *Death the Slayer*. Woodcut. London, Victoria and Albert Museum.

50. Rethel: *Death the Friend*. Woodcut. London, Victoria and Albert Museum.

51. BAUDELAIRE: '*Specimen of Antique Beauty, dedicated to Chenavard.*' Pen, pencil and wash. Private Collection.

52. CHENAVARD: *Augustus closes the Doors of the Temple of Janus.* Oil on canvas.
Lyons, Musée des Beaux-Arts.

53. KAULBACH: *The Madhouse*. Munich, Stadtmuseum.

and ambiguous quality rather than by one which is literal and precise, and often it is the translator who invents their *intentions*.

Philosophic Art is not so alien to the French mentality as one might think. France has a weakness for myths, morals and rebuses; or to put it better, being a country of reasoners, she has a weakness for mental effort.

The Romantic School has been particularly distinguished for its reaction against these rationalistic tendencies and its establishment of the glory of pure art; and certain tendencies—notably those of M. Chenavard, the rehabilitation of hieroglyphic art—are themselves a reaction against the school of art for art's sake.

Can it be that there are philosophic climates, as there are climates of love? Venice practised the love of art for art's sake; Lyons is a philosophic city. Lyons has her own philosophy, her own school of poetry, her own school of painting, and finally her own school of philosophic painting.

She is a strange city of bigotry and commerce, both Catholic and Protestant, full of fog and smoke, a city in which ideas sort themselves out with difficulty. Everything that comes from Lyons is meticulous, slowly thought out and timid; the Abbé Noireau, Laprade, Soulary, Chenavard, Janmot. You might suppose that everyone there was suffering from an intellectual cold in the nose. Even in Soulary I detect that categorizing habit of mind which is so conspicuous in the works of Chenavard and which betrays itself also in the songs of Pierre Dupont.[1]

Chenavard's[2] brain is itself not unlike the city of Lyons; it is foggy and sooty and bristles with spikes, like that city of blast-furnaces and spires. It is a brain in which things do not mirror themselves clearly; we see them only reflected through an atmosphere of fumes.

Chenavard is not a painter; he despises what we understand by painting. It would be unjust, however, to apply to him the fable of the fox and the grapes; for I think that even if Chenavard could paint with as much dexterity as anyone you care to mention, he would remain no less contemptuous of the sauces and spices of art.

[1] Baudelaire wrote an enthusiastic, if critical, article about Dupont; see *l'Art Romantique*.

[2] For the most complete account of this artist, see Joseph C. Sloane, *P. M. J. Chenavard, Artist of 1848*. University of North Carolina Press, 1962. Baudelaire and he had several friends in common, including Delacroix; see pp. 64-5.

Let it be said at once that Chenavard has an enormous superiority over all other artists; for if he is not sufficiently animal, they are far too lacking in spirituality.

Chenavard knows how to read and to reason, and has thereby made himself the friend of all who love reasoning; he is a remarkable scholar, and is experienced in the art of meditation.

A passion for libraries has been with him from his earliest years; accustomed while quite young to attach an idea to every plastic form, he has never rummaged in a portfolio of engravings or wandered round a picture-gallery without regarding them as storehouses of general human thought. Deeply interested in religions and gifted with an encyclopedic mind, he was naturally bound to end up by conceiving an impartially syncretic system.

Although heavy and difficult to manoeuvre, his mind has its charm which he knows how to put to good use, and if he has waited long before playing his part, rest assured that in spite of his apparent simplicity of nature, his ambitions have never been small.

(Chenavard's first pictures: *M. de Dreux-Brézé and Mirabeau—The Convention Voting the Death of Louis XVI.* Chenavard chose an excellent moment to show off his system of historical philosophy, expressed by means of the pencil.)

At this point we propose to divide our work into two parts, in the first of which we shall analyse the intrinsic merit of an artist gifted with an astonishing compositional skill, which is much greater than one would suspect if one took too seriously the scorn which he professes for the resources of his art—his skill at drawing women; in the second we shall examine that merit which I call 'extrinsic'—in other words, his philosophic system.

(M. Ledru-Rollin[1]—a general confusion of mind and a lively public preoccupation with the philosophy of history.)

Humanity is analogous to Man himself.

It has its ages, and its pleasures, its labours and its ideas which are analogous to its ages.

(An analysis of Chenavard's emblematic calendar.[2]—That certain arts belong to certain ages of humanity, just as certain passions belong to certain ages of man.)

[1] Minister of the Interior in the Government of 1848. [2] See p. 212.

The age of man himself can be divided into *childhood*, corresponding to the historical period from Adam until Babel; into *manhood*, corresponding to the period from Babel until Christ, who will be considered as representing the zenith of human life; into *middle age*, which corresponds to the period from Christ until Napoleon; and finally into *old age*, corresponding to the period which we are about to enter and whose beginning is marked by the supremacy of America and of industry.

The total age of humanity will be eight thousand four hundred years.

A consideration of some of Chenavard's specific notions: the absolute superiority of Pericles.

The inferiority of landscape—a sign of decadence.

The simultaneous supremacy of Music and Industry—a sign of decadence.

An analysis from the point of view of pure art of certain of his cartoons exhibited in 1855[1].

What puts the finishing touch to the essentially utopian and decadent quality of Chenavard himself is the fact that he wanted to enrol artists, like workmen, to execute his cartoons on a large scale under his direction, and to colour them barbarously.

Chenavard is a great mind of the decadence, and he will remain as a monstrous sign of the times.

M. Janmot too comes from Lyons.

He is a religious and elegiac spirit who must have been affected early in life by the bigotry of Lyons.

Rethel's poems are well constructed as poems.

Chenavard's historical calendar is a fantasy of an unimpeachable symmetry, but Janmot's *Histoire d'une âme*[2] is muddy and confused.

Their general character of religiosity gave to this series of compositions a great importance among clerical journalists at the time when they were shown in the Passage du Saumon; we saw them again later at the Exposition Universelle, when they were the object of a lofty contempt. The artist himself wrote a commentary in verse which can only

[1] See pl. 52.

[2] The subject of a series of pictures by Janmot exhibited in Paris in 1854; the catalogue was accompanied by a verse commentary by the artist himself. (Note by the 1868 editors.) The series, correctly entitled 'Le Poème de l'Ame', is now in the possession of the Faculté des Lettres, Lyons. A catalogue, including four plates and a valuable introduction by René Jullian, was published by the Lyons Museum in 1950.

have succeeded in demonstrating more clearly his uncertainty of purpose and in embarrassing more acutely the minds of the philosophical spectators to whom it was addressed.

The only thing that I was able to gather was that these pictures represented successive states of the soul at different ages; nevertheless, as there were always two characters on the stage at once, a boy and a girl, I found it quite impossible to decide whether the basic thought of the poem was not rather the parallel history of *two* young souls, or the history of the double male and female element in a single soul.

Putting aside all these criticisms, which only go to prove that M. Janmot is not a philosophically sound brain, it must be admitted that from the point of view of pure art the composition of these scenes, and even their acidity of colour, contained an infinite charm which is hard to describe—something of the sweetness of solitude, the sacristy, the church and the cloister; an unconscious and childlike quality of mysticism. I have felt something approaching it from certain works of Lesueur and certain Spanish pictures.

(An analysis of some of the subjects of the series, particularly the *Education of Evil* and the *Nightmare*, which revealed a remarkable understanding of the fantastic. The two young people going on a kind of *mystical walk* over the mountains, etc., etc.)

Everyone who is deeply sensitive and has a natural bent for the arts (it is important however not to confuse sensitivity of the imagination with sensitivity of the heart) will feel as I do that every art ought to be self-sufficient, and at the same time to remain within the limits set by providence; nevertheless it is man's privilege to be always capable of developing great talents within a false genre or while violating the natural constitution of art.

Although I regard Philosophic Artists as heretics, I have often come to admire their efforts by an effect of my own reason.

What seems to me finally to establish their heretical character is their inconsequence; for they draw very well and very inventively, and if they were logical when they came to put into practice an art which they put on the same footing as any other means of instruction, they ought to have the courage of their own convictions and revert to all the innumerable and barbaric conventions of hieratic art.

I

DIDACTIC PAINTING: NOTES ON CHENAVARD'S UTOPIA

There are two men in Chenavard, the *utopian* and the *artist*. He wishes to be praised for his utopias, and is sometimes an artist *in spite of* his utopias.

The birthplace of Painting was the Temple. Its roots are in Religion. The modern Temple and the modern Religion are the Revolution. Thus let us create the *Temple of the Revolution* and the painting of the Revolution. In other words, the modern Pantheon will contain the *History of Humanity*.

Pan must kill God. Pan is the people.

An aesthetic which is chimerical, in other words *a posteriori*, individual and artificial, substituted for the involuntary, spontaneous, fatal and vital aesthetic of the people.

Thus Wagner refashions Greek Tragedy, which was created spontaneously by Greece.

The Revolution is not a religion, since it has neither prophets, saints nor miracles, and its very aim is to deny all that.

If there is something good in Chenavard's thesis, it is simply a contempt for the trivial and a conviction that great painting is founded on great ideas.

A great degree of naiveté also, as with all utopians. He supposes that all men have an equal love of *justice* (holiness) and an equal humility. Honest man, excellent man!

Proud solitary, stranger to life!

II

Chenavard is a caricature of ancient wisdom traced by modern fantasy. Painters who think.

III

MEN OF LYONS

ARTISTS	LITERATI
Chenavard	Laprade
Janmot	Ballanche (for the smoke)
Révoil	A. Pommier
Bonnefonds	Soulary
Orsel	Blanc Saint-Bonnet
Perrin	Noirot
Compte-Calix	Pierre Dupont
Flandrin	De Gérando
Saint-Jean	J.-B. Say
Jacquand	Terrasson
Boissieu	

P. CHENAVARD: Calendrier d'une philosophie de l'Histoire.

See p. 208

NOTES ON THE ILLUSTRATIONS

NOTES ON THE ILLUSTRATIONS

Frontispiece. CONSTANTIN GUYS (1802–92): In the Row, Hyde Park. Pen and water-colour, $9\frac{1}{8} \times 7$ in. London, Mr. Tom Girtin.

This, and other drawings by the artist in the Girtin Collection, reminds us that in the 1840s Guys was employed as French tutor in the family of Dr. T. C. Girtin, son of the great English water-colourist. At this time it is recorded that 'while giving his lessons, he was quite unable to keep his fingers from "scribbling", as they called it, with whatever lay handy, pen or pencil: often with the butt end of either, dipped in the ink-pot, which he invariably upset in his zeal.'

1. Photograph of Guys as an old man, by Nadar. Paris, Bibliothèque Nationale.
2. GUYS: The Balaklava Railway reaching the Church of Kadiculi, Crimea. Dated 2 March 1855. Pen and ink, with sepia and water-colour, $8\frac{1}{8} \times 13$ in. Paris, Mme J. C. Prost.
3. GUYS: 'My humble self.' The artist in conversation with two sisters of mercy in the hospital at Pera. See p. 21. Pen and wash, $11\frac{5}{8} \times 15$ in. Paris, Musée des Arts Décoratifs.
4. GUYS: The Tchengoan Tower beyond the Tchernaya. Signed, and dated 20 July 1855. Pen and water-colour, $9 \times 14\frac{1}{4}$ in. Paris, Mme J. C. Prost. Signed drawings by Guys are rare, though many are elaborately inscribed.
5. GUYS: Two Prisoners or Deserters taken in the plain of Balaklava, brought to General Vinois by English dragoons. Pen and ink and water-colour, $8\frac{1}{2} \times 12\frac{1}{2}$ in. Paris, Mme J. C. Prost.
6. After GUYS: Procession of the Sultan at the Festival of the Bairam, Constantinople.

   This wood-engraving, published in the *Illustrated London News*, 29 July 1854, p. 97, is a typical example of the finished product, for which Guys's drawings were only intended as preliminaries. The Bairam is a three days' festival to mark the end of Ramadhan. See p. 21.
7. GUYS: Ramadhan in the Mosque of Top Hane, Constantinople. Pencil, pen and brown ink, and water-colour, $10\frac{1}{8} \times 13\frac{3}{8}$ in. London, British Museum.
8. GUYS: The Sultan's Wives in their Carriage. Pen and water-colour, $14\frac{1}{2} \times 21\frac{1}{4}$ in. Paris, Musée des Arts Décoratifs.
9. GUYS: A Turkish Woman with parasol. Pen and water-colour, $10\frac{1}{2} \times 7\frac{5}{8}$ in. Paris, Petit Palais.

   This drawing was given by Baudelaire to his mother as a New Year's present, 1860. After Baudelaire's death she gave it to Barbey d'Aurevilly, who had always admired it.

10. Guys: Mounted Soldiers. Pen and wash, $12\frac{1}{2}\times 19\frac{5}{8}$ in. London, British Museum.

11. Guys: Standing Soldiers. Pen and wash, $10\frac{1}{2}\times 14\frac{3}{8}$ in. London, British Museum.

    Mr. Bruno Streiff suggests that the uniforms are probably Spanish.

12. Guys: Meeting in the Park. Pen and water-colour, $9\frac{1}{2}\times 11\frac{3}{4}$ in. New York, Metropolitan Museum.

    This appears to be a French rather than an English scene.

13. Guys: Children playing horse and carriage. See p. 199. Pen and wash, $6\frac{1}{2}\times 9\frac{3}{8}$ in. New York, Metropolitan Museum.

14. Guys: A Family walking in the Park. Pen and ink and water-colour, $9\frac{1}{4}\times 7\frac{1}{2}$ in. Private Collection.

15. Guys: Taking the air. Pen and ink and water-colour, $7\frac{1}{4}\times 4\frac{5}{8}$ in. London, Mr. Tom Girtin.

    This is probably a London scene, especially in view of the provenance. See note on the frontispiece, above.

16. Guys: Two Spanish Girls on their Balcony. Wash, $17\frac{1}{4}\times 14\frac{1}{4}$ in. Paris, Musée des Arts Décoratifs.

17. Guys: Two Courtesans. Water-colour, $13\frac{1}{8}\times 9\frac{7}{8}$ in. Paris, Mme Ronald Davis.

    This drawing belonged to Baudelaire; after his death it passed to Ancelle, his legal guardian, from whose heirs it was acquired by Jacques Crépet, the great Baudelairean scholar. It was given to its present owner by M. Crépet.

18. Guys: Rue Maubué, 1840. Inscribed and dated by the artist. Pencil, pen and black ink, brush and water-colour, $8\times 5\frac{1}{4}$ in. Private Collection.

19. Guys: Three Women by a Bar. See p. 38. Pen and wash and water-colour, $10\times 7\frac{1}{8}$ in. Paris, Petit Palais.

20. Guys: Napoleon III and his staff on horseback. Pen and wash touched with water-colour, $7\frac{1}{4}\times 10\frac{1}{4}$ in. Private Collection.

21. Guys: Carriage and four. Pen and wash, $7\frac{3}{4}\times 12$ in. Private Collection.

    This drawing was formerly in the Nadar Collection, as is shown by the mark.

22. Guys: Greetings in the Bois de Boulogne. Pen and wash, $9\frac{1}{4}\times 14\frac{3}{4}$ in. Paris, Mme J. C. Prost.

23. Guys: The Brighton Coach. Pen and ink and water-colour, $5\frac{1}{2}\times 7\frac{1}{2}$ in. London, Mr. Tom Girtin.

24. Guys: The Morning Ride. Signed, and dated 1853. Pen and ink and wash, $8\frac{3}{4}\times 13$ in. Private Collection.

25 EUGÈNE LAMI (1809–90): Portrait of Delacroix. Water-colour after a pastel by Eugène Giraud. France, Private Collection.

26. EUGÈNE DELACROIX (1798–1863): The Massacre at Chios. Oil on canvas, 13 ft. 8 in. × 11 ft. 8 in. Salon of 1824. Paris, Louvre.

Delacroix took the subject of this masterpiece of his early period from an actual event which had taken place in 1822, during the Greek War of Independence. He is said to have modified the execution of this painting as a result of seeing the paintings by Constable which were shown at the same Salon.

27. DELACROIX: The Death of Sardanapalus (detail). Oil on canvas, 12 ft. 11 in. × 16 ft. Salon of 1827. Paris, Louvre.

For Delacroix's preoccupation with themes of violence and brutality, see p. 59.

28. DELACROIX: The Expulsion of Heliodorus from the Temple. Paris, Church of St. Sulpice.

Delacroix's last great mural commission was for the Chapelle des Anges at St. Sulpice, and was executed between 1856 and 1861. See pp. 50 ff.

29. DELACROIX: Apollo Victorious over the Serpent Python (sketch). Brussels, Musée des Beaux-Arts.

This is a sketch for the ceiling in the Galerie d'Apollon at the Louvre, which was executed between 1849 and 1852. See p. 55.

30. DELACROIX: Study for the figure of Liberty. Pencil $12\frac{3}{4} \times 9$ in. Paris, Louvre.

This is a study for the main figure in the painting, 'Liberty guiding the People: the 28th July 1830', which was exhibited at the Salon in 1831. It is a characteristic example of Delacroix's pencil technique, and at one time was in the collection of Edgar Degas.

31. DELACROIX: Portrait of Jenny Le Guillou. Oil on canvas, $18 \times 14\frac{3}{4}$ in. Paris, Louvre.

On the sitter, see p. 62. This portrait, executed *c.* 1840, was bequeathed to her by Delacroix and did not come to light again until 1930.

32. ERNEST MEISSONIER (1851–91): The Barricade. Oil on canvas, $11\frac{1}{2} \times 8\frac{3}{4}$ in. Salon of 1850–1 (Souvenir de guerre civile). See p. 64. Paris, Musée du Louvre.

The scene is set in the rue de la Mortellerie, Paris, which no longer exists.

33. EDGAR ALLAN POE. From a daguerreotype.

34. ALPHONSE LEGROS (1837–1911): The Pit and the Pendulum. Etching, touched with wash, $10\frac{1}{4} \times 14\frac{1}{2}$ in. London, Victoria and Albert Museum.

One of Legros's illustrations to the stories of Poe, as is the next illustration.

35. LEGROS: Berenice. Signed, and dated 1862. Etching, touched with wash, $10\frac{5}{8} \times 14\frac{3}{4}$ in. London, Victoria and Albert Museum.

36. RICHARD WAGNER. From a photograph by Nadar.

37. TANNHÄUSER—the décor for Act I, scene 2, designed by Desplechin, for the Paris Opéra production: from a wood-engraving in *l'Illustration*, 16 March 1861, p. 165.

38. NICOLAS-TOUSSAINT CHARLET (1792–1845): Valentin decorated by Marshal Gérard. Lithograph, $5\frac{1}{4} \times 5\frac{7}{8}$ in. London, Victoria and Albert Museum.

    No. 40 of a set of fifty lithographs entitled 'Vie Civile, Politique et Militaire du Caporal Valentin'. On Charlet, see pp. 167–171.

39. GAVARNI (1804–66): After the Ball. Lithograph. Paris, Bibliothèque Nationale.

    A posthumous work, No. 2691 in Armelhault and Bocher's *Oeuvre de Gavarni*, 1873. The two girls are dressed in the costume of 'débardeurs'. On Gavarni, see pp. 182–3.

40. EDMÉ-JEAN PIGAL (1798–1872): 'The other foot, Sir, Please!' Lithograph ('L'aut' pied, not' maître'). London, Victoria and Albert Museum.

    No. 7 of the series, 'Miroir de Paris', published in *Le Charivari*. On Pigal, see pp. 167-8.

41. HONORÉ DAUMIER (1808–79): Robert Macaire—Barrister. Lithograph (Delteil 362). See p. 178. Private Collection.

    No. 9 of the series, 'Caricaturiana'. The following is a translation of the caption: 'My dear Bertrand, give me a hundred crowns and I'll have you acquitted on the spot!'—'I haven't got a shilling.'—'Very well, a hundred *francs*!'—'I haven't got a penny.'—'Haven't you got *ten* francs?'—'Not a farthing.'—'Then give me your shoes, and I'll plead extenuating circumstances.' On Daumier, see pp. 171–180.

42. DAUMIER: Dido and Aeneas. Lithograph (Delteil 939). See pp. 178-9. Private Collection.

    No. 15 of the series, 'Histoire Ancienne'. The following is a translation of the caption, which is a comic adaptation from Virgil:

    A protective fog obscured the heavens; and as they both happened to have come out without their umbrellas, Aeneas guided his lady-friend into a dim grotto, there on this fine day to crown his passion.

43. CHARLES-JOSEPH TRAVIÈS (1804–59): Liard—The Philosopher Tramp. Lithograph (Liard—chiffonnier philosophe). See pp. 184-6. London, Victoria and Albert Museum.

    Published in *Le Charivari*: Béraldi, *Le Graveur du XIXe siècle*, vol. XII (1892), p. 151, No. 4.

44. WILLIAM HOGARTH (1697–1764): The Reward of Cruelty. Engraving. See pp. 187-8. London, Victoria and Albert Museum.

    No. 4 of the series, 'The Four Stages of Cruelty' (1751).

45. FRANCISCO GOYA (1746–1828): 'Who would have believed it?' Aquatint (Quien lo creyera!). See p. 191. London, Victoria and Albert Museum.

    No. 62 of *Los Caprichos*. On Goya, see pp. 190-193.

46. GEORGE CRUIKSHANK (1792–1878): 'A Skaiting Party'. Etching, 9 × 5⅜ in. London, Victoria and Albert Museum. Published Nov. 1st, 1841.

47. BARTOLOMEO PINELLI (1781–1835): Roman Carnival. Water-colour, 20⅛ × 26⅛ in. London, Victoria and Albert Museum.

    On Pinelli, see pp. 194-5.

48. ALFRED RETHEL (1816–59): Dance of Death for the year 1848. Woodcut, 8¾ × 12½ in. London, Victoria and Albert Museum.

    Rethel's set of woodcuts, of which this is plate 2, was entitled *Ein Todtentanz aus dem Jahre 1848*: each plate was accompanied by a text in verse by R. Reinick. The following is a translation of the text for the plate reproduced here:—

    'The morning shines down from the vault of heaven, as brightly as usual on town and countryside. See, the people's friend, the man with a scythe, as he rides along with eager haste. He directs his steed towards the city, with high hopes of a rich harvest to be garnered there. The cock's plume waving on his hat glows red with blood in the sun. His scythe flashes like a thunder-gleam, his steed whinnies and the ravens screech.' See p. 205.

49. RETHEL: Death the Slayer. Woodcut, 12¼ × 10⅞ in. London, Victoria and Albert Museum. See p. 206.

50. RETHEL: Death the Friend. Woodcut, 12¼ × 10⅞ in. London, Victoria and Albert Museum. See p. 206.

51. BAUDELAIRE: 'Specimen of Antique Beauty, dedicated to Chenavard.' Pen, pencil and wash, 7⅜ × 5 in. Private Collection.

    Inscribed in Baudelaire's hand: 'échantillon de *Beauté antique*, dédié à *Chenavard*.' See pp. 20–79 for Baudelaire's opinions on Chenavard.

52. PAUL CHENAVARD (1807–95): Augustus closes the doors of the Temple of Janus. Oil on canvas, 14 ft 11½ in. × 11 ft. 4⅝ in. Lyons, Musée des Beaux-Arts.

    This is one of the large grisaille panels intended for the decoration of the Panthéon. J. C. Sloane (*Art Bulletin*, vol. XXXIII, 1951, p. 247) records this as No. 29 in his list of the Panthéon decorations, and interprets it as representing the end of civil strife and the start of the Augustan Age.

53. WILHELM KAULBACH (1805–74): The Madhouse. Munich, Stadtmuseum. Baudelaire would have known Kaulbach's *Narrenhaus* from this engraving by H. Merz, published a year after the original drawing, in 1836. See p. 205.

ROBERT SEYMOUR (1798–1836): 'Oh! the deep, deep sea!'
See pp. 188-9.

INDEX